DICTIONARY

THEME−BASED

British English Collection

ENGLISH-
ARABIC

The most useful words
To expand your lexicon and sharpen
your language skills

9000 words

Theme-based dictionary British English-Arabic - 9000 words

By Andrey Taranov

T&P Books vocabularies are intended for helping you learn, memorize and review foreign words. The dictionary is divided into themes, covering all major spheres of everyday activities, business, science, culture, etc.

The process of learning words using T&P Books' theme-based dictionaries gives you the following advantages:

- Correctly grouped source information predetermines success at subsequent stages of word memorization
- Availability of words derived from the same root allowing memorization of word units (rather than separate words)
- Small units of words facilitate the process of establishing associative links needed for consolidation of vocabulary
- Level of language knowledge can be estimated by the number of learned words

T&P Books Publishing
www.tpbooks.com

This book is also available in E-book formats.
Please visit www.tpbooks.com or the major online bookstores.

ARABIC THEME-BASED DICTIONARY
British English collection

T&P Books vocabularies are intended to help you learn, memorize, and review foreign words. The vocabulary contains over 9000 commonly used words arranged thematically.

- Vocabulary contains the most commonly used words
- Recommended as an addition to any language course
- Meets the needs of beginners and advanced learners of foreign languages
- Convenient for daily use, revision sessions, and self-testing activities
- Allows you to assess your vocabulary

Special features of the vocabulary

- Words are organized according to their meaning, not alphabetically
- Words are presented in three columns to facilitate the reviewing and self-testing processes
- Words in groups are divided into small blocks to facilitate the learning process
- The vocabulary offers a convenient and simple transcription of each foreign word

The vocabulary has 256 topics including:

Basic Concepts, Numbers, Colors, Months, Seasons, Units of Measurement, Clothing & Accessories, Food & Nutrition, Restaurant, Family Members, Relatives, Character, Feelings, Emotions, Diseases, City, Town, Sightseeing, Shopping, Money, House, Home, Office, Working in the Office, Import & Export, Marketing, Job Search, Sports, Education, Computer, Internet, Tools, Nature, Countries, Nationalities and more ...

TABLE OF CONTENTS

PRONUNCIATION GUIDE

T&P phonetic alphabet	Arabic example	English example
[a]	طَفَّى [ṭaffa]	shorter than in 'ask'
[ā]	إختار [ixtār]	calf, palm
[e]	هامبورجر [hamburger]	elm, medal
[i]	زِفاف [zifāf]	shorter than in 'feet'
[ī]	أبريل [abrīl]	feet, meter
[u]	كلكتا [kalkutta]	book
[ū]	جاموس [ʒāmūs]	fuel, tuna
[b]	بِداية [bidāya]	baby, book
[d]	سعادة [sa'āda]	day, doctor
[ḍ]	وَضع [waḍ']	[d] pharyngeal
[ʒ]	الأرجنتين [arʒantīn]	forge, pleasure
[ð]	تِذكار [tiðkār]	weather, together
[ẓ]	ظهر [ẓahar]	[z] pharyngeal
[f]	خفيف [xafīf]	face, food
[g]	جولف [gūlf]	game, gold
[h]	إتّجاه [ittiʒāh]	home, have
[ḥ]	أحبّ [aḥabb]	[h] pharyngeal
[y]	ذهبيّ [ðahabiy]	yes, New York
[k]	كرسيّ [kursiy]	clock, kiss
[l]	لمح [lamaḥ]	lace, people
[m]	مرصد [marṣad]	magic, milk
[n]	جنوب [ʒanūb]	sang, thing
[p]	كابتشينو [kaputʃīnu]	pencil, private
[q]	وثيق [waθiq]	king, club
[r]	روح [rūḥ]	rice, radio
[s]	سُخريّة [suxriyya]	city, boss
[ṣ]	معصم [mi'ṣam]	[s] pharyngeal
[ʃ]	عشاء ['aʃā']	machine, shark
[t]	تنّوب [tannūb]	tourist, trip
[ṭ]	خريطة [xarīṭa]	[t] pharyngeal
[θ]	ماموث [mamūθ]	month, tooth
[v]	فيتنام [vitnām]	very, river
[w]	ودّع [wadda']	vase, winter
[x]	بخيل [baxīl]	as in Scots 'loch'
[ɣ]	تغدّى [taɣadda]	between [g] and [h]
[z]	ماعز [mā'iz]	zebra, please
['] (ayn)	سبعة [sab'a]	voiced pharyngeal fricative
['] (hamza)	سأل [sa'al]	glottal stop

ABBREVIATIONS
used in the dictionary

Arabic abbreviations

du	-	plural noun (double)
f	-	feminine noun
m	-	masculine noun
pl	-	plural

English abbreviations

ab.	-	about
adj	-	adjective
adv	-	adverb
anim.	-	animate
as adj	-	attributive noun used as adjective
e.g.	-	for example
etc.	-	et cetera
fam.	-	familiar
fem.	-	feminine
form.	-	formal
inanim.	-	inanimate
masc.	-	masculine
math	-	mathematics
mil.	-	military
n	-	noun
pl	-	plural
pron.	-	pronoun
sb	-	somebody
sing.	-	singular
sth	-	something
v aux	-	auxiliary verb
vi	-	intransitive verb
vi, vt	-	intransitive, transitive verb
vt	-	transitive verb

BASIC CONCEPTS

Basic concepts. Part 1

1. Pronouns

I, me	ana	أنا
you (masc.)	anta	أنت
you (fem.)	anti	أنت
he	huwa	هو
she	hiya	هي
we	naḥnu	نحن
you (to a group)	antum	أنتم
they	hum	هم

2. Greetings. Salutations. Farewells

Hello! (form.)	as salāmu ʿalaykum!	السلام عليكم!
Good morning!	ṣabāḥ al xayr!	صباح الخير!
Good afternoon!	nahārak saʿīd!	نهارك سعيد!
Good evening!	masāʾ al xayr!	مساء الخير!
to say hello	sallam	سلّم
Hi! (hello)	salām!	سلام!
greeting (n)	salām (m)	سلام
to greet (vt)	sallam ʿala	سلّم على
How are you?	kayfa ḥāluka?	كيف حالك؟
What's new?	ma axbārak?	ما أخبارك؟
Bye-Bye! Goodbye!	maʿ as salāma!	مع السلامة!
See you soon!	ilal liqāʾ!	إلى اللقاء!
Farewell!	maʿ as salāma!	مع السلامة!
to say goodbye	waddaʿ	ودّع
Cheers!	bay bay!	باي باي!
Thank you! Cheers!	ʃukran!	شكرًا!
Thank you very much!	ʃukran ʒazīlan!	شكرًا جزيلًا!
My pleasure!	ʿafwan	عفوا
Don't mention it!	la ʃukr ʿala wāʒib	لا شكر على واجب
It was nothing	al ʿafw	العفو
Excuse me! (fam.)	ʿan iðnak!	عن أذنك!
Excuse me! (form.)	ʿafwan!	عفوًا!!
to excuse (forgive)	ʿaðar	عذر
to apologize (vi)	iʿtaðar	إعتذر
My apologies	ana ʾāsif	أنا آسف

I'm sorry!	la tu'āχiðni!	لا تؤاخذني!
to forgive (vt)	'afa	عفا
please (adv)	min faḍlak	من فضلك

Don't forget!	la tansa!	لا تنس!
Certainly!	ṭab'an!	طبعًا!
Of course not!	abadan!	أبدًا!
Okay! (I agree)	ittafaqna!	إتفقنا!
That's enough!	kifāya!	كفاية!

3. How to address

mister, sir	ya sayyid	يا سيّد
madam	ya sayyida	يا سيدة
miss	ya 'ānisa	يا آنسة
young man	ya ustāð	يا أستاذ
young man (little boy)	ya bni	يا بني
miss (little girl)	ya binti	يا بنتي

4. Cardinal numbers. Part 1

0 zero	ṣifr	صفر
1 one	wāḥid	واحد
1 one (fem.)	wāḥida	واحدة
2 two	iθnān	إثنان
3 three	θalāθa	ثلاثة
4 four	arba'a	أربعة

5 five	χamsa	خمسة
6 six	sitta	ستّة
7 seven	sab'a	سبعة
8 eight	θamāniya	ثمانية
9 nine	tis'a	تسعة

10 ten	'aʃara	عشرة
11 eleven	aḥad 'aʃar	أحد عشر
12 twelve	iθnā 'aʃar	إثنا عشر
13 thirteen	θalāθat 'aʃar	ثلاثة عشر
14 fourteen	arba'at 'aʃar	أربعة عشر

15 fifteen	χamsat 'aʃar	خمسة عشر
16 sixteen	sittat 'aʃar	ستّة عشر
17 seventeen	sab'at 'aʃar	سبعة عشر
18 eighteen	θamāniyat 'aʃar	ثمانية عشر
19 nineteen	tis'at 'aʃar	تسعة عشر

20 twenty	'iʃrūn	عشرون
21 twenty-one	wāḥid wa 'iʃrūn	واحد وعشرون
22 twenty-two	iθnān wa 'iʃrūn	إثنان وعشرون
23 twenty-three	θalāθa wa 'iʃrūn	ثلاثة وعشرون
30 thirty	θalāθīn	ثلاثون
31 thirty-one	wāḥid wa θalāθūn	واحد وثلاثون

| 32 thirty-two | iθnān wa θalāθūn | إثنان وثلاثون |
| 33 thirty-three | θalāθa wa θalāθūn | ثلاثة وثلاثون |

40 forty	arbaʿūn	أربعون
41 forty-one	wāḥid wa arbaʿūn	واحد وأربعون
42 forty-two	iθnān wa arbaʿūn	إثنان وأربعون
43 forty-three	θalāθa wa arbaʿūn	ثلاثة وأربعون

50 fifty	xamsūn	خمسون
51 fifty-one	wāḥid wa xamsūn	واحد وخمسون
52 fifty-two	iθnān wa xamsūn	إثنان وخمسون
53 fifty-three	θalāθa wa xamsūn	ثلاثة وخمسون

60 sixty	sittūn	ستّون
61 sixty-one	wāḥid wa sittūn	واحد وستّون
62 sixty-two	iθnān wa sittūn	إثنان وستّون
63 sixty-three	θalāθa wa sittūn	ثلاثة وستّون

70 seventy	sabʿūn	سبعون
71 seventy-one	wāḥid wa sabʿūn	واحد وسبعون
72 seventy-two	iθnān wa sabʿūn	إثنان وسبعون
73 seventy-three	θalāθa wa sabʿūn	ثلاثة وسبعون

80 eighty	θamānūn	ثمانون
81 eighty-one	wāḥid wa θamānūn	واحد وثمانون
82 eighty-two	iθnān wa θamānūn	إثنان وثمانون
83 eighty-three	θalāθa wa θamānūn	ثلاثة وثمانون

90 ninety	tisʿūn	تسعون
91 ninety-one	wāḥid wa tisʿūn	واحد وتسعون
92 ninety-two	iθnān wa tisʿūn	إثنان وتسعون
93 ninety-three	θalāθa wa tisʿūn	ثلاثة وتسعون

5. Cardinal numbers. Part 2

100 one hundred	mi'a	مائة
200 two hundred	mi'atān	مائتان
300 three hundred	θalāθumi'a	ثلاثمائة
400 four hundred	rubʿumi'a	أربعمائة
500 five hundred	xamsumi'a	خمسمائة

600 six hundred	sittumi'a	ستّمائة
700 seven hundred	sabʿumi'a	سبعمائة
800 eight hundred	θamānimi'a	ثمانمائة
900 nine hundred	tisʿumi'a	تسعمائة

1000 one thousand	alf	ألف
2000 two thousand	alfān	ألفان
3000 three thousand	θalāθat 'ālāf	ثلاثة آلاف
10000 ten thousand	'aʃarat 'ālāf	عشرة آلاف
one hundred thousand	mi'at alf	مائة ألف

| million | milyūn (m) | مليون |
| billion | milyār (m) | مليار |

6. Ordinal numbers

first (adj)	awwal	أوّل
second (adj)	θāni	ثان
third (adj)	θāliθ	ثالث
fourth (adj)	rābiʿ	رابع
fifth (adj)	χāmis	خامس
sixth (adj)	sādis	سادس
seventh (adj)	sābiʿ	سابع
eighth (adj)	θāmin	ثامن
ninth (adj)	tāsiʿ	تاسع
tenth (adj)	ʿāʃir	عاشر

7. Numbers. Fractions

fraction	kasr (m)	كسر
one half	niṣf	نصف
one third	θulθ	ثلث
one quarter	rubʿ	ربع
one eighth	θumn	ثمن
one tenth	ʿuʃr	عشر
two thirds	θulθān	ثلثان
three quarters	talātit arbāʿ	ثلاثة أرباع

8. Numbers. Basic operations

subtraction	ṭarḥ (m)	طرح
to subtract (vi, vt)	ṭaraḥ	طرح
division	qisma (f)	قسمة
to divide (vt)	qasam	قسم
addition	ʒamʿ (m)	جمع
to add up (vt)	ʒamaʿ	جمع
to add (vi)	ʒamaʿ	جمع
multiplication	ḍarb (m)	ضرب
to multiply (vt)	ḍarab	ضرب

9. Numbers. Miscellaneous

digit, figure	raqm (m)	رقم
number	ʿadad (m)	عدد
numeral	ism al ʿadad (m)	إسم العدد
minus sign	nāqiṣ (m)	ناقص
plus sign	zāʾid (m)	زائد
formula	ṣīɣa (f)	صيغة
calculation	ḥisāb (m)	حساب
to count (vi, vt)	ʿadd	عدّ

| to count up | ḥasab | حسب |
| to compare (vt) | qāran | قارن |

How much?	kam?	كم؟
sum, total	maʒmūʿ (m)	مجموع
result	natīʒa (f)	نتيجة
remainder	al bāqi (m)	الباقي

a few (e.g., ~ years ago)	ʿiddat	عدّة
little (I had ~ time)	qalīl	قليل
the rest	al bāqi (m)	الباقي
one and a half	wāḥid wa niṣf (m)	واحد ونصف
dozen	iθnā ʿaʃar (f)	إثنا عشر

in half (adv)	ila ʃaṭrayn	إلى شطرين
equally (evenly)	bit tasāwi	بالتساوى
half	niṣf (m)	نصف
time (three ~s)	marra (f)	مرّة

10. The most important verbs. Part 1

to advise (vt)	naṣaḥ	نصح
to agree (say yes)	ittafaq	إتّفق
to answer (vi, vt)	aʒāb	أجاب
to apologize (vi)	iʿtaðar	إعتذر
to arrive (vi)	waṣal	وصل

to ask (~ oneself)	sa'al	سأل
to ask (~ sb to do sth)	ṭalab	طلب
to be (vi)	kān	كان

to be afraid	χāf	خاف
to be hungry	arād an ya'kul	أراد أن يأكل
to be interested in ...	ihtamm	إهتمّ
to be needed	kān maṭlūb	كان مطلوبا
to be surprised	indahaʃ	إندهش

to be thirsty	arād an yaʃrab	أراد أن يشرب
to begin (vt)	bada'	بدأ
to belong to ...	χaṣṣ	خصّ
to boast (vi)	tabāha	تباهى
to break (split into pieces)	kasar	كسر
to call (~ for help)	istaɣāθ	إستغاث

can (v aux)	istaṭāʿ	إستطاع
to catch (vt)	amsak	أمسك
to change (vt)	ɣayyar	غيّر
to choose (select)	iχtār	إختار
to come down (the stairs)	nazil	نزل

to compare (vt)	qāran	قارن
to complain (vi, vt)	ʃaka	شكا
to confuse (mix up)	iχtalaṭ	إختلط
to continue (vt)	istamarr	إستمرّ

| to control (vt) | taḥakkam | تَحَكَّمَ |
| to cook (dinner) | ḥaḍḍar | حَضَّرَ |

to cost (vt)	kallaf	كَلَّفَ
to count (add up)	ʿadd	عَدَّ
to count on …	iʿtamad ʿala …	إعتَمَد على...
to create (vt)	χalaq	خلق
to cry (weep)	baka	بكى

11. The most important verbs. Part 2

to deceive (vi, vt)	χadaʿ	خَدَع
to decorate (tree, street)	zayyan	زَيَّن
to defend (a country, etc.)	dāfaʿ	دافع
to demand (request firmly)	ṭālib	طالَب
to dig (vt)	ḥafar	حفر

to discuss (vt)	nāqaʃ	ناقَش
to do (vt)	ʿamal	عمِل
to doubt (have doubts)	ʃakk fi	شكَّ في
to drop (let fall)	awqaʿ	أوقَع
to enter (room, house, etc.)	daχal	دخَل

to exist (vi)	kān mawʒūd	كان موجودًا
to expect (foresee)	tanabbaʾ	تنبَّأ
to explain (vt)	ʃaraḥ	شرح
to fall (vi)	saqaṭ	سقَط

to fancy (vt)	aʿʒab	أعجب
to find (vt)	waʒad	وجَد
to finish (vt)	atamm	أتمَّ
to fly (vi)	ṭār	طار
to follow … (come after)	tabaʿ	تبِع

to forget (vi, vt)	nasiy	نسِي
to forgive (vt)	ʿafa	عفا
to give (vt)	aʿṭa	أعطى
to give a hint	aʿṭa talmīḥ	أعطى تلميحًا
to go (on foot)	maʃa	مشى
to go for a swim	sabaḥ	سبَح
to go out (for dinner, etc.)	χaraʒ	خرَج
to guess (the answer)	χamman	خمَّن

to have (vt)	malak	ملك
to have breakfast	afṭar	أفطر
to have dinner	taʿaʃʃa	تعشَّى
to have lunch	tayadda	تغدَّى
to hear (vt)	samiʿ	سمِع

to help (vt)	sāʿad	ساعد
to hide (vt)	χabaʾ	خبَّأ
to hope (vi, vt)	tamanna	تمنَّى
to hunt (vi, vt)	iṣṭād	إصطاد
to hurry (vi)	istaʿʒal	إستعجل

12. The most important verbs. Part 3

to inform (vt)	axbar	أَخبَر
to insist (vi, vt)	aṣarr	أصَرّ
to insult (vt)	ahān	أهان
to invite (vt)	da'a	دعا
to joke (vi)	mazaḥ	مزح

to keep (vt)	ḥafaẓ	حفظ
to keep silent, to hush	sakat	سكت
to kill (vt)	qatal	قتل
to know (sb)	'araf	عرف
to know (sth)	'araf	عرف
to laugh (vi)	ḍaḥik	ضحك

to liberate (city, etc.)	ḥarrar	حرّر
to look for ... (search)	baḥaθ	بحث
to love (sb)	aḥabb	أحَبّ
to make a mistake	axṭa'	أخطأ
to manage, to run	adār	أدار

to mean (signify)	'ana	عنى
to mention (talk about)	ðakar	ذكَر
to miss (school, etc.)	ɣāb	غاب
to notice (see)	lāḥaẓ	لاحظ
to object (vi, vt)	i'taraḍ	إعترض

to observe (see)	rāqab	راقب
to open (vt)	fataḥ	فتح
to order (meal, etc.)	ṭalab	طلب
to order (mil.)	amar	أمر
to own (possess)	malak	ملك

to participate (vi)	iʃtarak	إشترك
to pay (vi, vt)	dafa'	دفع
to permit (vt)	raxxaṣ	رخّص
to plan (vt)	xaṭṭaṭ	خطّط
to play (children)	la'ib	لعب

to pray (vi, vt)	ṣalla	صلّى
to prefer (vt)	faḍḍal	فضّل
to promise (vt)	wa'ad	وعد
to pronounce (vt)	naṭaq	نطق
to propose (vt)	iqtaraḥ	إقترح
to punish (vt)	'āqab	عاقب

13. The most important verbs. Part 4

to read (vi, vt)	qara'	قرأ
to recommend (vt)	naṣaḥ	نصح
to refuse (vi, vt)	rafaḍ	رفض
to regret (be sorry)	nadim	ندم
to rent (sth from sb)	ista'ʒar	إستأجر

to repeat (say again)	karrar	كرّر
to reserve, to book	ḥaʒaz	حجز
to run (vi)	ʒara	جرى
to save (rescue)	anqað	أنقذ

to say (~ thank you)	qāl	قال
to scold (vt)	wabbaχ	وبّخ
to see (vt)	ra'a	رأى
to sell (vt)	bā'	باع

to send (vt)	arsal	أرسل
to shoot (vi)	aṭlaq an nār	أطلق النار
to shout (vi)	ṣaraχ	صرخ
to show (vt)	'araḍ	عرض
to sign (document)	waqqa'	وقّع

to sit down (vi)	ʒalas	جلس
to smile (vi)	ibtasam	إبتسم
to speak (vi, vt)	takallam	تكلّم
to steal (money, etc.)	saraq	سرق
to stop (for pause, etc.)	waqaf	وقف

to stop (please ~ calling me)	tawaqqaf	توقّف
to study (vt)	daras	درس
to swim (vi)	sabaḥ	سبح
to take (vt)	aχað	أخذ
to think (vi, vt)	ẓann	ظنّ

to threaten (vt)	haddad	هدّد
to touch (with hands)	lamas	لمس
to translate (vt)	tarʒam	ترجم
to trust (vt)	waθiq	وثق
to try (attempt)	ḥāwal	حاول

to turn (e.g., ~ left)	in'aṭaf	إنعطف
to underestimate (vt)	istaχaff	إستخفّ
to understand (vt)	fahim	فهم
to unite (vt)	waḥḥad	وحّد
to wait (vt)	intaẓar	إنتظر

to want (wish, desire)	arād	أراد
to warn (vt)	ḥaððar	حذّر
to work (vi)	'amal	عمل
to write (vt)	katab	كتب
to write down	katab	كتب

14. Colours

colour	lawn (m)	لون
shade (tint)	daraʒat al lawn (m)	درجة اللون
hue	ṣabɣit lūn (f)	لون
rainbow	qaws quzaḥ (m)	قوس قزح
white (adj)	abyaḍ	أبيض
black (adj)	aswad	أسود

grey (adj)	ramādiy	رمادي
green (adj)	axḍar	أخضر
yellow (adj)	aṣfar	أصفر
red (adj)	ahmar	أحمر

blue (adj)	azraq	أزرق
light blue (adj)	azraq fātiḥ	أزرق فاتح
pink (adj)	wardiy	وردي
orange (adj)	burtuqāliy	برتقالي
violet (adj)	banafsaʒiy	بنفسجي
brown (adj)	bunniy	بني

| golden (adj) | ðahabiy | ذهبي |
| silvery (adj) | fiḍḍiy | فضي |

beige (adj)	bɛ:ʒ	بيج
cream (adj)	ʿāʒiy	عاجي
turquoise (adj)	fayrūziy	فيروزي
cherry red (adj)	karaziy	كرزي
lilac (adj)	laylakiy	ليلكي
crimson (adj)	qirmiziy	قرمزي

light (adj)	fātiḥ	فاتح
dark (adj)	ɣāmiq	غامق
bright, vivid (adj)	zāhi	زاه

coloured (pencils)	mulawwan	ملون
colour (e.g. ~ film)	mulawwan	ملون
black-and-white (adj)	abyaḍ wa aswad	أبيض وأسود
plain (one-coloured)	waḥīd al lawn, sāda	وحيد اللون، سادة
multicoloured (adj)	mutaʿaddid al alwān	متعدد الألوان

15. Questions

Who?	man?	من؟
What?	māða?	ماذا؟
Where? (at, in)	ayna?	أين؟
Where (to)?	ila ayna?	إلى أين؟
From where?	min ayna?	من أين؟
When?	mata?	متى؟
Why? (What for?)	li māða?	لماذا؟
Why? (~ are you crying?)	li māða?	لماذا؟

What for?	li māða?	لماذا؟
How? (in what way)	kayfa?	كيف؟
What? (What kind of ...?)	ay?	أي؟
Which?	ay?	أي؟

To whom?	li man?	لمن؟
About whom?	ʿamman?	عمن؟
About what?	ʿamma?	عمّا؟
With whom?	maʿ man?	مع من؟
How many? How much?	kam?	كم؟
Whose?	li man?	لمن؟

16. Prepositions

with (accompanied by)	ma'	مع
without	bi dūn	بدون
to (indicating direction)	ila	إلى
about (talking ~ ...)	'an	عن
before (in time)	qabl	قبل
in front of ...	amām	أمام
under (beneath, below)	taḥt	تحت
above (over)	fawq	فوق
on (atop)	'ala	على
from (off, out of)	min	من
of (made from)	min	من
in (e.g. ~ ten minutes)	ba'd	بعد
over (across the top of)	'abr	عبر

17. Function words. Adverbs. Part 1

Where? (at, in)	ayna?	أين؟
here (adv)	huna	هنا
there (adv)	hunāk	هناك
somewhere (to be)	fi makānin ma	في مكان ما
nowhere (not in any place)	la fi ay makān	لا في أي مكان
by (near, beside)	bi ʒānib	بجانب
by the window	bi ʒānib aʃ ʃubbāk	بجانب الشبّاك
Where (to)?	ila ayna?	إلى أين؟
here (e.g. come ~!)	huna	هنا
there (e.g. to go ~)	hunāk	هناك
from here (adv)	min huna	من هنا
from there (adv)	min hunāk	من هناك
close (adv)	qarīban	قريبًا
far (adv)	ba'īdan	بعيدًا
near (e.g. ~ Paris)	'ind	عند
nearby (adv)	qarīban	قريبًا
not far (adv)	ɣayr ba'īd	غير بعيد
left (adj)	al yasār	اليسار
on the left	'alaʃ ʃimāl	على الشمال
to the left	ilaʃ ʃimāl	إلى الشمال
right (adj)	al yamīn	اليمين
on the right	'alal yamīn	على اليمين
to the right	llal yamīn	إلى اليمين
in front (adv)	min al amām	من الأمام
front (as adj)	amāmiy	أمامي

ahead (the kids ran ~)	ilal amām	إلى الأمام
behind (adv)	warā'	وراء
from behind	min al warā'	من الوراء
back (towards the rear)	ilal warā'	إلى الوراء

middle	wasaṭ (m)	وسط
in the middle	fil wasat	في الوسط

at the side	bi ʒānib	بجانب
everywhere (adv)	fi kull makān	في كل مكان
around (in all directions)	ḥawl	حول

from inside	min ad dāχil	من الداخل
somewhere (to go)	ila ayy makān	إلى أيّ مكان
straight (directly)	bi aqṣar ṭarīq	بأقصر طريق
back (e.g. come ~)	'īyāban	إيابًا

from anywhere	min ayy makān	من أي مكان
from somewhere	min makānin ma	من مكان ما

firstly (adv)	awwalan	أوّلًا
secondly (adv)	θāniyan	ثانيًا
thirdly (adv)	θāliθan	ثالثًا

suddenly (adv)	faʒ'a	فجأة
at first (in the beginning)	fil bidāya	في البداية
for the first time	li 'awwal marra	لأوّل مرّة
long before …	qabl … bi mudda ṭawīla	قبل...بمدّة طويلة
anew (over again)	min ʒadīd	من جديد
for good (adv)	ilal abad	إلى الأبد

never (adv)	abadan	أبدًا
again (adv)	min ʒadīd	من جديد
now (at present)	al 'ān	الآن
often (adv)	kaθīran	كثيرًا
then (adv)	fi ðalika al waqt	في ذلك الوقت
urgently (quickly)	'āʒilan	عاجلًا
usually (adv)	kal 'āda	كالعادة

by the way, …	'ala fikra …	على فكرة...
possibly	min al mumkin	من الممكن
probably (adv)	la'alla	لعلّ
maybe (adv)	min al mumkin	من الممكن
besides …	bil iḍāfa ila ðalik …	بالإضافة إلى...
that's why …	li ðalik	لذلك
in spite of …	bir raɣm min …	بالرغم من...
thanks to …	bi faḍl …	بفضل...

what (pron.)	allaði	الذي
that (conj.)	anna	أنّ
something	ʃay' (m)	شيء
anything (something)	ʃay' (m)	شيء
nothing	la ʃay'	لا شيء

who (pron.)	allaði	الذي
someone	aḥad	أحد

somebody	aḥad	أحد
nobody	la aḥad	لا أحد
nowhere (a voyage to ~)	la ila ay makān	لا إلى أي مكان
nobody's	la yaχuṣṣ aḥad	لا يخص أحداً
somebody's	li aḥad	لأحد

so (I'm ~ glad)	hakaða	هكذا
also (as well)	kaðalika	كذلك
too (as well)	ayḍan	أيضاً

18. Function words. Adverbs. Part 2

Why?	li māða?	لماذا؟
for some reason	li sababin ma	لسبب ما
because ...	li'anna ...	لأنّ...
for some purpose	li amr mā	لأمر ما

and	wa	و
or	aw	أو
but	lakin	لكن
for (e.g. ~ me)	li	لـ

too (excessively)	kaθīran ʒiddan	كثير جداً
only (exclusively)	faqaṭ	فقط
exactly (adv)	biḍ ḍabṭ	بالضبط
about (more or less)	naḥw	نحو

approximately (adv)	taqrīban	تقريباً
approximate (adj)	taqrībiy	تقريبي
almost (adv)	taqrīban	تقريباً
the rest	al bāqi (m)	الباقي

each (adj)	kull	كلّ
any (no matter which)	ayy	أيّ
many, much (a lot of)	kaθīr	كثير
many people	kaθīr min an nās	كثير من الناس
all (everyone)	kull an nās	كل الناس

in return for ...	muqābil ...	مقابل...
in exchange (adv)	muqābil	مقابل

by hand (made)	bil yad	باليد
hardly (negative opinion)	hayhāt	هيهات

probably (adv)	la'alla	لعلّ
on purpose (intentionally)	qaṣdan	قصداً
by accident (adv)	ṣudfa	صدفة

very (adv)	ʒiddan	جداً
for example (adv)	maθalan	مثلاً
between	bayn	بين
among	bayn	بين
so much (such a lot)	haðihi al kammiyya	هذه الكمية
especially (adv)	χāṣṣa	خاصّة

Basic concepts. Part 2

19. Opposites

rich (adj)	ɣaniy	غنيّ
poor (adj)	faqīr	فقير
ill, sick (adj)	marīḍ	مريض
well (not sick)	salīm	سليم
big (adj)	kabīr	كبير
small (adj)	ṣaɣīr	صغير
quickly (adv)	bi surʿa	بسرعة
slowly (adv)	bi buṭʾ	ببطء
fast (adj)	sarīʿ	سريع
slow (adj)	baṭīʾ	بطيء
glad (adj)	farḥān	فرحان
sad (adj)	ḥazīn	حزين
together (adv)	maʿan	معًا
separately (adv)	bi mufradih	بمفرده
aloud (to read)	bi ṣawt ʿāli	بصوت عال
silently (to oneself)	sirran	سرًّا
tall (adj)	ʿāli	عال
low (adj)	munχafiḍ	منخفض
deep (adj)	ʿamīq	عميق
shallow (adj)	ḍaḥl	ضحل
yes	naʿam	نعم
no	la	لا
distant (in space)	baʿīd	بعيد
nearby (adj)	qarīb	قريب
far (adv)	baʿīdan	بعيدًا
nearby (adv)	qarīban	قريبًا
long (adj)	ṭawīl	طويل
short (adj)	qaṣīr	قصير
good (kindhearted)	ṭayyib	طيّب
evil (adj)	ʃarīr	شرير

| married (adj) | mutazawwiʒ | متزوّج |
| single (adj) | aʿzab | أعزب |

| to forbid (vt) | manaʿ | منع |
| to permit (vt) | samaḥ | سمح |

| end | nihāya (f) | نهاية |
| beginning | bidāya (f) | بداية |

| left (adj) | al yasār | اليسار |
| right (adj) | al yamīn | اليمين |

| first (adj) | awwal | أوّل |
| last (adj) | 'āχir | آخر |

| crime | ʒarīma (f) | جريمة |
| punishment | ʿuqūba (f), ʿiqāb (m) | عقوبة, عقاب |

| to order (vt) | amar | أمر |
| to obey (vi, vt) | ṭāʿ | طاع |

| straight (adj) | mustaqīm | مستقيم |
| curved (adj) | munḥani | منحن |

| paradise | al ʒanna (f) | الجنّة |
| hell | al ʒaḥīm (f) | الجحيم |

| to be born | wulid | وُلد |
| to die (vi) | māt | مات |

| strong (adj) | qawiy | قويّ |
| weak (adj) | daʿīf | ضعيف |

| old (adj) | ʿaʒūz | عجوز |
| young (adj) | ʃābb | شابّ |

| old (adj) | qadīm | قديم |
| new (adj) | ʒadīd | جديد |

| hard (adj) | ṣalb | صلب |
| soft (adj) | ṭariy | طريّ |

| warm (tepid) | dāfi' | دافئ |
| cold (adj) | bārid | بارد |

| fat (adj) | θaχīn | ثخين |
| thin (adj) | naḥīf | نحيف |

| narrow (adj) | dayyiq | ضيّق |
| wide (adj) | wāsiʿ | واسع |

| good (adj) | ʒayyid | جيّد |
| bad (adj) | sayyi' | سيئ |

| brave (adj) | ʃuʒāʿ | شجاع |
| cowardly (adj) | ʒabān | جبان |

20. Weekdays

Monday	yawm al iθnayn (m)	يوم الإثنين
Tuesday	yawm aθ θulāθā' (m)	يوم الثلاثاء
Wednesday	yawm al arbi'ā' (m)	يوم الأربعاء
Thursday	yawm al χamīs (m)	يوم الخميس
Friday	yawm al ʒum'a (m)	يوم الجمعة
Saturday	yawm as sabt (m)	يوم السبت
Sunday	yawm al aḥad (m)	يوم الأحد

today (adv)	al yawm	اليوم
tomorrow (adv)	ɣadan	غداً
the day after tomorrow	ba'd ɣad	بعد غد
yesterday (adv)	ams	أمس
the day before yesterday	awwal ams	أوّل أمس

day	yawm (m)	يوم
working day	yawm 'amal (m)	يوم عمل
public holiday	yawm al 'uṭla ar rasmiyya (m)	يوم العطلة الرسمية
day off	yawm 'uṭla (m)	يوم عطلة
weekend	ayyām al 'uṭla (pl)	أيام العطلة

all day long	ṭūl al yawm	طول اليوم
the next day (adv)	fil yawm at tāli	في اليوم التالي
two days ago	min yawmayn	قبل يومين
the day before	fil yawm as sābiq	في اليوم السابق
daily (adj)	yawmiy	يومي
every day (adv)	yawmiyyan	يومياً

week	usbū' (m)	أسبوع
last week (adv)	fil isbū' al māḍi	في الأسبوع الماضي
next week (adv)	fil isbū' al qādim	في الأسبوع القادم
weekly (adj)	usbū'iy	أسبوعي
every week (adv)	usbū'iyyan	أسبوعياً
twice a week	marratayn fil usbū'	مرّتين في الأسبوع
every Tuesday	kull yawm aθ θulaθā'	كل يوم الثلاثاء

21. Hours. Day and night

morning	ṣabāḥ (m)	صباح
in the morning	fiṣ ṣabāḥ	في الصباح
noon, midday	ẓuhr (m)	ظهر
in the afternoon	ba'd aẓ ẓuhr	بعد الظهر

evening	masā' (m)	مساء
in the evening	fil masā'	في المساء
night	layl (m)	ليل
at night	bil layl	بالليل
midnight	muntaṣif al layl (m)	منتصف الليل

second	θāniya (f)	ثانية
minute	daqīqa (f)	دقيقة
hour	sā'a (f)	ساعة

half an hour	niṣf sā'a (m)	نصف ساعة
a quarter-hour	rub' sā'a (f)	ربع ساعة
fifteen minutes	χamsat 'aʃar daqīqa	خمس عشرة دقيقة
24 hours	yawm kāmil (m)	يوم كامل

sunrise	ʃurūq aʃ ʃams (m)	شروق الشمس
dawn	faʒr (m)	فجر
early morning	ṣabāḥ bākir (m)	صباح باكر
sunset	ɣurūb aʃ ʃams (m)	غروب الشمس

early in the morning	fis ṣabāḥ al bākir	في الصباح الباكر
this morning	al yawm fiṣ ṣabāḥ	اليوم في الصباح
tomorrow morning	ɣadan fiṣ ṣabāḥ	غدًا في الصباح

this afternoon	al yawm ba'd aẓ ẓuhr	اليوم بعد الظهر
in the afternoon	ba'd aẓ ẓuhr	بعد الظهر
tomorrow afternoon	ɣadan ba'd aẓ ẓuhr	غدًا بعد الظهر

| tonight (this evening) | al yawm fil masā' | اليوم في المساء |
| tomorrow night | ɣadan fil masā' | غدًا في المساء |

at 3 o'clock sharp	fis sā'a aθ θāliθa tamāman	في الساعة الثالثة تماما
about 4 o'clock	fis sā'a ar rābi'a taqrīban	في الساعة الرابعة تقريبا
by 12 o'clock	ḥattas sā'a aθ θāniya 'aʃara	حتى الساعة الثانية عشرة
in 20 minutes	ba'd 'iʃrīn daqīqa	بعد عشرين دقيقة
in an hour	ba'd sā'a	بعد ساعة
on time (adv)	fi maw'idih	في موعده

a quarter to ...	illa rub'	إلا ربع
within an hour	ṭiwāl sā'a	طوال الساعة
every 15 minutes	kull rub' sā'a	كل ربع ساعة
round the clock	layl nahār	ليل نهار

22. Months. Seasons

January	yanāyir (m)	يناير
February	fibrāyir (m)	فبراير
March	māris (m)	مارس
April	abrīl (m)	أبريل
May	māyu (m)	مايو
June	yūnyu (m)	يونيو

July	yūlyu (m)	يوليو
August	aɣustus (m)	أغسطس
September	sibtambar (m)	سبتمبر
October	uktūbir (m)	أكتوبر
November	nuvimbar (m)	نوفمبر
December	disimbar (m)	ديسمبر

spring	rabī' (m)	ربيع
in spring	fir rabī'	في الربيع
spring (as adj)	rabī'iy	ربيعي
summer	ṣayf (m)	صيف
in summer	fiṣ ṣayf	في الصيف

summer (as adj)	ṣayfiy	صيفي
autumn	χarīf (m)	خريف
in autumn	fil χarīf	في الخريف
autumn (as adj)	χarīfiy	خريفي
winter	ʃitā' (m)	شتاء
in winter	fiʃ ʃitā'	في الشتاء
winter (as adj)	ʃitawiy	شتوي
month	ʃahr (m)	شهر
this month	fi haða aʃ ʃahr	في هذا الشهر
next month	fiʃ ʃahr al qādim	في الشهر القادم
last month	fiʃ ʃahr al māḍi	في الشهر الماضي
a month ago	qabl ʃahr	قبل شهر
in a month (a month later)	ba'd ʃahr	بعد شهر
in 2 months (2 months later)	ba'd ʃahrayn	بعد شهرين
the whole month	ṭūl aʃ ʃahr	طول الشهر
all month long	ʃahr kāmil	شهر كامل
monthly (~ magazine)	ʃahriy	شهري
monthly (adv)	kull ʃahr	كل شهر
every month	kull ʃahr	كل شهر
twice a month	marratayn fiʃ ʃahr	مرّتين في الشهر
year	sana (f)	سنة
this year	fi haðihi as sana	في هذه السنة
next year	fis sana al qādima	في السنة القادمة
last year	fis sana al māḍiya	في السنة الماضية
a year ago	qabla sana	قبل سنة
in a year	ba'd sana	بعد سنة
in two years	ba'd sanatayn	بعد سنتين
the whole year	ṭūl as sana	طول السنة
all year long	sana kāmila	سنة كاملة
every year	kull sana	كل سنة
annual (adj)	sanawiy	سنوي
annually (adv)	kull sana	كل سنة
4 times a year	arba' marrāt fis sana	أربع مرّات في السنة
date (e.g. today's ~)	tarīχ (m)	تاريخ
date (e.g. ~ of birth)	tarīχ (m)	تاريخ
calendar	taqwīm (m)	تقويم
half a year	niṣf sana (m)	نصف سنة
six months	niṣf sana (m)	نصف سنة
season (summer, etc.)	faṣl (m)	فصل
century	qarn (m)	قرن

23. Time. Miscellaneous

time	waqt (m)	وقت
moment	laḥẓa (f)	لحظة

instant (n)	laḥẓa (f)	لمظة
instant (adj)	xāṭif	خاطف
lapse (of time)	fatra (f)	فترة
life	ḥayāt (f)	حياة
eternity	abadiyya (f)	أبديّة

epoch	'ahd (m)	عهد
era	'aṣr (m)	عصر
cycle	dawra (f)	دورة
period	fatra (f)	فترة
term (short-~)	fatra (f)	فترة

the future	al mustaqbal (m)	المستقبل
future (as adj)	qādim	قادم
next time	fil marra al qādima	في المرّة القادمة
the past	al māḍi (m)	الماضي
past (recent)	māḍi	ماض
last time	fil marra al māḍiya	في المرّة الماضية

later (adv)	fima ba'd	فيما بعد
after (prep.)	ba'd	بعد
nowadays (adv)	fi haðihi al ayyām	في هذه الأيام
now (at this moment)	al 'ān	الآن
immediately (adv)	ḥālan	حالاً
soon (adv)	qarīban	قريباً
in advance (beforehand)	muqaddaman	مقدّماً

a long time ago	min zamān	من زمان
recently (adv)	min zaman qarīb	من زمان قريب
destiny	maṣīr (m)	مصير
recollections	ðikra (f)	ذكرى
archives	arʃīf (m)	أرشيف
during ...	aθnā'...	أثناء...
long, a long time (adv)	li mudda ṭawīla	لمدّة طويلة
not long (adv)	li mudda qaṣīra	لمدّة قصيرة
early (in the morning)	bākiran	باكراً
late (not early)	muta'axxiran	متأخّراً

forever (for good)	lil abad	للأبد
to start (begin)	bada'	بدأ
to postpone (vt)	aʒʒal	أجّل

at the same time	fi nafs al waqt	في نفس الوقت
permanently (adv)	dā'iman	دائماً
constant (noise, pain)	mustamirr	مستمرّ
temporary (adj)	mu'aqqat	مؤقّت
sometimes (adv)	min ḥīn li 'āxar	من حين لآخر
rarely (adv)	nādiran	نادراً
often (adv)	kaθīran	كثيراً

24. Lines and shapes

square	murabba' (m)	مربّع
square (as adj)	murabba'	مربّع

circle	dā'ira (f)	دائرة
round (adj)	mudawwar	مدور
triangle	muθallaθ (m)	مثلث
triangular (adj)	muθallaθ	مثلث

oval	baydawiy (m)	بيضوي
oval (as adj)	baydawiy	بيضوي
rectangle	mustaṭīl (m)	مستطيل
rectangular (adj)	mustaṭīliy	مستطيلي

pyramid	haram (m)	هرم
rhombus	mu'ayyan (m)	معين
trapezium	murabba' munḥarif (m)	مربع منحرف
cube	muka''ab (m)	مكعب
prism	manʃūr (m)	منشور

circumference	muḥīṭ munḥanan muɣlaq (m)	محيط منحنى مغلق
sphere	kura (f)	كرة
ball (solid sphere)	kura (f)	كرة
diameter	quṭr (m)	قطر
radius	niṣf qaṭr (m)	نصف قطر
perimeter (circle's ~)	muḥīṭ (m)	محيط
centre	wasaṭ (m)	وسط

horizontal (adj)	ufuqiy	أفقي
vertical (adj)	'amūdiy	عمودي
parallel (n)	χaṭṭ mutawāzi (m)	خط متواز
parallel (as adj)	mutawāzi	متواز

line	χaṭṭ (m)	خط
stroke	ḥaraka (m)	حركة
straight line	χaṭṭ mustaqīm (m)	خط مستقيم
curve (curved line)	χaṭṭ munḥani (m)	خط منحن
thin (line, etc.)	rafī'	رقيع
contour (outline)	kuntūr (m)	كنتور

intersection	taqāṭu' (m)	تقاطع
right angle	zāwya mustaqīma (f)	زاوية مستقيمة
segment	qiṭ'a (f)	قطعة
sector (circular ~)	qiṭā' (m)	قطاع
side (of a triangle)	ḍil' (m)	ضلع
angle	zāwiya (f)	زاوية

25. Units of measurement

weight	wazn (m)	وزن
length	ṭūl (m)	طول
width	'arḍ (m)	عرض
height	irtifā' (m)	إرتفاع
depth	'umq (m)	عمق
volume	ḥaʒm (m)	حجم
area	misāḥa (f)	مساحة
gram	grām (m)	جرام
milligram	milliɣrām (m)	مليغرام

kilogram	kiluɣrām (m)	كيلوغرام
ton	ṭunn (m)	طنّ
pound	raṭl (m)	رطل
ounce	ūnṣa (f)	أونصة

metre	mitr (m)	متر
millimetre	millimitr (m)	مليمتر
centimetre	santimitr (m)	سنتيمتر
kilometre	kilumitr (m)	كيلومتر
mile	mīl (m)	ميل

inch	būṣa (f)	بوصة
foot	qadam (f)	قدم
yard	yārda (f)	ياردة

| square metre | mitr murabbaʿ (m) | متر مربّع |
| hectare | hiktār (m) | هكتار |

litre	litr (m)	لتر
degree	daraʒa (f)	درجة
volt	vūlt (m)	فولت
ampere	ambīr (m)	أمبير
horsepower	ḥiṣān (m)	حصان

quantity	kammiyya (f)	كمّية
a little bit of ...	qalīl ...	قليل...
half	niṣf (m)	نصف
dozen	iθnā ʿaʃar (f)	إثنا عشر
piece (item)	waḥda (f)	وحدة

| size | ḥaʒm (m) | حجم |
| scale (map ~) | miqyās (m) | مقياس |

minimal (adj)	al adna	الأدنى
the smallest (adj)	al aṣɣar	الأصغر
medium (adj)	mutawassiṭ	متوسّط
maximal (adj)	al aqṣa	الأقصى
the largest (adj)	al akbar	الأكبر

26. Containers

canning jar (glass ~)	barṭamān (m)	برطمان
tin, can	tanaka (f)	تنكة
bucket	ʒardal (m)	جردل
barrel	barmīl (m)	برميل

wash basin (e.g., plastic ~)	ḥawḍ lil ɣasīl (m)	حوض للغسيل
tank (100L water ~)	χazzān (m)	خزّان
hip flask	zamzamiyya (f)	زمزمية
jerrycan	ʒirikan (m)	جركن
tank (e.g., tank car)	χazzān (m)	خزّان

| mug | māgg (m) | ماجّ |
| cup (of coffee, etc.) | finʒān (m) | فنجان |

saucer	ṭabaq finʒān (m)	طبق فنجان
glass (tumbler)	kubbāya (f)	كبّاية
wine glass	ka's (f)	كأس
stock pot (soup pot)	kassirūlla (f)	كاسرولة

| bottle (~ of wine) | zuʒāʒa (f) | زجاجة |
| neck (of the bottle, etc.) | 'unq (m) | عنق |

carafe (decanter)	dawraq zuʒāʒiy (m)	دورق زجاجيّ
pitcher	ibrīq (m)	إبريق
vessel (container)	inā' (m)	إناء
pot (crock, stoneware ~)	aṣīṣ (m)	أصيص
vase	vāza (f)	فازة

flacon, bottle (perfume ~)	zuʒāʒa (f)	زجاجة
vial, small bottle	zuʒāʒa (f)	زجاجة
tube (of toothpaste)	umbūba (f)	أنبوبة

sack (bag)	kīs (m)	كيس
bag (paper ~, plastic ~)	kīs (m)	كيس
packet (of cigarettes, etc.)	'ulba (f)	علبة

box (e.g. shoebox)	'ulba (f)	علبة
crate	ṣundū' (m)	صندوق
basket	salla (f)	سلّة

27. Materials

material	mādda (f)	مادّة
wood (n)	xaʃab (m)	خشب
wood-, wooden (adj)	xaʃabiy	خشبيّ

| glass (n) | zuʒāʒ (m) | زجاج |
| glass (as adj) | zuʒāʒiy | زجاجيّ |

| stone (n) | ḥaʒar (m) | حجر |
| stone (as adj) | ḥaʒariy | حجريّ |

| plastic (n) | blastīk (m) | بلاستيك |
| plastic (as adj) | min al blastīk | من البلاستيك |

| rubber (n) | maṭṭāṭ (m) | مطّاط |
| rubber (as adj) | maṭṭāṭiy | مطّاطيّ |

| cloth, fabric (n) | qumāʃ (m) | قماش |
| fabric (as adj) | min al qumāʃ | من القماش |

| paper (n) | waraq (m) | ورق |
| paper (as adj) | waraqiy | ورقيّ |

cardboard (n)	kartūn (m)	كرتون
cardboard (as adj)	kartūniy	كرتونيّ
polyethylene	buli iθilīn (m)	بولي إيئيلين
cellophane	silufān (m)	سيلوفان

plywood	ablakāʃ (m)	أبلكاش
porcelain (n)	bursilān (m)	بورسلان
porcelain (as adj)	min il bursilān	من البورسلان
clay (n)	ṭīn (m)	طين
clay (as adj)	faxxāry	فخّاري
ceramic (n)	siramīk (m)	سيراميك
ceramic (as adj)	siramīkiy	سيراميكيّ

28. Metals

metal (n)	maʿdan (m)	معدن
metal (as adj)	maʿdaniy	معدنيّ
alloy (n)	sabīka (f)	سبيكة

gold (n)	ðahab (m)	ذهب
gold, golden (adj)	ðahabiy	ذهبيّ
silver (n)	fiḍḍa (f)	فضّة
silver (as adj)	fiḍḍiy	فضّيّ

iron (n)	ḥadīd (m)	حديد
iron-, made of iron (adj)	ḥadīdiy	حديديّ
steel (n)	fūlāð (m)	فولاذ
steel (as adj)	fulāðiy	فولاذيّ
copper (n)	nuḥās (m)	نحاس
copper (as adj)	nuḥāsiy	نحاسيّ

aluminium (n)	alumīniyum (m)	الومينيوم
aluminium (as adj)	alumīniyum	الومينيوم
bronze (n)	brūnz (m)	برونز
bronze (as adj)	brūnziy	برونزيّ

brass	nuḥās aṣfar (m)	نحاس أصفر
nickel	nikil (m)	نيكل
platinum	blatīn (m)	بلاتين
mercury	ziʾbaq (m)	زئبق
tin	qaṣdīr (m)	قصدير
lead	ruṣāṣ (m)	رصاص
zinc	zink (m)	زنك

HUMAN BEING

Human being. The body

29. Humans. Basic concepts

human being	insān (m)	إنسان
man (adult male)	raʒul (m)	رجل
woman	imraʾa (f)	إمرأة
child	ṭifl (m)	طفل
girl	bint (f)	بنت
boy	walad (m)	ولد
teenager	murāhiq (m)	مراهق
old man	ʿaʒūz (m)	عجوز
old woman	ʿaʒūza (f)	عجوزة

30. Human anatomy

organism (body)	ʒism (m)	جسم
heart	qalb (m)	قلب
blood	dam (m)	دم
artery	ʃaryān (m)	شريان
vein	ʿirq (m)	عرق
brain	muxx (m)	مخّ
nerve	ʿaṣab (m)	عصب
nerves	aʿṣāb (pl)	أعصاب
vertebra	faqra (f)	فقرة
spine (backbone)	ʿamūd faqriy (m)	عمود فقريّ
stomach (organ)	maʿida (f)	معدة
intestines, bowels	amʿāʾ (pl)	أمعاء
intestine (e.g. large ~)	miʿan (m)	معى
liver	kibd (f)	كبد
kidney	kilya (f)	كلية
bone	ʿaẓm (m)	عظم
skeleton	haykal ʿaẓmiy (m)	هيكل عظميّ
rib	ḍilʿ (m)	ضلع
skull	ʒumʒuma (f)	جمجمة
muscle	ʿaḍala (f)	عضلة
biceps	ʿaḍala ðāt raʾsayn (f)	عضلة ذات رأسين
triceps	ʿaḍla θulāθiyyat ar ruʾūs (f)	عضلة ثلاثيّة الرؤوس
tendon	watar (m)	وتر
joint	mafṣil (m)	مفصل

lungs	ri'atān (du)	رئتان
genitals	a'ḍā' ʒinsiyya (pl)	أعضاء جنسيّة
skin	buʃra (m)	بشرة

31. Head

head	ra's (m)	رأس
face	waʒh (m)	وجه
nose	anf (m)	أنف
mouth	fam (m)	فم

eye	'ayn (f)	عين
eyes	'uyūn (pl)	عيون
pupil	ḥadaqa (f)	حدقة
eyebrow	ḥāʒib (m)	حاجب
eyelash	rimʃ (m)	رمش
eyelid	ʒafn (m)	جفن

tongue	lisān (m)	لسان
tooth	sinn (f)	سِن
lips	ʃifāh (pl)	شفاه
cheekbones	'iẓām waʒhiyya (pl)	عظام وجهيّة
gum	liθθa (f)	لثّة
palate	ḥanak (m)	حنك

nostrils	minxarān (du)	منخران
chin	ðaqan (m)	ذقن
jaw	fakk (m)	فكّ
cheek	xadd (m)	خدّ

forehead	ʒabha (f)	جبهة
temple	ṣudɣ (m)	صدغ
ear	uðun (f)	أذن
back of the head	qafa (m)	قفا
neck	raqaba (f)	رقبة
throat	ḥalq (m)	حلق

hair	ʃa'r (m)	شعر
hairstyle	tasrīḥa (f)	تسريحة
haircut	tasrīḥa (f)	تسريحة
wig	barūka (f)	باروكة

moustache	ʃawārib (pl)	شوارب
beard	liḥya (f)	لحية
to have (a beard, etc.)	'indahu	عنده
plait	difīra (f)	ضفيرة
sideboards	sawālif (pl)	سوالف

red-haired (adj)	aḥmar aʃ ʃa'r	أحمر الشعر
grey (hair)	abyaḍ	أبيض
bald (adj)	aṣla'	أصلع
bald patch	ṣala' (m)	صلع
ponytail	ðayl ḥiṣān (m)	ذيل حصان
fringe	quṣṣa (f)	قصّة

32. Human body

| hand | yad (m) | يد |
| arm | ðirā' (f) | ذراع |

finger	işba' (m)	إصبع
toe	işba' al qadam (m)	إصبع القدم
thumb	ibhām (m)	إبهام
little finger	xunşur (m)	خنصر
nail	zufr (m)	ظفر

fist	qabḍa (f)	قبضة
palm	kaff (f)	كفّ
wrist	mi'şam (m)	معصم
forearm	sā'id (m)	ساعد
elbow	mirfaq (m)	مرفق
shoulder	katf (f)	كتف

leg	riʒl (f)	رجل
foot	qadam (f)	قدم
knee	rukba (f)	ركبة
calf	sammāna (f)	سمّانة
hip	faxð (f)	فخذ
heel	'aqb (m)	عقب

body	ʒism (m)	جسم
stomach	baṭn (m)	بطن
chest	şadr (m)	صدر
breast	θady (m)	ثدي
flank	ʒamb (m)	جنب
back	zahr (m)	ظهر
lower back	asfal az zahr (m)	أسفل الظهر
waist	xaşr (m)	خصر

navel (belly button)	surra (f)	سرّة
buttocks	ardāf (pl)	أرداف
bottom	dubr (m)	دبر

beauty spot	ʃāma (f)	شامة
birthmark (café au lait spot)	waḥma	وحمة
tattoo	waʃm (m)	وشم
scar	nadba (f)	ندبة

Clothing & Accessories

33. Outerwear. Coats

clothes	malābis (pl)	ملابس
outerwear	malābis fawqāniyya (pl)	ملابس فوقانيّة
winter clothing	malābis ʃitawiyya (pl)	ملابس شتويّة
coat (overcoat)	miʿṭaf (m)	معطف
fur coat	miʿṭaf farw (m)	معطف فرو
fur jacket	ʒakīt farw (m)	جاكيت فرو
down coat	haʃiyyat rīʃ (m)	حشبة ريش
jacket (e.g. leather ~)	ʒākīt (m)	جاكيت
raincoat (trenchcoat, etc.)	miʿṭaf lil maṭar (m)	معطف للمطر
waterproof (adj)	ṣāmid lil māʾ	صامد للماء

34. Men's & women's clothing

shirt (button shirt)	qamīṣ (m)	قميص
trousers	banṭalūn (m)	بنطلون
jeans	ʒīnz (m)	جينز
suit jacket	sutra (f)	سترة
suit	badla (f)	بدلة
dress (frock)	fustān (m)	فستان
skirt	tannūra (f)	تنّورة
blouse	blūza (f)	بلوزة
knitted jacket (cardigan, etc.)	kardigān (m)	كارديجان
jacket (of a woman's suit)	ʒākīt (m)	جاكيت
T-shirt	ti ʃirt (m)	تي شيرت
shorts (short trousers)	ʃūrt (m)	شورت
tracksuit	badlat at tadrīb (f)	بدلة التدريب
bathrobe	θawb hammām (m)	ثوب حمّام
pyjamas	biʒāma (f)	بيجاما
jumper (sweater)	bulūvir (m)	بلوفر
pullover	bulūvir (m)	بلوفر
waistcoat	ṣudayriy (m)	صديريّ
tailcoat	badlat sahra (f)	بدلة سهرة
dinner suit	smūkin (m)	سموكن
uniform	zayy muwaḥḥad (m)	زي موحّد
workwear	θiyāb al ʿamal (m)	ثياب العمل
boiler suit	uvirūl (m)	اوفرول
coat (e.g. doctor's smock)	θawb (m)	ثوب

35. Clothing. Underwear

underwear	malābis dāχiliyya (pl)	ملابس داخليّة
pants	sirwāl dāχiliy riӡāliy (m)	سروال داخلي رجالي
panties	sirwāl dāχiliy nisā'iy (m)	سروال داخلي نسائي
vest (singlet)	qamīṣ bila aqmām (m)	قميص بلا أكمام
socks	ӡawārib (pl)	جوارب
nightdress	qamīṣ nawm (m)	قميص نوم
bra	ḥammālat ṣadr (f)	حمّالة صدر
knee highs (knee-high socks)	ӡawārib ṭawīla (pl)	جوارب طويلة
tights	ӡawārib kulūn (pl)	جوارب كولون
stockings (hold ups)	ӡawārib nisā'iyya (pl)	جوارب نسائية
swimsuit, bikini	libās sibāḥa (m)	لباس سباحة

36. Headwear

hat	qubba'a (f)	قبّعة
trilby hat	burnayṭa (f)	برنيطة
baseball cap	kāb baysbūl (m)	كاب بيسبول
flatcap	qubba'a musaṭṭaḥa (f)	قبّعة مسطحة
beret	birīh (m)	بيريه
hood	ɣiṭā' (m)	غطاء
panama hat	qubba'at banāma (f)	قبّعة بناما
knit cap (knitted hat)	qubbā'a maḥbūka (m)	قبّعة محبوكة
headscarf	ʿiӡārb (m)	إيشارب
women's hat	burnayṭa (f)	برنيطة
hard hat	χūða (f)	خوذة
forage cap	kāb (m)	كاب
helmet	χūða (f)	خوذة
bowler	qubba'at dirbi (f)	قبّعة ديربي
top hat	qubba'a 'āliya (f)	قبّعة عالية

37. Footwear

footwear	aḥðiya (pl)	أحذية
shoes (men's shoes)	ӡazma (f)	جزمة
shoes (women's shoes)	ӡazma (f)	جزمة
boots (e.g., cowboy ~)	būt (m)	بوت
carpet slippers	ʃibʃib (m)	شبشب
trainers	ḥiðā' riyāḍiy (m)	حذاء رياضيّ
trainers	kutʃi (m)	كوتشي
sandals	ṣandal (pl)	صندل
cobbler (shoe repairer)	iskāfiy (m)	إسكافيّ
heel	ka'b (m)	كعب

pair (of shoes)	zawӡ (m)	زوج
lace (shoelace)	ʃarīṭ (m)	شريط
to lace up (vt)	rabaṭ	ربط
shoehorn	labbāsat ḥiðā' (f)	لبّاسة حذاء
shoe polish	warnīʃ al ḥiðā' (m)	ورنيش الحذاء

38. Textile. Fabrics

cotton (n)	quṭn (m)	قطن
cotton (as adj)	min al quṭn	من القطن
flax (n)	kattān (m)	كتّان
flax (as adj)	min il kattān	من الكتّان
silk (n)	ḥarīr (m)	حرير
silk (as adj)	min al ḥarīr	من الحرير
wool (n)	ṣūf (m)	صوف
wool (as adj)	min aṣ ṣūf	من الصوف
velvet	muӽmal (m)	مخمل
suede	ӡild ʃāmwāh (m)	جلد شامواه
corduroy	quṭn qaṭīfa (f)	قطن قطيفة
nylon (n)	naylūn (m)	نايلون
nylon (as adj)	min an naylūn	من النيلون
polyester (n)	bulyistir (m)	بوليستر
polyester (as adj)	min al bulyastar	من البوليستر
leather (n)	ӡild (m)	جلد
leather (as adj)	min al ӡild	من الجلد
fur (n)	farw (m)	فرو
fur (e.g. ~ coat)	min al farw	من الفرو

39. Personal accessories

gloves	quffāz (m)	قفّاز
mittens	quffāz muӽlaq (m)	قفّاز مغلق
scarf (muffler)	'īʃārb (m)	إيشارب
glasses	naẓẓāra (f)	نظّارة
frame (eyeglass ~)	iṭār (m)	إطار
umbrella	ʃamsiyya (f)	شمسيّة
walking stick	'aṣa (f)	عصا
hairbrush	furʃat ʃaʻr (f)	فرشة شعر
fan	mirwaḥa yadawiyya (f)	مروحة يدويّة
tie (necktie)	karavatta (f)	كرافتة
bow tie	babyūn (m)	ببيون
braces	ḥammāla (f)	حمّالة
handkerchief	mandīl (m)	منديل
comb	miʃṭ (m)	مشط
hair slide	dabbūs (m)	دبّوس

| hairpin | bansa (m) | بنسة |
| buckle | bukla (f) | بكلة |

| belt | ḥizām (m) | حزام |
| shoulder strap | ḥammalat al katf (f) | حمّالة الكتف |

bag (handbag)	ʃanṭa (f)	شنطة
handbag	ʃanṭat yad (f)	شنطة يد
rucksack	ḥaqībat ẓahr (f)	حقيبة ظهر

40. Clothing. Miscellaneous

fashion	mūḍa (f)	موضة
in vogue (adj)	fil mūḍa	في الموضة
fashion designer	muṣammim azyāʾ (m)	مصمّم أزياء

collar	yāqa (f)	ياقة
pocket	ʒayb (m)	جيب
pocket (as adj)	ʒayb	جيب
sleeve	kumm (m)	كمّ
hanging loop	ʿallāqa (f)	علّاقة
flies (on trousers)	lisān (m)	لسان

zip (fastener)	zimām munzaliq (m)	زمام منزلق
fastener	miʃbak (m)	مشبك
button	zirr (m)	زرّ
buttonhole	ʿurwa (f)	عروة
to come off (ab. button)	waqaʿ	وقع

to sew (vi, vt)	χāṭ	خاط
to embroider (vi, vt)	ṭarraz	طرّز
embroidery	taṭrīz (m)	تطريز
sewing needle	ibra (f)	إبرة
thread	χayṭ (m)	خيط
seam	darz (m)	درز

to get dirty (vi)	tawassaχ	توسّخ
stain (mark, spot)	buqʿa (f)	بقعة
to crease, to crumple	takarmaʃ	تكرمش
to tear, to rip (vt)	qaṭṭaʿ	قطّع
clothes moth	ʿuθθa (f)	عثّة

41. Personal care. Cosmetics

toothpaste	maʿʒūn asnān (m)	معجون أسنان
toothbrush	furʃat asnān (f)	فرشة أسنان
to clean one's teeth	naẓẓaf al asnān	نظّف الأسنان

razor	mūs ḥilāqa (m)	موس حلاقة
shaving cream	krīm ḥilāqa (m)	كريم حلاقة
to shave (vi)	ḥalaq	حلق
soap	ṣābūn (m)	صابون

shampoo	ʃāmbū (m)	شامبو
scissors	maqaṣṣ (m)	مقصّ
nail file	mibrad (m)	مبرد
nail clippers	milqaṭ (m)	ملقط
tweezers	milqaṭ (m)	ملقط
cosmetics	mawādd at taʒmīl (pl)	موادّ التجميل
face mask	mask (m)	ماسك
manicure	manikūr (m)	مانيكور
to have a manicure	'amal manikūr	عمل مانيكور
pedicure	badikīr (m)	باديكير
make-up bag	ḥaqībat adawāt at taʒmīl (f)	حقيبة أدوات التجميل
face powder	budrat waʒh (f)	بودرة وجه
powder compact	'ulbat būdra (f)	علبة بودرة
blusher	aḥmar xudūd (m)	أحمر خدود
perfume (bottled)	'iṭr (m)	عطر
toilet water (lotion)	kulūnya (f)	كولونيا
lotion	lusiyun (m)	لوسيون
cologne	kulūniya (f)	كولونيا
eyeshadow	ay ʃaduw (m)	اي شادو
eyeliner	kuḥl al 'uyūn (m)	كحل العيون
mascara	maskara (f)	ماسكارا
lipstick	aḥmar ʃifāh (m)	أحمر شفاه
nail polish	mulammi' al azāfir (m)	ملمّع الاظافر
hair spray	muθabbit aʃ ʃa'r (m)	مثبّت الشعر
deodorant	muzīl rawā'iḥ (m)	مزيل روائح
cream	krīm (m)	كريم
face cream	krīm lil waʒh (m)	كريم للوجه
hand cream	krīm lil yadayn (m)	كريم لليدين
anti-wrinkle cream	krīm muḍādd lit taʒāʿīd (m)	كريم مضادّ للتجاعيد
day cream	krīm an nahār (m)	كريم النهار
night cream	krīm al layl (m)	كريم الليل
day (as adj)	nahāriy	نهاريّ
night (as adj)	layliy	ليلي
tampon	tambūn (m)	تامبون
toilet paper (toilet roll)	waraq ḥammām (m)	ورق حمّام
hair dryer	muʒaffif ʃa'r (m)	مجفّف شعر

42. Jewellery

jewellery, jewels	muʒawharāt (pl)	مجوهرات
precious (e.g. ~ stone)	karīm	كريم
hallmark stamp	damya (f)	دمغة
ring	xātim (m)	خاتم
wedding ring	diblat al xuṭūba (m)	دبلة الخطوبة
bracelet	siwār (m)	سوار
earrings	ḥalaq (m)	حلق

necklace (~ of pearls)	'aqd (m)	عقد
crown	tāʒ (m)	تاج
bead necklace	'aqd χaraz (m)	عقد خرز

diamond	almās (m)	الماس
emerald	zumurrud (m)	زمرّد
ruby	yāqūt aḥmar (m)	ياقوت أحمر
sapphire	yāqūt azraq (m)	ياقوت أزرق
pearl	lu'lu' (m)	لؤلؤ
amber	kahramān (m)	كهرمان

43. Watches. Clocks

watch (wristwatch)	sā'a (f)	ساعة
dial	waʒh as sā'a (m)	وجه الساعة
hand (clock, watch)	'aqrab as sā'a (m)	عقرب الساعة
metal bracelet	siwār sā'a ma'daniyya (m)	سوار ساعة معدنية
watch strap	siwār sā'a (m)	سوار ساعة

battery	baṭṭāriyya (f)	بطّاريّة
to be flat (battery)	tafarraχ	تفرّغ
to change a battery	χayyar al baṭṭāriyya	غيّر البطّاريّة
to run fast	sabaq	سبق
to run slow	ta'aχχar	تأخّر

wall clock	sā'at ḥā'iṭ (f)	ساعة حائط
hourglass	sā'a ramliyya (f)	ساعة رمليّة
sundial	sā'a ʃamsiyya (f)	ساعة شمسيّة
alarm clock	munabbih (m)	منبّه
watchmaker	sa'ātiy (m)	ساعاتي
to repair (vt)	aṣlaḥ	أصلح

Food. Nutricion

44. Food

meat	laḥm (m)	لحم
chicken	daʒāʒ (m)	دجاج
poussin	farrūʒ (m)	فروج
duck	baṭṭa (f)	بطة
goose	iwazza (f)	إوزة
game	ṣayd (m)	صيد
turkey	daʒāʒ rūmiy (m)	دجاج رومي

pork	laḥm al xinzīr (m)	لحم الخنزير
veal	laḥm il 'iʒl (m)	لحم العجل
lamb	laḥm aḍ ḍa'n (m)	لحم الضأن
beef	laḥm al baqar (m)	لحم البقر
rabbit	arnab (m)	أرنب

sausage (bologna, etc.)	suʒuq (m)	سجق
vienna sausage (frankfurter)	suʒuq (m)	سجق
bacon	bikūn (m)	بيكن
ham	hām (m)	هام
gammon	faxð xinzīr (m)	فخذ خنزير

pâté	ma'ʒūn laḥm (m)	معجون لحم
liver	kibda (f)	كبدة
mince (minced meat)	ḥaʃwa (f)	حشوة
tongue	lisān (m)	لسان

egg	bayḍa (f)	بيضة
eggs	bayḍ (m)	بيض
egg white	bayāḍ al bayḍ (m)	بياض البيض
egg yolk	ṣafār al bayḍ (m)	صفار البيض

fish	samak (m)	سمك
seafood	fawākih al baḥr (pl)	فواكه البحر
caviar	kaviyār (m)	كافيار

crab	salṭa'ūn (m)	سلطعون
prawn	ʒambari (m)	جمبري
oyster	maḥār (m)	محار
spiny lobster	karkand ʃāik (m)	كركند شائك
octopus	uxtubūṭ (m)	أخطبوط
squid	kalmāri (m)	كالماري

sturgeon	samak al ḥaʃʃ (m)	سمك الحفش
salmon	salmūn (m)	سلمون
halibut	samak al halbūt (m)	سمك الهلبوت
cod	samak al qudd (m)	سمك القد
mackerel	usqumriy (m)	أسقمري

| tuna | tūna (f) | تونة |
| eel | ḥankalīs (m) | حنكليس |

trout	salmūn muraqqaṭ (m)	سلمون مرقط
sardine	sardīn (m)	سردين
pike	samak al karāki (m)	سمك الكراكي
herring	rinʒa (f)	رنجة

bread	χubz (m)	خبز
cheese	ʒubna (f)	جبنة
sugar	sukkar (m)	سكّر
salt	milḥ (m)	ملح

rice	urz (m)	أرز
pasta (macaroni)	makarūna (f)	مكرونة
noodles	nūdlis (f)	نودلز

butter	zubda (f)	زبدة
vegetable oil	zayt (m)	زيت
sunflower oil	zayt ʿabīd aʃ ʃams (m)	زيت عبيد الشمس
margarine	marɣarīn (m)	مرغرين

| olives | zaytūn (m) | زيتون |
| olive oil | zayt az zaytūn (m) | زيت الزيتون |

milk	ḥalīb (m)	حليب
condensed milk	ḥalīb mukaθθaf (m)	حليب مكثف
yogurt	yūɣurt (m)	يوغرت
soured cream	krīma ḥāmiḍa (f)	كريمة حامضة
cream (of milk)	krīma (f)	كريمة

| mayonnaise | mayunīz (m) | مايونيز |
| buttercream | krīmat zubda (f) | كريمة زبدة |

groats (barley ~, etc.)	ḥubūb (pl)	حبوب
flour	daqīq (m)	دقيق
tinned food	muʿallabāt (pl)	معلبات

cornflakes	kurn fliks (m)	كورن فليكس
honey	ʿasal (m)	عسل
jam	murabba (m)	مربّى
chewing gum	ʿilk (m)	علك

45. Drinks

water	mā' (m)	ماء
drinking water	mā' ʃurb (m)	ماء شرب
mineral water	mā' maʿdaniy (m)	ماء معدنيّ

still (adj)	bi dūn ɣāz	بدون غاز
carbonated (adj)	mukarban	مكربن
sparkling (adj)	bil ɣāz	بالغاز
ice	θalʒ (m)	ثلج
with ice	biθ θalʒ	بالثلج

non-alcoholic (adj)	bi dūn kuḥūl	بدون كحول
soft drink	maʃrūb ɣāziy (m)	مشروب غازي
refreshing drink	maʃrūb muθallaʒ (m)	مشروب مثلج
lemonade	ʃarāb laymūn (m)	شراب ليمون

spirits	maʃrūbāt kuḥūliyya (pl)	مشروبات كحوليّة
wine	nabīð (f)	نبيذ
white wine	nibīð abyaḍ (m)	نبيذ أبيض
red wine	nabīð aḥmar (m)	نبيذ أحمر

liqueur	liqiūr (m)	ليكيور
champagne	ʃambāniya (f)	شمبانيا
vermouth	virmut (m)	فيرموث

whisky	wiski (m)	وسكي
vodka	vudka (f)	فودكا
gin	ʒīn (m)	جين
cognac	kunyāk (m)	كونياك
rum	rum (m)	رم

coffee	qahwa (f)	قهوة
black coffee	qahwa sāda (f)	قهوة سادة
white coffee	qahwa bil ḥalīb (f)	قهوة بالحليب
cappuccino	kaputʃīnu (m)	كابتشينو
instant coffee	niskafi (m)	نيسكافيه

milk	ḥalīb (m)	حليب
cocktail	kuktayl (m)	كوكتيل
milkshake	milk ʃiyk (m)	ميلك شيك

juice	ʿaṣīr (m)	عصير
tomato juice	ʿaṣīr ṭamāṭim (m)	عصير طماطم
orange juice	ʿaṣīr burtuqāl (m)	عصير برتقال
freshly squeezed juice	ʿaṣīr ṭāziʒ (m)	عصير طازج

beer	bīra (f)	بيرة
lager	bīra xafīfa (f)	بيرة خفيفة
bitter	bīra ɣāmiqa (f)	بيرة غامقة

tea	ʃāy (m)	شاي
black tea	ʃāy aswad (m)	شاي أسود
green tea	ʃāy axḍar (m)	شاي أخضر

46. Vegetables

| vegetables | xuḍār (pl) | خضار |
| greens | xuḍrawāt waraqiyya (pl) | خضروات ورقيّة |

tomato	ṭamāṭim (f)	طماطم
cucumber	xiyār (m)	خيار
carrot	ʒazar (m)	جزر
potato	baṭāṭis (f)	بطاطس
onion	baṣal (m)	بصل
garlic	θūm (m)	ثوم

cabbage	kurumb (m)	كرنب
cauliflower	qarnabīṭ (m)	قرنبيط
Brussels sprouts	kurumb brūksil (m)	كرنب بروكسل
broccoli	brukuli (m)	بركولي

beetroot	banʒar (m)	بنجر
aubergine	bātinʒān (m)	باذنجان
courgette	kūsa (f)	كوسة
pumpkin	qarʻ (m)	قرع
turnip	lift (m)	لفت

parsley	baqdūnis (m)	بقدونس
dill	ʃabat (m)	شبت
lettuce	χass (m)	خسّ
celery	karafs (m)	كرفس
asparagus	halyūn (m)	هليون
spinach	sabāniχ (m)	سبانخ

pea	bisilla (f)	بسلّة
beans	fūl (m)	فول
maize	ðura (f)	ذرَة
kidney bean	faṣūliya (f)	فاصوليا

sweet paper	filfil (m)	فلفل
radish	fiʒl (m)	فجل
artichoke	χurʃūf (m)	خرشوف

47. Fruits. Nuts

fruit	fākiha (f)	فاكهة
apple	tuffāḥa (f)	تفّاحة
pear	kummaθra (f)	كمّثرى
lemon	laymūn (m)	ليمون
orange	burtuqāl (m)	برتقال
strawberry (garden ~)	farawla (f)	فراولة

tangerine	yūsufiy (m)	يوسفي
plum	barqūq (m)	برقوق
peach	durrāq (m)	دراق
apricot	miʃmiʃ (f)	مشمش
raspberry	tūt al ʻullayq al aḥmar (m)	توت العلّيق الأحمر
pineapple	ananās (m)	أناناس

banana	mawz (m)	موز
watermelon	baṭṭīχ aḥmar (m)	بطّيخ أحمر
grape	ʻinab (m)	عنب
cherry	karaz (m)	كرز
melon	baṭṭīχ aṣfar (f)	بطّيخ أصفر

grapefruit	zinbāʻ (m)	زنباع
avocado	avukādu (f)	افوكاتو
papaya	babāya (m)	بابايا
mango	mangu (m)	مانجو
pomegranate	rummān (m)	رمان

redcurrant	kiʃmiʃ aħmar (m)	كشمش أحمر
blackcurrant	ʿinab aθ θaʿlab al aswad (m)	عنب الثعلب الأسود
gooseberry	ʿinab aθ θaʿlab (m)	عنب الثعلب
bilberry	ʿinab al aħrāʒ (m)	عنب الأحراج
blackberry	θamar al ʿullayk (m)	ثمر العليّق

raisin	zabīb (m)	زبيب
fig	tīn (m)	تين
date	tamr (m)	تمر

peanut	fūl sudāniy (m)	فول سودانيّ
almond	lawz (m)	لوز
walnut	ʿayn al ʒamal (f)	عين الجمل
hazelnut	bunduq (m)	بندق
coconut	ʒawz al hind (m)	جوز هند
pistachios	fustuq (m)	فستق

48. Bread. Sweets

bakers' confectionery (pastry)	ħalawiyyāt (pl)	حلويّات
bread	xubz (m)	خبز
biscuits	baskawīt (m)	بسكويت

chocolate (n)	ʃukulāta (f)	شكولاتة
chocolate (as adj)	biʃ ʃukulāta	بالشكولاتة
candy (wrapped)	bumbūn (m)	بونبون
cake (e.g. cupcake)	kaʿk (m)	كعك
cake (e.g. birthday ~)	tūrta (f)	تورتة

pie (e.g. apple ~)	faṭīra (f)	فطيرة
filling (for cake, pie)	ħaʃwa (f)	حشوة

jam (whole fruit jam)	murabba (m)	مربّى
marmalade	marmalād (f)	مرملاد
wafers	wāfil (m)	وافل
ice-cream	muθallaʒāt (pl)	مثلّجات
pudding (Christmas ~)	būding (m)	بودنج

49. Cooked dishes

course, dish	waʒba (f)	وجبة
cuisine	maṭbax (m)	مطبخ
recipe	waṣfa (f)	وصفة
portion	waʒba (f)	وجبة

salad	sulṭa (f)	سلطة
soup	ʃūrba (f)	شوربة

clear soup (broth)	maraq (m)	مرق
sandwich (bread)	sandawitʃ (m)	ساندويتش
fried eggs	bayḍ maqliy (m)	بيض مقليّ
hamburger (beefburger)	hamburger (m)	هامبورجر

beefsteak	biftīk (m)	بفتيك
side dish	ṭabaq ʒānibiy (m)	طبق جانبيّ
spaghetti	spayitti (m)	سباغيتي
mash	harīs baṭāṭis (m)	هريس بطاطس
pizza	bītza (f)	بيتزا
porridge (oatmeal, etc.)	ʿaṣīda (f)	عصيدة
omelette	bayḍ maxfūq (m)	بيض مخفوق

boiled (e.g. ~ beef)	maslūq	مسلوق
smoked (adj)	mudaxxin	مدخّن
fried (adj)	maqliy	مقليّ
dried (adj)	muʒaffaf	مجفّف
frozen (adj)	muʒammad	مجمّد
pickled (adj)	muxallil	مخلّل

sweet (sugary)	musakkar	مسكّر
salty (adj)	māliḥ	مالح
cold (adj)	bārid	بارد
hot (adj)	sāxin	ساخن
bitter (adj)	murr	مرّ
tasty (adj)	laðīð	لذيذ

to cook in boiling water	ṭabax	طبخ
to cook (dinner)	haḍḍar	حضّر
to fry (vt)	qala	قلى
to heat up (food)	saxxan	سخّن

to salt (vt)	mallaḥ	ملّح
to pepper (vt)	falfal	فلفل
to grate (vt)	baʃar	بشر
peel (n)	qiʃra (f)	قشرة
to peel (vt)	qaʃʃar	قشّر

50. Spices

salt	milḥ (m)	ملح
salty (adj)	māliḥ	مالح
to salt (vt)	mallaḥ	ملّح

black pepper	filfil aswad (m)	فلفل أسود
red pepper (milled ~)	filfil ahmar (m)	فلفل أحمر
mustard	ṣalṣat al xardal (f)	صلصة الخردل
horseradish	fiʒl ḥārr (m)	فجل حارّ

condiment	tābil (m)	تابل
spice	bahār (m)	بهار
sauce	ṣalṣa (f)	صلصة
vinegar	xall (m)	خلّ

anise	yānsūn (m)	يانسون
basil	rīhān (m)	ريحان
cloves	qurumful (m)	قرنفل
ginger	zanʒabīl (m)	زنجبيل
coriander	kuzbara (f)	كزبرة

cinnamon	qirfa (f)	قرفة
sesame	simsim (m)	سمسم
bay leaf	awrāq al ɣār (pl)	أوراق الغار
paprika	babrika (f)	بابريكا
caraway	karāwiya (f)	كراوية
saffron	za'farān (m)	زعفران

51. Meals

| food | akl (m) | أكل |
| to eat (vi, vt) | akal | أكل |

breakfast	fuţūr (m)	فطور
to have breakfast	afţar	أفطر
lunch	ɣadā' (m)	غداء
to have lunch	taɣadda	تغدّى
dinner	'aʃā' (m)	عشاء
to have dinner	ta'aʃʃa	تعشّى

| appetite | ʃahiyya (f) | شهيّة |
| Enjoy your meal! | hanī'an marī'an! | هنيئًا مريئًا! |

to open (~ a bottle)	fataḥ	فتح
to spill (liquid)	dalaq	دلق
to spill out (vi)	indalaq	إندلق
to boil (vi)	ɣala	غلى
to boil (vt)	ɣala	غلى
boiled (~ water)	maɣliy	مغلي
to chill, cool down (vt)	barrad	برّد
to chill (vi)	tabarrad	تبرّد

| taste, flavour | ţa'm (m) | طعم |
| aftertaste | al maðāq al 'āliq fil fam (m) | المذاق العالق فى الفم |

to slim down (lose weight)	faqad al wazn	فقد الوزن
diet	ḥimya ɣaðā'iyya (f)	حمية غذائية
vitamin	vitamīn (m)	فيتامين
calorie	su'ra ḥarāriyya (f)	سعرة حرارية
vegetarian (n)	nabātiy (m)	نباتي
vegetarian (adj)	nabātiy	نباتي

fats (nutrient)	duhūn (pl)	دهون
proteins	brutināt (pl)	بروتينات
carbohydrates	naʃawiyyāt (pl)	نشويّات
slice (of lemon, ham)	ʃarīḥa (f)	شريحة
piece (of cake, pie)	qit'a (f)	قطعة
crumb (of bread, cake, etc.)	futāta (f)	فتاتة

52. Table setting

| spoon | mil'aqa (f) | ملعقة |
| knife | sikkīn (m) | سكّين |

fork	ʃawka (f)	شوكة
cup (e.g., coffee ~)	finʒān (m)	فنجان
plate (dinner ~)	ṭabaq (m)	طبق
saucer	ṭabaq finʒān (m)	طبق فنجان
serviette	mandīl (m)	منديل
toothpick	χallat asnān (f)	خلة أسنان

53. Restaurant

restaurant	maṭ'am (m)	مطعم
coffee bar	kafé (m), maqha (m)	كافيه, مقهى
pub, bar	bār (m)	بار
tearoom	ṣālun ʃāy (m)	صالون شاي
waiter	nādil (m)	نادل
waitress	nādila (f)	نادلة
barman	bārman (m)	بارمان
menu	qā'imat aṭ ṭa'ām (f)	قائمة طعام
wine list	qā'imat al χumūr (f)	قائمة خمور
to book a table	ḥaʒaz mā'ida	حجز مائدة
course, dish	waʒba (f)	وجبة
to order (meal)	ṭalab	طلب
to make an order	ṭalab	طلب
aperitif	ʃarāb (m)	شراب
starter	muqabbilāt (pl)	مقبّلات
dessert, pudding	ḥalawiyyāt (pl)	حلويّات
bill	ḥisāb (m)	حساب
to pay the bill	dafa' al ḥisāb	دفع الحساب
to give change	a'ṭa al bāqi	أعطى الباقي
tip	baqʃīʃ (m)	بقشيش

Family, relatives and friends

54. Personal information. Forms

name (first name)	ism (m)	إسم
surname (last name)	ism al 'ā'ila (m)	إسم العائلة
date of birth	tarīχ al mīlād (m)	تاريخ الميلاد
place of birth	makān al mīlād (m)	مكان الميلاد
nationality	ʒinsiyya (f)	جنسية
place of residence	maqarr al iqāma (m)	مقر الإقامة
country	balad (m)	بلد
profession (occupation)	mihna (f)	مهنة
gender, sex	ʒins (m)	جنس
height	ṭūl (m)	طول
weight	wazn (m)	وزن

55. Family members. Relatives

mother	umm (f)	أمّ
father	ab (m)	أب
son	ibn (m)	إبن
daughter	ibna (f)	إبنة
younger daughter	al ibna aṣ ṣaɣīra (f)	الإبنة الصغيرة
younger son	al ibn aṣ ṣaɣīr (m)	الابن الصغير
eldest daughter	al ibna al kabīra (f)	الإبنة الكبيرة
eldest son	al ibn al kabīr (m)	الإبن الكبير
brother	aχ (m)	أخ
elder brother	al aχ al kabīr (m)	الأخ الكبير
younger brother	al aχ aṣ ṣaɣīr (m)	الأخ الصغير
sister	uχt (f)	أخت
elder sister	al uχt al kabīra (f)	الأخت الكبيرة
younger sister	al uχt aṣ ṣaɣīra (f)	الأخت الصغيرة
cousin (masc.)	ibn 'amm (m), ibn χāl (m)	إبن عمّ، إبن خال
cousin (fem.)	ibnat 'amm (f), ibnat χāl (f)	إبنة عمّ، إبنة خال
mummy	mama (f)	ماما
dad, daddy	baba (m)	بابا
parents	wālidān (du)	والدان
child	ṭifl (m)	طفل
children	aṭfāl (pl)	أطفال
grandmother	ʒidda (f)	جدّة
grandfather	ʒadd (m)	جدّ
grandson	ḥafīd (m)	حفيد

| granddaughter | ḥafīda (f) | حفيدة |
| grandchildren | aḥfād (pl) | أحفاد |

uncle	'amm (m), χāl (m)	عمّ, خال
aunt	'amma (f), χāla (f)	عمّة, خالة
nephew	ibn al aχ (m), ibn al uχt (m)	إبن الأخ, إبن الأخت
niece	ibnat al aχ (f), ibnat al uχt (f)	إبنة الأخ, إبنة الأخت
mother-in-law (wife's mother)	ḥamātt (f)	حماة
father-in-law (husband's father)	ḥamm (m)	حم
son-in-law (daughter's husband)	zawʒ al ibna (m)	زوج الأبنة
stepmother	zawʒat al ab (f)	زوجة الأب
stepfather	zawʒ al umm (m)	زوج الأمّ

infant	ṭifl raḍīʿ (m)	طفل رضيع
baby (infant)	mawlūd (m)	مولود
little boy, kid	walad ṣaɣīr (m)	ولد صغير

wife	zawʒa (f)	زوجة
husband	zawʒ (m)	زوج
spouse (husband)	zawʒ (m)	زوج
spouse (wife)	zawʒa (f)	زوجة

married (masc.)	mutazawwiʒ	متزوّج
married (fem.)	mutazawwiʒa	متزوّجة
single (unmarried)	aʿzab	أعزب
bachelor	aʿzab (m)	أعزب
divorced (masc.)	muṭallaq (m)	مطلّق
widow	armala (f)	أرملة
widower	armal (m)	أرمل

relative	qarīb (m)	قريب
close relative	nasīb qarīb (m)	نسيب قريب
distant relative	nasīb baʿīd (m)	نسيب بعيد
relatives	aqārib (pl)	أقارب

orphan (boy or girl)	yatīm (m)	يتيم
guardian (of a minor)	waliyy amr (m)	وليّ أمر
to adopt (a boy)	tabanna	تبنّى
to adopt (a girl)	tabanna	تبنّى

56. Friends. Colleagues

friend (masc.)	ṣadīq (m)	صديق
friend (fem.)	ṣadīqa (f)	صديقة
friendship	ṣadāqa (f)	صداقة
to be friends	ṣādaq	صادق

pal (masc.)	ṣāḥib (m)	صاحب
pal (fem.)	ṣaḥiba (f)	صاحبة
partner	rafīq (m)	رفيق
chief (boss)	raʾīs (m)	رئيس

superior (n)	ra'īs (m)	رئيس
owner, proprietor	ṣāḥib (m)	صاحب
subordinate (n)	tābi' (m)	تابع
colleague	zamīl (m)	زميل

acquaintance (person)	ma'ruf (m)	معروف
fellow traveller	rafīq safar (m)	رفيق سفر
classmate	zamīl fiṣ ṣaff (m)	زميل في الصفّ

neighbour (masc.)	ʒār (m)	جار
neighbour (fem.)	ʒāra (f)	جارة
neighbours	ʒirān (pl)	جيران

57. Man. Woman

woman	imra'a (f)	إمرأة
girl (young woman)	fatāt (f)	فتاة
bride	'arūsa (f)	عروسة

beautiful (adj)	ʒamīla	جميلة
tall (adj)	ṭawīla	طويلة
slender (adj)	raʃīqa	رشيقة
short (adj)	qaṣīra	قصيرة

| blonde (n) | ʃaqrā' (f) | شقراء |
| brunette (n) | sawdā' aʃ ʃa'r (f) | سوداء الشعر |

ladies' (adj)	sayyidāt	سيّدات
virgin (girl)	'aðrā' (f)	عذراء
pregnant (adj)	ḥāmil	حامل

man (adult male)	raʒul (m)	رجل
blonde haired man	aʃqar (m)	أشقر
dark haired man	aswad aʃ ʃa'r (m)	أسود الشعر
tall (adj)	ṭawīl	طويل
short (adj)	qaṣīr	قصير

rude (rough)	waqiḥ	وقح
stocky (adj)	malyān	مليان
robust (adj)	matīn	متين
strong (adj)	qawiy	قويّ
strength	quwwa (f)	قوّة

plump, fat (adj)	θaxīn	ثخين
swarthy (dark-skinned)	asmar	أسمر
slender (well-built)	raʃīq	رشيق
elegant (adj)	anīq	أنيق

58. Age

| age | 'umr (m) | عمر |
| youth (young age) | ʃabāb (m) | شباب |

young (adj)	ʃābb	شابّ
younger (adj)	aṣɣar	أصغر
older (adj)	akbar	أكبر

young man	ʃābb (m)	شابّ
teenager	murāhiq (m)	مراهق
guy, fellow	ʃābb (m)	شابّ

| old man | ʿaʒūz (m) | عجوز |
| old woman | ʿaʒūza (f) | عجوزة |

adult (adj)	bāliɣ (m)	بالغ
middle-aged (adj)	fi muntaṣaf al ʿumr	في منتصف العمر
elderly (adj)	ʿaʒūz	عجوز
old (adj)	ʿaʒūz	عجوز

retirement	maʿāʃ (m)	معاش
to retire (from job)	uḥīl ʿalal maʿāʃ	أحيل على المعاش
retiree, pensioner	mutaqāʿid (m)	متقاعد

59. Children

child	ṭifl (m)	طفل
children	aṭfāl (pl)	أطفال
twins	taw'amān (du)	توأمان

cradle	mahd (m)	مهد
rattle	xaʃxīʃa (f)	خشخيشة
nappy	ḥifāẓ aṭfāl (m)	حفاظ أطفال

dummy, comforter	bazzāza (f)	بزّازة
pram	ʿarabat aṭfāl (f)	عربة أطفال
nursery	rawḍat aṭfāl (f)	روضة أطفال
babysitter	murabbiyat aṭfāl (f)	مربّية الأطفال

childhood	ṭufūla (f)	طفولة
doll	dumya (f)	دمية
toy	luʿba (f)	لعبة
construction set (toy)	mukaʿʿabāt (pl)	مكعّبات
well-bred (adj)	mu'addab	مؤدّب
ill-bred (adj)	qalīl al adab	قليل الأدب
spoilt (adj)	mutdalliʿ	متدلّع

to be naughty	laʿib	لعب
mischievous (adj)	laʿūb	لعوب
mischievousness	izʿāʒ (m)	إزعاج
mischievous child	ṭifl laʿūb (m)	طفل لعوب

| obedient (adj) | muṭīʿ | مطيع |
| disobedient (adj) | ʿāq | عاقّ |

docile (adj)	ʿāqil	عاقل
clever (intelligent)	ðakiy	ذكيّ
child prodigy	ṭifl muʿʒiza (m)	طفل معجزة

60. Married couples. Family life

to kiss (vt)	bās	باس
to kiss (vi)	bās	باس
family (n)	'ā'ila (f)	عائلة
family (as adj)	'ā'iliy	عائليّ
couple	zawʒān (du)	زوجان
marriage (state)	zawāʒ (m)	زواج
hearth (home)	bayt (m)	بيت
dynasty	sulāla (f)	سلالة
date	maw'id (m)	موعد
kiss	būsa (f)	بوسة
love (for sb)	ḥubb (m)	حبّ
to love (sb)	aḥabb	أحبّ
beloved	ḥabīb	حبيب
tenderness	ḥanān (m)	حنان
tender (affectionate)	ḥanūn	حنون
faithfulness	iχlāṣ (m)	إخلاص
faithful (adj)	muχliṣ	مخلص
care (attention)	'ināya (f)	عناية
caring (~ father)	muhtamm	مهتمّ
newlyweds	'arūsān (du)	عروسان
honeymoon	ʃahr al 'asal (m)	شهر العسل
to get married (ab. woman)	tazawwaʒ	تزوّج
to get married (ab. man)	tazawwaʒ	تزوّج
wedding	zifāf (m)	زفاف
golden wedding	al yubīl að ðahabiy liz zawāʒ (m)	اليوبيل الذهبي للزواج
anniversary	ðikra sanawiyya (f)	ذكرى سنويّة
lover (masc.)	ḥabīb (m)	حبيب
mistress (lover)	ḥabība (f)	حبيبة
adultery	χiyāna zawʒiyya (f)	خيانة زوجية
to cheat on ... (commit adultery)	χān	خان
jealous (adj)	ɣayūr	غيور
to be jealous	ɣār	غار
divorce	ṭalāq (m)	طلاق
to divorce (vi)	ṭallaq	طلّق
to quarrel (vi)	taʃāʒar	تشاجر
to be reconciled (after an argument)	taṣālaḥ	تصالح
together (adv)	ma'an	معًا
sex	ʒins (m)	جنس
happiness	sa'āda (f)	سعادة
happy (adj)	sa'īd	سعيد
misfortune (accident)	muṣība (m)	مصيبة
unhappy (adj)	ta'is	تعس

Character. Feelings. Emotions

61. Feelings. Emotions

feeling (emotion)	ʃuʿūr (m)	شعور
feelings	maʃāʿir (pl)	مشاعر
to feel (vt)	ʃaʿar	شعر
hunger	ʒawʿ (m)	جوع
to be hungry	arād an yaʼkul	أراد أن يأكل
thirst	ʿataʃ (m)	عطش
to be thirsty	arād an yaʃrab	أراد أن يشرب
sleepiness	nuʿās (m)	نعاس
to feel sleepy	arād an yanām	أراد أن ينام
tiredness	taʿab (m)	تعب
tired (adj)	taʿbān	تعبان
to get tired	taʿib	تعب
mood (humour)	ḥāla nafsiyya, mazāʒ (m)	حالة نفسيّة، مزاج
boredom	malal (m)	ملل
to be bored	ʃaʿar bil malal	شعر بالملل
seclusion	ʿuzla (f)	عزلة
to seclude oneself	inzawa	إنزوى
to worry (make anxious)	aqlaq	أقلق
to be worried	qalaq	قلق
worrying (n)	qalaq (m)	قلق
anxiety	qalaq (m)	قلق
preoccupied (adj)	maʃɣūl al bāl	مشغول البال
to be nervous	qalaq	قلق
to panic (vi)	uṣīb bið ðaʿr	أصيب بالذعر
hope	amal (m)	أمل
to hope (vi, vt)	tamanna	تمنّى
certainty	yaqīn (m)	يقين
certain, sure (adj)	mutaʼakkid	متأكّد
uncertainty	ʿadam at taʼakkud (m)	عدم التأكّد
uncertain (adj)	ɣayr mutaʼakkid	غير متأكّد
drunk (adj)	sakrān	سكران
sober (adj)	ṣāḥi	صاح
weak (adj)	ḍaʿīf	ضعيف
happy (adj)	saʿīd	سعيد
to scare (vt)	arhab	أرهب
fury (madness)	ɣaḍab ʃadīd (m)	غضب شديد
rage (fury)	ɣaḍab (m)	غضب
depression	iktiʼāb (m)	إكتئاب
discomfort (unease)	ʿadam irtiyāḥ (m)	عدم إرتياح

comfort	rāḥa (f)	راحة
to regret (be sorry)	nadim	ندم
regret	nadam (m)	ندم
bad luck	sūʾ al ḥazz (m)	سوء الحظ
sadness	ḥuzn (f)	حزن

shame (remorse)	xaʒal (m)	خجل
gladness	faraḥ (m)	فرح
enthusiasm, zeal	ḥamās (m)	حماس
enthusiast	mutaḥammis (m)	متحمس
to show enthusiasm	taḥammas	تحمس

62. Character. Personality

character	ṭabʿ (m)	طبع
character flaw	ʿayb (m)	عيب
mind, reason	ʿaql (m)	عقل

conscience	ḍamīr (m)	ضمير
habit (custom)	ʿāda (f)	عادة
ability (talent)	qudra (f)	قدرة
can (e.g. ~ swim)	ʿaraf	عرف

patient (adj)	ṣābir	صابر
impatient (adj)	qalīl aṣ ṣabr	قليل الصبر
curious (inquisitive)	fuḍūliy	فضولي
curiosity	fuḍūl (m)	فضول

modesty	tawāḍuʿ (m)	تواضع
modest (adj)	mutawāḍiʿ	متواضع
immodest (adj)	ɣayr mutawāḍiʿ	غير متواضع

laziness	kasal (m)	كسل
lazy (adj)	kaslān	كسلان
lazy person (masc.)	kaslān (m)	كسلان

cunning (n)	makr (m)	مكر
cunning (as adj)	mākir	ماكر
distrust	ʿadam aθ θiqa (m)	عدم الثقة
distrustful (adj)	ʃakūk	شكوك

generosity	karam (m)	كرم
generous (adj)	karīm	كريم
talented (adj)	mawhūb	موهوب
talent	mawhiba (f)	موهبة

courageous (adj)	ʃuʒāʿ	شجاع
courage	ʃaʒāʿa (f)	شجاعة
honest (adj)	amīn	أمين
honesty	amāna (f)	أمانة

careful (cautious)	ḥāðir	حاذر
brave (courageous)	ʃuʒāʿ	شجاع
serious (adj)	ʒādd	جاد

strict (severe, stern)	ṣārim	صارم
decisive (adj)	ḥazīm	حزيم
indecisive (adj)	mutaraddid	متردد
shy, timid (adj)	ҳaʒūl	خجول
shyness, timidity	ҳaʒal (m)	خجل

confidence (trust)	θiqa (f)	ثقة
to believe (trust)	waθiq	وثق
trusting (credulous)	sarī' at taṣdīq	سريع التصديق

sincerely (adv)	bi ṣarāḥa	بصراحة
sincere (adj)	muҳliṣ	مخلص
sincerity	iҳlāṣ (m)	إخلاص
open (person)	ṣarīḥ	صريح

calm (adj)	hādi'	هادئ
frank (sincere)	ṣarīḥ	صريح
naïve (adj)	sāðiʒ	ساذج
absent-minded (adj)	ʃārid al fikr	شارد الفكر
funny (odd)	mudḥik	مضحك

greed, stinginess	buҳl (m)	بخل
greedy, stingy (adj)	baҳīl	بخيل
stingy (adj)	baҳīl	بخيل
evil (adj)	ʃarīr	شرير
stubborn (adj)	'anīd	عنيد
unpleasant (adj)	karīh	كريه

selfish person (masc.)	anāniy (m)	أنانيّ
selfish (adj)	anāniy	أنانيّ
coward	ʒabān (m)	جبان
cowardly (adj)	ʒabān	جبان

63. Sleep. Dreams

to sleep (vi)	nām	نام
sleep, sleeping	nawm (m)	نوم
dream	ḥulm (m)	حلم
to dream (in sleep)	ḥalam	حلم
sleepy (adj)	na'sān	نعسان

bed	sarīr (m)	سرير
mattress	martaba (f)	مرتبة
blanket (eiderdown)	baṭṭāniyya (f)	بطّانيّة
pillow	wisāda (f)	وسادة
sheet	milāya (f)	ملاية

insomnia	araq (m)	أرق
sleepless (adj)	ariq	أرق
sleeping pill	munawwim (m)	منوّم
to take a sleeping pill	tanāwal munawwim	تناول منوّمًا

to feel sleepy	arād an yanām	أراد أن ينام
to yawn (vi)	taθā'ab	تثاءب

to go to bed	ðahab ila n nawm	ذهب إلى النوم
to make up the bed	a'add as sarīr	أعدّ السرير
to fall asleep	nām	نام

nightmare	kābūs (m)	كابوس
snore, snoring	ʃaxīr (m)	شخير
to snore (vi)	ʃaxxar	شخّر

alarm clock	munabbih (m)	منبّه
to wake (vt)	ayqaẓ	أيقظ
to wake up	istayqaẓ	إستيقظ
to get up (vi)	qām	قام
to have a wash	ɣasal waʒhah	غسل وجهه

64. Humour. Laughter. Gladness

humour (wit, fun)	fukāha (f)	فكاهة
sense of humour	ḥiss (m)	حس
to enjoy oneself	istamta'	إستمتع
cheerful (merry)	farḥān	فرحان
merriment (gaiety)	faraḥ (m)	فرح

smile	ibtisāma (f)	إبتسامة
to smile (vi)	ibtasam	إبتسم
to start laughing	ḍaḥik	ضحك
to laugh (vi)	ḍaḥik	ضحك
laugh, laughter	ḍaḥka (f)	ضحكة

anecdote	ḥikāya muḍḥika (f)	حكاية مضحكة
funny (anecdote, etc.)	muḍḥik	مضحك
funny (odd)	muḍḥik	مضحك

to joke (vi)	mazaḥ	مزح
joke (verbal)	nukta (f)	نكتة
joy (emotion)	sa'āda (f)	سعادة
to rejoice (vi)	mariḥ	مرح
joyful (adj)	saʿīd	سعيد

65. Discussion, conversation. Part 1

| communication | tawāṣul (m) | تواصل |
| to communicate | tawāṣal | تواصل |

conversation	muḥādaθa (f)	محادثة
dialogue	ḥiwār (m)	حوار
discussion (discourse)	munāqaʃa (f)	مناقشة
dispute (debate)	munāẓara (f)	مناظرة
to dispute, to debate	xālaf	خالف

interlocutor	muḥāwir (m)	محاور
topic (theme)	mawḍū' (m)	موضوع
point of view	wiʒhat naẓar (f)	وجهة نظر

opinion (point of view)	ra'y (m)	رأي
speech (talk)	xiṭāb (m)	خطاب
discussion (of a report, etc.)	munāqaʃa (f)	مناقشة
to discuss (vt)	nāqaʃ	ناقش
talk (conversation)	ḥadīs (m)	حديث
to talk (to chat)	tahādaθ	تحادث
meeting (encounter)	liqā' (m)	لقاء
to meet (vi, vt)	qābal	قابل
proverb	maθal (m)	مثل
saying	qawl ma'θūr (m)	قول مأثور
riddle (poser)	luɣz (m)	لغز
to pose a riddle	alqa luɣz	ألقى لغزًا
password	kalimat al murūr (f)	كلمة مرور
secret	sirr (m)	سرّ
oath (vow)	qasam (m)	قسم
to swear (an oath)	aqsam	أقسم
promise	wa'd (m)	وعد
to promise (vt)	wa'ad	وعد
advice (counsel)	naṣīḥa (f)	نصيحة
to advise (vt)	naṣaḥ	نصح
to follow one's advice	intaṣaḥ	إنتصح
to listen to ... (obey)	aṭā'	أطاع
news	xabar (m)	خبر
sensation (news)	daʒʒa (f)	ضجّة
information (report)	ma'lūmāt (pl)	معلومات
conclusion (decision)	istintāʒ (f)	إستنتاج
voice	ṣawt (m)	صوت
compliment	madḥ (m)	مدح
kind (nice)	laṭīf	لطيف
word	kalima (f)	كلمة
phrase	'ibāra (f)	عبارة
answer	ʒawāb (m)	جواب
truth	ḥaqīqa (f)	حقيقة
lie	kiðb (m)	كذب
thought	fikra (f)	فكرة
idea (inspiration)	fikra (f)	فكرة
fantasy	xayāl (m)	خيال

66. Discussion, conversation. Part 2

respected (adj)	muḥtaram	محترم
to respect (vt)	iḥtaram	إحترم
respect	iḥtirām (m)	إحترام
Dear ... (letter)	'azīzi ...	عزيزي...
to introduce (sb to sb)	'arraf	عرّف
to make acquaintance	ta'arraf	تعرّف

intention	niyya (f)	نيّة
to intend (have in mind)	nawa	نوى
wish	tamanni (m)	تمنٍ
to wish (~ good luck)	tamanna	تمنّى

surprise (astonishment)	'aʒab (m)	عجب
to surprise (amaze)	adhaʃ	أدهش
to be surprised	indahaʃ	إندهش

to give (vt)	a'ṭa	أعطى
to take (get hold of)	aχað	أخذ
to give back	radd	ردّ
to return (give back)	arʒa'	أرجع

to apologize (vi)	i'taðar	إعتذر
apology	i'tiðār (m)	إعتذار
to forgive (vt)	'afa	عفا

to talk (speak)	taḥaddaθ	تحدّث
to listen (vi)	istama'	إستمع
to hear out	sami'	سمع
to understand (vt)	fahim	فهم

to show (to display)	'araḍ	عرض
to look at ...	naẓar	نظر
to call (yell for sb)	nāda	نادى
to distract (disturb)	ʃaɣal	شغل
to disturb (vt)	az'aʒ	أزعج
to pass (to hand sth)	sallam	سلّم
demand (request)	ṭalab (m)	طلب
to request (ask)	ṭalab	طلب
demand (firm request)	maṭlab (m)	مطلب
to demand (request firmly)	ṭālib	طالب

to tease (call names)	ɣāẓ	غاظ
to mock (make fun of)	saχar	سخر
mockery, derision	suχriyya (f)	سخريّة
nickname	laqab (m)	لقب

insinuation	talmīḥ (m)	تلميح
to insinuate (imply)	lamaḥ	لمح
to mean (vt)	qaṣad	قصد

description	waṣf (m)	وصف
to describe (vt)	waṣaf	وصف
praise (compliments)	madḥ (m)	مدح
to praise (vt)	madaḥ	مدح

disappointment	χaybat amal (f)	خيبة أمل
to disappoint (vt)	χayyab	خيّب
to be disappointed	χābat 'āmāluh	خابت آماله

supposition	iftirāḍ (m)	إفتراض
to suppose (assume)	iftaraḍ	إفترض
warning (caution)	taḥðīr (m)	تحذير
to warn (vt)	ḥaððar	حذّر

67. Discussion, conversation. Part 3

to talk into (convince)	aqna'	أقنع
to calm down (vt)	ṭam'an	طمأن
silence (~ is golden)	sukūt (m)	سكوت
to be silent (not speaking)	sakat	سكت
to whisper (vi, vt)	hamas	همس
whisper	hamsa (f)	همسة
frankly, sincerely (adv)	bi ṣarāḥa	بصراحة
in my opinion ...	fi ra'yi ...	في رأيي...
detail (of the story)	tafṣīl (m)	تفصيل
detailed (adj)	mufaṣṣal	مفصّل
in detail (adv)	bit tafāṣīl	بالتفاصيل
hint, clue	iʃāra (f), talmīḥ (m)	إشارة, تلميح
to give a hint	a'ṭa talmīḥ	أعطى تلميحاً
look (glance)	naẓra (f)	نظرة
to have a look	alqa naẓra	ألقى نظرة
fixed (look)	θābit	ثابت
to blink (vi)	ramaʃ	رمش
to wink (vi)	ɣamaz	غمز
to nod (in assent)	hazz ra'sah	هزّ رأسه
sigh	tanahhuda (f)	تنهّدة
to sigh (vi)	tanahhad	تنهّد
to shudder (vi)	irta'aʃ	إرتعش
gesture	iʃārat yad (f)	إشارة يد
to touch (one's arm, etc.)	lamas	لمس
to seize (e.g., ~ by the arm)	amsak	أمسك
to tap (on the shoulder)	ṣafaq	صفق
Look out!	xuð bālak!	خذ بالك!
Really?	wallahi?	والله؟
Are you sure?	hal anta muta'akkid?	هل أنت متأكّد؟
Good luck!	bit tawfīq!	بالتوفيق!
I see!	wāḍiḥ!	واضح!
What a pity!	ya lil asaf!	يا للأسف!

68. Agreement. Refusal

consent	muwāfaqa (f)	موافقة
to consent (vi)	wāfa'	وافق
approval	istiḥsān (m)	إستحسان
to approve (vt)	istiḥsan	إستحسن
refusal	rafḍ (m)	رفض
to refuse (vi, vt)	rafaḍ	رفض
Great!	'aẓīm!	عظيم!
All right!	ittafaqna!	إتّفقنا!

Okay! (I agree)	ittafaqna!	إتَفقنا!
forbidden (adj)	mamnūʿ	ممنوع
it's forbidden	mamnūʿ	ممنوع
it's impossible	mustaḥīl	مستحيل
incorrect (adj)	ɣalaṭ	غلط

to reject (~ a demand)	rafaḍ	رفض
to support (cause, idea)	ayyad	أيّد
to accept (~ an apology)	qabil	قبل

| to confirm (vt) | aθbat | أثبت |
| confirmation | iθbāt (m) | إثبات |

permission	samāḥ (m)	سماح
to permit (vt)	samaḥ	سمح
decision	qarār (m)	قرار
to say nothing (hold one's tongue)	ṣamat	صمت

condition (term)	ʃarṭ (m)	شرط
excuse (pretext)	ʿuðr (m)	عذر
praise (compliments)	madḥ (m)	مدح
to praise (vt)	madaḥ	مدح

69. Success. Good luck. Failure

success	naʒāḥ (m)	نجاح
successfully (adv)	bi naʒāḥ	بنجاح
successful (adj)	nāʒiḥ	ناجح

| luck (good luck) | ḥazz (m) | حظ |
| Good luck! | bit tawfīq! | بالتوفيق! |

| lucky (e.g. ~ day) | murawaffiq | متوفّق |
| lucky (fortunate) | maḥzūz | محظوظ |

failure	faʃl (m)	فشل
misfortune	sūʾ al ḥazz (m)	سوء الحظ
bad luck	sūʾ al ḥazz (m)	سوء الحظ

| unsuccessful (adj) | fāʃil | فاشل |
| catastrophe | kāriθa (f) | كارثة |

pride	faxr (m)	فخر
proud (adj)	faxūr	فخور
to be proud	iftaxar	إفتخر

| winner | fāʾiz (m) | فائز |
| to win (vi) | fāz | فاز |

to lose (not win)	xasir	خسر
try	muḥāwala (f)	محاولة
to try (vi)	ḥāwal	حاول
chance (opportunity)	furṣa (f)	فرصة

70. Quarrels. Negative emotions

shout (scream)	ṣarχa (f)	صرخة
to shout (vi)	ṣaraχ	صرخ
to start to cry out	ṣaraχ	صرخ

quarrel	muʃāȝara (f)	مشاجرة
to quarrel (vi)	taʃāȝar	تشاجر
fight (squabble)	muʃāȝara (f)	مشاجرة
to make a scene	taʃāȝar	تشاجر
conflict	χilāf (m)	خلاف
misunderstanding	sū'at tafāhum (m)	سوء التفاهم

insult	ihāna (f)	إهانة
to insult (vt)	ahān	أهان
insulted (adj)	muhān	مهان
resentment	ḍaym (m)	ضيم
to offend (vt)	asā'	أساء
to take offence	istā'	إستاء

indignation	istiyā' (m)	إستياء
to be indignant	istā'	إستاء
complaint	ʃakwa (f)	شكوى
to complain (vi, vt)	ʃaka	شكا

apology	i'tiðār (m)	إعتذار
to apologize (vi)	i'taðar	إعتذر
to beg pardon	i'taðar	إعتذر

criticism	naqd (m)	نقد
to criticize (vt)	naqad	نقد
accusation (charge)	ittihām (m)	إتهام
to accuse (vt)	ittaham	إتهم

revenge	intiqām (m)	إنتقام
to avenge (get revenge)	intaqam	إنتقم
to pay back	radd	رد

disdain	iḥtiqār (m)	إحتقار
to despise (vt)	iḥtaqar	إحتقر
hatred, hate	karāha (f)	كراهة
to hate (vt)	karah	كره

nervous (adj)	'aṣabiy	عصبيّ
to be nervous	qalaq	قلق
angry (mad)	za'lān	زعلان
to make angry	az'al	أزعل

humiliation	iðlāl (m)	إذلال
to humiliate (vt)	ðallal	ذلل
to humiliate oneself	taðallal	تذلل

shock	ṣadma (f)	صدمة
to shock (vt)	ṣadam	صدم
trouble (e.g. serious ~)	muʃkila (f)	مشكلة

unpleasant (adj)	karīh	كريه
fear (dread)	χawf (m)	خوف
terrible (storm, heat)	ʃadīd	شديد
scary (e.g. ~ story)	muχīf	مخيف
horror	ruʿb (m)	رعب
awful (crime, news)	murʿib	مرعب

to begin to tremble	irtaʿaʃ	إرتعش
to cry (weep)	baka	بكى
to start crying	baka	بكى
tear	damaʿa (f)	دمعة

fault	yalṭa (f)	غلطة
guilt (feeling)	ðamb (m)	ذنب
dishonor (disgrace)	ʿār (m)	عار
protest	iḥtiʒāʒ (m)	إحتجاج
stress	tawattur (m)	توتّر

to disturb (vt)	azʿaʒ	أزعج
to be furious	yaḍib	غضب
angry (adj)	yaḍbān	غضبان
to end (~ a relationship)	anha	أنهى
to swear (at sb)	ʃātam	شاتم

to scare (become afraid)	χāf	خاف
to hit (strike with hand)	ḍarab	ضرب
to fight (street fight, etc.)	taʿārak	تعارك

to settle (a conflict)	sawwa	سوّى
discontented (adj)	yayr rāḍi	غير راض
furious (adj)	ʿanīf	عنيف

It's not good!	laysa haða amr ʒayyid!	ليس هذا أمرًا جيّدًا!
It's bad!	haða amr sayyiʾ!	هذا أمر سيّء!

Medicine

illness	maraḍ (m)	مرض
to be ill	maraḍ	مرض
health	ṣiḥḥa (f)	صحّة
runny nose (coryza)	zukām (m)	زكام
tonsillitis	iltihāb al lawzatayn (m)	التهاب اللوزتين
cold (illness)	bard (m)	برد
to catch a cold	aṣābahu al bard	أصابه البرد
bronchitis	iltihāb al qaṣabāt (m)	إلتهاب القصبات
pneumonia	iltihāb ar ri'atayn (m)	إلتهاب الرئتين
flu, influenza	inflūnza (f)	إنفلونزا
shortsighted (adj)	qaṣīr an naẓar	قصير النظر
longsighted (adj)	ba'īd an naẓar	بعيد النظر
strabismus (crossed eyes)	ḥawal (m)	حول
squint-eyed (adj)	aḥwal	أحول
cataract	katarakt (f)	كاتاراكت
glaucoma	glawkūma (f)	جلوكوما
stroke	sakta (f)	سكتة
heart attack	iḥtijā' (m)	إحتشاء
myocardial infarction	nawba qalbiya (f)	نوبة قلبية
paralysis	ʃalal (m)	شلل
to paralyse (vt)	ʃall	شلّ
allergy	ḥassāsiyya (f)	حسّاسيّة
asthma	rabw (m)	ربو
diabetes	ad dā' as sukkariy (m)	الداء السكّريّ
toothache	alam al asnān (m)	ألم الأسنان
caries	naxar al asnān (m)	نخر الأسنان
diarrhoea	ishāl (m)	إسهال
constipation	imsāk (m)	إمساك
stomach upset	'usr al haḍm (m)	عسر الهضم
food poisoning	tasammum (m)	تسمّم
to get food poisoning	tasammam	تسمّم
arthritis	iltihāb al mafāṣil (m)	إلتهاب المفاصل
rickets	kusāḥ al aṭfāl (m)	كساح الأطفال
rheumatism	riumatizm (m)	روماتزم
atherosclerosis	taṣṣallub aʃ ʃarayīn (m)	تصلّب الشرايين
gastritis	iltihāb al ma'ida (m)	إلتهاب المعدة
appendicitis	iltihāb az zā'ida ad dūdiyya (m)	إلتهاب الزائدة الدوديّة

cholecystitis	iltihāb al marāra (m)	إلتهاب المرارة
ulcer	qurḥa (f)	قرحة
measles	maraḍ al ḥaṣba (m)	مرض الحصبة
rubella (German measles)	ḥaṣba almāniyya (f)	حصبة ألمانية
jaundice	yaraqān (m)	يرقان
hepatitis	iltihāb al kabd al vayrūsiy (m)	إلتهاب الكبد الفيروسيّ
schizophrenia	ʃizufrīniya (f)	شيزوفرينيا
rabies (hydrophobia)	dāʾ al kalb (m)	داء الكلب
neurosis	ʿiṣāb (m)	عصاب
concussion	irtiʒāʒ al muxx (m)	إرتجاج المخ
cancer	saraṭān (m)	سرطان
sclerosis	taṣṣallub (m)	تصلّب
multiple sclerosis	taṣṣallub mutaʿaddid (m)	تصلّب متعدد
alcoholism	idmān al xamr (m)	إدمان الخمر
alcoholic (n)	mudmin al xamr (m)	مدمن الخمر
syphilis	sifilis az zuhariy (m)	سفلس الزهري
AIDS	al aydz (m)	الايدز
tumour	waram (m)	ورم
malignant (adj)	xabīθ	خبيث
benign (adj)	ḥamīd (m)	حميد
fever	ḥumma (f)	حمّى
malaria	malāriya (f)	ملاريا
gangrene	ɣanɣrīna (f)	غنغرينا
seasickness	duwār al baḥr (m)	دوار البحر
epilepsy	maraḍ aṣ ṣarʿ (m)	مرض الصرع
epidemic	wabāʾ (m)	وباء
typhus	tīfus (m)	تيفوس
tuberculosis	maraḍ as sull (m)	مرض السلّ
cholera	kulīra (f)	كوليرا
plague (bubonic ~)	ṭāʿūn (m)	طاعون

72. Symptoms. Treatments. Part 1

symptom	ʿaraḍ (m)	عرض
temperature	ḥarāra (f)	حرارة
high temperature (fever)	ḥumma (f)	حمّى
pulse (heartbeat)	nabḍ (m)	نبض
dizziness (vertigo)	dawxa (f)	دوخة
hot (adj)	ḥārr	حارّ
shivering	nafaḍān (m)	نفضان
pale (e.g. ~ face)	aṣfar	أصفر
cough	suʿāl (m)	سعال
to cough (vi)	saʿal	سعل
to sneeze (vi)	ʿaṭas	عطس
faint	iɣmāʾ (m)	إغماء

to faint (vi)	γumiya ʿalayh	غمي عليه
bruise (hématome)	kadma (f)	كدمة
bump (lump)	tawarrum (m)	تورّم
to bang (bump)	iṣṭadam	إصطدم
contusion (bruise)	raḍḍ (m)	رضّ
to get a bruise	taraḍḍaḍ	ترضّض

to limp (vi)	ʿaraʒ	عرج
dislocation	χalʿ (m)	خلع
to dislocate (vt)	χalaʿ	خلع
fracture	kasr (m)	كسر
to have a fracture	inkasar	إنكسر

cut (e.g. paper ~)	ʒurḥ (m)	جرح
to cut oneself	ʒaraḥ nafsah	جرح نفسه
bleeding	nazf (m)	نزف

burn (injury)	ḥarq (m)	حرق
to get burned	taʃayyaṭ	تشيّط

to prick (vt)	waχaz	وخز
to prick oneself	waχaz nafsah	وخز نفسه
to injure (vt)	aṣāb	أصاب
injury	iṣāba (f)	إصابة
wound	ʒurḥ (m)	جرح
trauma	ṣadma (f)	صدمة

to be delirious	haða	هذى
to stutter (vi)	talaʿsam	تلعثم
sunstroke	ḍarbat ʃams (f)	ضربة شمس

73. Symptoms. Treatments. Part 2

pain, ache	alam (m)	ألم
splinter (in foot, etc.)	ʃaẓiyya (f)	شظيّة

sweat (perspiration)	ʿirq (m)	عرق
to sweat (perspire)	ʿariq	عرق
vomiting	taqayyuʿ (m)	تقيّؤ
convulsions	taʃannuʒāt (pl)	تشنّجات

pregnant (adj)	ḥāmil	حامل
to be born	wulid	وُلد
delivery, labour	wilāda (f)	ولادة
to deliver (~ a baby)	walad	ولد
abortion	iʒhāḍ (m)	إجهاض

breathing, respiration	tanaffus (m)	تنفّس
in-breath (inhalation)	istinʃāq (m)	إستنشاق
out-breath (exhalation)	zafīr (m)	زفير
to exhale (breathe out)	zafar	زفر
to inhale (vi)	istanʃaq	إستنشق
disabled person	muʿāq (m)	معاق
cripple	muqʿad (m)	مقعد

drug addict	mudmin muxaddirāt (m)	مدمن مخدّرات
deaf (adj)	aṭraʃ	أطرش
mute (adj)	axras	أخرس
deaf mute (adj)	aṭraʃ axras	أطرش أخرس

mad, insane (adj)	maʒnūn	مجنون
madman (demented person)	maʒnūn (m)	مجنون
madwoman	maʒnūna (f)	مجنونة
to go insane	ʒunn	جنّ

gene	ʒīn (m)	جين
immunity	manāʿa (f)	مناعة
hereditary (adj)	wirāθiy	وراثيّ
congenital (adj)	xilqiy munð al wilāda	خلقيّ منذ الولادة

virus	virūs (m)	فيروس
microbe	mikrūb (m)	ميكروب
bacterium	ʒurθūma (f)	جرثومة
infection	ʿadwa (f)	عدوى

74. Symptoms. Treatments. Part 3

hospital	mustaʃfa (m)	مستشفى
patient	marīḍ (m)	مريض

diagnosis	taʃxīṣ (m)	تشخيص
cure	ʿilāʒ (m)	علاج
medical treatment	ʿilāʒ (m)	علاج
to get treatment	taʿālaʒ	تعالج
to treat (~ a patient)	ʿālaʒ	عالج
to nurse (look after)	marraḍ	مرّض
care (nursing ~)	ʿināya (f)	عناية

operation, surgery	ʿamaliyya ʒaraḥiyya (f)	عمليّة جرحيّة
to bandage (head, limb)	ḍammad	ضمّد
bandaging	taḍmīd (m)	تضميد

vaccination	talqīḥ (m)	تلقيح
to vaccinate (vt)	laqqaḥ	لقّح
injection	ḥuqna (f)	حقنة
to give an injection	ḥaqan ibra	حقن إبرة

attack	nawba (f)	نوبة
amputation	batr (m)	بتر
to amputate (vt)	batar	بتر
coma	ɣaybūba (f)	غيبوبة
to be in a coma	kān fi ḥālat ɣaybūba	كان في حالة غيبوبة
intensive care	al ʿināya al murakkaza (f)	العناية المركّزة

to recover (~ from flu)	ʃufiy	شفي
condition (patient's ~)	ḥāla (f)	حالة
consciousness	waʿy (m)	وعي
memory (faculty)	ðākira (f)	ذاكرة

to pull out (tooth)	χalaʿ	خلع
filling	ḥaʃw (m)	حشو
to fill (a tooth)	ḥaʃa	حشا

| hypnosis | at tanwīm al maɣnaṭīsiy (m) | التنويم المغناطيسيّ |
| to hypnotize (vt) | nawwam | نوّم |

75. Doctors

doctor	ṭabīb (m)	طبيب
nurse	mumarriḍa (f)	ممرّضة
personal doctor	duktūr ʃaχṣiy (m)	دكتور شخصيّ

dentist	ṭabīb al asnān (m)	طبيب الأسنان
optician	ṭabīb al ʿuyūn (m)	طبيب العيون
general practitioner	ṭabīb bāṭiniy (m)	طبيب باطنيّ
surgeon	ʒarrāḥ (m)	جرّاح

psychiatrist	ṭabīb nafsiy (m)	طبيب نفسيّ
paediatrician	ṭabīb al aṭfāl (m)	طبيب الأطفال
psychologist	sikulūʒiy (m)	سيكولوجيّ
gynaecologist	ṭabīb an nisāʾ (m)	طبيب النساء
cardiologist	ṭabīb al qalb (m)	طبيب القلب

76. Medicine. Drugs. Accessories

medicine, drug	dawāʾ (m)	دواء
remedy	ʿilāʒ (m)	علاج
to prescribe (vt)	waṣaf	وصف
prescription	waṣfa (f)	وصفة

tablet, pill	qurṣ (m)	قرص
ointment	marham (m)	مرهم
ampoule	ambūla (f)	أمبولة
mixture, solution	dawāʾ ʃarāb (m)	دواء شراب
syrup	ʃarāb (m)	شراب
capsule	ḥabba (f)	حبّة
powder	ðarūr (m)	ذرور

gauze bandage	ḍammāda (f)	ضمادة
cotton wool	quṭn (m)	قطن
iodine	yūd (m)	يود

plaster	blāstir (m)	بلاستر
eyedropper	māṣṣat al bastara (f)	ماصّة البسترة
thermometer	tirmūmitr (m)	ترمومتر
syringe	miḥqana (f)	محقنة

wheelchair	kursiy mutaḥarrik (m)	كرسيّ متحرّك
crutches	ʿukkāzān (du)	عكّازان
painkiller	musakkin (m)	مسكّن
laxative	mulayyin (m)	ملّين

spirits (ethanol)	iθanūl (m)	إيثانول
medicinal herbs	a'ʃāb ṭibbiyya (pl)	أعشاب طبية
herbal (~ tea)	'uʃbiy	عشبيّ

77. Smoking. Tobacco products

tobacco	tabɣ (m)	تبغ
cigarette	sīʒāra (f)	سيجارة
cigar	sīʒār (m)	سيجار
pipe	ɣalyūn (m)	غليون
packet (of cigarettes)	'ulba (f)	علبة

matches	kibrīt (m)	كبريت
matchbox	'ulbat kibrīt (f)	علبة كبريت
lighter	wallā'a (f)	ولّاعة
ashtray	ṭaqṭūqa (f)	طقطوقة
cigarette case	'ulbat saʒā'ir (f)	علبة سجائر

| cigarette holder | ḥamilat siʒāra (f) | حاملة سيجارة |
| filter (cigarette tip) | filtir (m) | فلتر |

to smoke (vi, vt)	daxxan	دخّن
to light a cigarette	aʃal siʒāra	أشعل سيجارة
smoking	tadxīn (m)	تدخين
smoker	mudaxxin (m)	مدخّن

cigarette end	'uqb siʒāra (m)	عقب سيجارة
smoke, fumes	duxān (m)	دخان
ash	ramād (m)	رماد

HUMAN HABITAT

City

78. City. Life in the city

city, town	madīna (f)	مدينة
capital city	ʿāṣima (f)	عاصمة
village	qarya (f)	قرية
city map	xarīṭat al madīna (f)	خريطة المدينة
city centre	markaz al madīna (m)	مركز المدينة
suburb	ḍāḥiya (f)	ضاحية
suburban (adj)	aḍ ḍawāḥi	الضواحي
outskirts	aṭrāf al madīna (pl)	أطراف المدينة
environs (suburbs)	ḍawāḥi al madīna (pl)	ضواحي المدينة
city block	ḥayy (m)	حي
residential block (area)	ḥayy sakaniy (m)	حي سكني
traffic	ḥarakat al murūr (f)	حركة المرور
traffic lights	iʃārāt al murūr (pl)	إشارات المرور
public transport	wasāʾil an naql (pl)	وسائل النقل
crossroads	taqāṭuʿ (m)	تقاطع
zebra crossing	maʿbar al muʃāt (m)	معبر المشاة
pedestrian subway	nafaq muʃāt (m)	نفق مشاة
to cross (~ the street)	ʿabar	عبر
pedestrian	māʃi (m)	ماش
pavement	raṣīf (m)	رصيف
bridge	ʒisr (m)	جسر
embankment (river walk)	kurnīʃ (m)	كورنيش
fountain	nāfūra (f)	نافورة
allée (garden walkway)	mamʃa (m)	ممشى
park	ḥadīqa (f)	حديقة
boulevard	bulvār (m)	بولفار
square	maydān (m)	ميدان
avenue (wide street)	ʃāriʿ (m)	شارع
street	ʃāriʿ (m)	شارع
side street	zuqāq (m)	زقاق
dead end	ṭarīq masdūd (m)	طريق مسدود
house	bayt (m)	بيت
building	mabna (m)	مبنى
skyscraper	nāṭiḥat saḥāb (f)	ناطحة سحاب
facade	wāʒiha (f)	واجهة
roof	saqf (m)	سقف

window	ʃubbāk (m)	شبّاك
arch	qaws (m)	قوس
column	ʻamūd (m)	عمود
corner	zāwiya (f)	زاوية

shop window	vatrīna (f)	فترينة
signboard (store sign, etc.)	lāfita (f)	لافتة
poster (e.g., playbill)	mulṣaq (m)	ملصق
advertising poster	mulṣaq iʻlāniy (m)	ملصق إعلاني
hoarding	lawḥat iʻlānāt (f)	لوحة إعلانات

rubbish	zubāla (f)	زبالة
rubbish bin	ṣundūq zubāla (m)	صندوق زبالة
to litter (vi)	rama zubāla	رمى زبالة
rubbish dump	mazbala (f)	مزبلة

telephone box	kuʃk tilifūn (m)	كشك تليفون
lamppost	ʻamūd al miṣbāḥ (m)	عمود المصباح
bench (park ~)	dikka (f), kursiy (m)	دكّة, كرسي

police officer	ʃurṭiy (m)	شرطيّ
police	ʃurṭa (f)	شرطة
beggar	ʃaḥḥāð (m)	شحّاذ
homeless (n)	mutaʃarrid (m)	متشرّد

79. Urban institutions

shop	maḥall (m)	محلّ
chemist, pharmacy	ṣaydaliyya (f)	صيدليّة
optician (spectacles shop)	al adawāt al baṣariyya (pl)	الأدوات البصريّة
shopping centre	markaz tiȝāriy (m)	مركز تجاريّ
supermarket	subirmarkit (m)	سوبرماركت

bakery	maxbaz (m)	مخبز
baker	xabbāz (m)	خبّاز
cake shop	dukkān ḥalawāniy (m)	دكّان حلوانيّ
grocery shop	baqqāla (f)	بقّالة
butcher shop	malḥama (f)	ملحمة

| greengrocer | dukkān xuḍār (m) | دكّان خضار |
| market | sūq (f) | سوق |

coffee bar	kafé (m), maqha (m)	كافيه, مقهى
restaurant	maṭʻam (m)	مطعم
pub, bar	ḥāna (f)	حانة
pizzeria	maṭʻam pizza (m)	مطعم بيتزا

hairdresser	ṣālūn ḥilāqa (m)	صالون حلاقة
post office	maktab al barīd (m)	مكتب البريد
dry cleaners	tanzīf ȝaff (m)	تنظيف جافّ
photo studio	istūdiyu taṣwīr (m)	إستوديو تصوير

| shoe shop | maḥall aḥðiya (m) | محلّ أحذية |
| bookshop | maḥall kutub (m) | محلّ كتب |

sports shop	maḥall riyāḍiy (m)	محلّ رياضيّ
clothes repair shop	maḥall xiyāṭat malābis (m)	محلّ خياطة ملابس
formal wear hire	maḥall ta'ʒīr malābis rasmiyya (m)	محلّ تأجير ملابس رسمية
video rental shop	maḥal ta'ʒīr vidiyu (m)	محلّ تأجير فيديو
circus	sirk (m)	سيرك
zoo	ḥadīqat al ḥayawān (f)	حديقة حيوان
cinema	sinima (f)	سينما
museum	matḥaf (m)	متحف
library	maktaba (f)	مكتبة
theatre	masraḥ (m)	مسرح
opera (opera house)	ubra (f)	أوبرا
nightclub	malha layliy (m)	ملهى ليليّ
casino	kazinu (m)	كازينو
mosque	masʒid (m)	مسجد
synagogue	kanīs ma'bad yahūdiy (m)	كنيس معبد يهوديّ
cathedral	katidrā'iyya (f)	كاتدرائيّة
temple	ma'bad (m)	معبد
church	kanīsa (f)	كنيسة
college	kulliyya (m)	كلّيّة
university	ʒāmi'a (f)	جامعة
school	madrasa (f)	مدرسة
prefecture	muqāṭa'a (f)	مقاطعة
town hall	baladiyya (f)	بلديّة
hotel	funduq (m)	فندق
bank	bank (m)	بنك
embassy	safāra (f)	سفارة
travel agency	ʃarikat siyāḥa (f)	شركة سياحة
information office	maktab al isti'lāmāt (m)	مكتب الإستعلامات
currency exchange	ṣarrāfa (f)	صرّافة
underground, tube	mitru (m)	مترو
hospital	mustaʃfa (m)	مستشفى
petrol station	maḥaṭṭat banzīn (f)	محطّة بنزين
car park	mawqif as sayyārāt (m)	موقف السيّارات

80. Signs

signboard (store sign, etc.)	lāfita (f)	لافتة
notice (door sign, etc.)	bayān (m)	بيان
poster	mulṣaq i'lāniy (m)	ملصق إعلانيّ
direction sign	'alāmat ittiʒāh (f)	علامة إتّجاه
arrow (sign)	'alāmat iʃāra (f)	علامة إشارة
caution	taḥðīr (m)	تحذير
warning sign	lāfitat taḥðīr (f)	لافتة تحذير
to warn (vt)	ḥaððar	حذّر

rest day (weekly ~)	yawm 'utla (m)	يوم عطلة
timetable (schedule)	ʒadwal (m)	جدول
opening hours	awqāt al 'amal (pl)	أوقات العمل

WELCOME!	ahlan wa sahlan!	أهلًا وسهلًا
ENTRANCE	duxūl	دخول
WAY OUT	xurūʒ	خروج

PUSH	idfa'	إدفع
PULL	isḥab	إسحب
OPEN	maftūḥ	مفتوح
CLOSED	muɣlaq	مغلق

| WOMEN | lis sayyidāt | للسيدات |
| MEN | lir riʒāl | للرجال |

DISCOUNTS	xaṣm	خصم
SALE	taxfīḍāt	تخفيضات
NEW!	ʒadīd!	جديد!
FREE	maʒʒānan	مجّانًا

ATTENTION!	intibāh!	إنتباه!
NO VACANCIES	kull al amākin maḥʒūza	كل الأماكن محجوزة
RESERVED	maḥʒūz	محجوز

| ADMINISTRATION | idāra | إدارة |
| STAFF ONLY | lil 'āmilīn faqaṭ | للعاملين فقط |

BEWARE OF THE DOG!	iḥðar wuʒūd al kalb	إحذر وجود الكلب
NO SMOKING	mamnū' at tadxīn	ممنوع التدخين
DO NOT TOUCH!	'adam al lams	عدم اللمس

DANGEROUS	xaṭīr	خطير
DANGER	xaṭar	خطر
HIGH VOLTAGE	tayyār 'āli	تيّار عالي
NO SWIMMING!	as sibāḥa mamnū'a	السباحة ممنوعة
OUT OF ORDER	mu'aṭṭal	معطّل

FLAMMABLE	sarī' al iʃti'āl	سريع الإشتعال
FORBIDDEN	mamnū'	ممنوع
NO TRESPASSING!	mamnū' al murūr	ممنوع المرور
WET PAINT	iḥðar ṭilā' ɣayr ʒāff	إحذر طلاء غير جاف

81. Urban transport

bus, coach	bāṣ (m)	باص
tram	trām (m)	ترام
trolleybus	truli bāṣ (m)	ترولي باص
route (bus ~)	xaṭṭ (m)	خطّ
number (e.g. bus ~)	raqm (m)	رقم

to go by ...	rakib ...	ركب...
to get on (~ the bus)	rakib	ركب
to get off ...	nazil min	نزل من

stop (e.g. bus ~)	mawqif (m)	موقف
next stop	al mahaṭṭa al qādima (f)	المحطة القادمة
terminus	āxir mahaṭṭa (f)	آخر محطة
timetable	ʒadwal (m)	جدول
to wait (vt)	intazar	إنتظر

| ticket | taðkira (f) | تذكرة |
| fare | uʒra (f) | أجرة |

cashier (ticket seller)	ṣarrāf (m)	صرّاف
ticket inspection	taftīʃ taðkira (m)	تفتيش تذكرة
ticket inspector	mufattiʃ taðākir (m)	مفتّش تذاكر

to be late (for ...)	ta'axxar	تأخّر
to miss (~ the train, etc.)	ta'axxar	تأخّر
to be in a hurry	ista'ʒal	إستعجل

taxi, cab	taksi (m)	تاكسي
taxi driver	sā'iq taksi (m)	سائق تاكسي
by taxi	bit taksi	بالتاكسي
taxi rank	mawqif taksi (m)	موقف تاكسي
to call a taxi	kallam tāksi	كلّم تاكسي
to take a taxi	axað taksi	أخذ تاكسي

traffic	ḥarakat al murūr (f)	حركة المرور
traffic jam	zaḥmat al murūr (f)	زحمة المرور
rush hour	sā'at að ðurwa (f)	ساعة الذروة
to park (vi)	awqaf	أوقف
to park (vt)	awqaf	أوقف
car park	mawqif as sayyārāt (m)	موقف السيارات

underground, tube	mitru (m)	مترو
station	maḥaṭṭa (f)	محطة
to take the tube	rakib al mitru	ركب المترو
train	qiṭār (m)	قطار
train station	maḥaṭṭat qiṭār (f)	محطة قطار

82. Sightseeing

monument	timθāl (m)	تمثال
fortress	qalʕa (f), ḥiṣn (m)	قلعة، حصن
palace	qaṣr (m)	قصر
castle	qalʕa (f)	قلعة
tower	burʒ (m)	برج
mausoleum	ḍarīḥ (m)	ضريح

architecture	handasa mi'māriyya (f)	هندسة معماريّة
medieval (adj)	min al qurūn al wusṭa	من القرون الوسطى
ancient (adj)	qadīm	قديم
national (adj)	waṭaniy	وطني
famous (monument, etc.)	maʃhūr	مشهور

| tourist | sā'iḥ (m) | سائح |
| guide (person) | murʃid (m) | مرشد |

excursion, sightseeing tour	ʒawla (f)	جولة
to show (vt)	ʻaraḍ	عرض
to tell (vt)	ḥaddaθ	حدث

to find (vt)	waʒad	وجد
to get lost (lose one's way)	ḍāʻ	ضاع
map (e.g. underground ~)	xarīṭa (f)	خريطة
map (e.g. city ~)	xarīṭa (f)	خريطة

souvenir, gift	tiðkār (m)	تذكار
gift shop	maḥall hadāya (m)	محلّ هدايا
to take pictures	ṣawwar	صوّر
to have one's picture taken	taṣawwar	تصوّر

83. Shopping

to buy (purchase)	iʃtara	إشترى
shopping	ʃay' (m)	شيء
to go shopping	iʃtara	إشترى
shopping	ʃubinɣ (m)	شوبينغ

to be open (ab. shop)	maftūḥ	مفتوح
to be closed	muɣlaq	مغلق

footwear, shoes	aḥðiya (pl)	أحذية
clothes, clothing	malābis (pl)	ملابس
cosmetics	mawādd at taʒmīl (pl)	موادّ التجميل
food products	ma'kūlāt (pl)	مأكولات
gift, present	hadiyya (f)	هديّة

shop assistant (masc.)	bā'iʻ (m)	بائع
shop assistant (fem.)	bā'iʻa (f)	بائعة

cash desk	ṣundū' ad daf' (m)	صندوق الدفع
mirror	mir'āt (f)	مرآة
counter (shop ~)	minḍada (f)	منضدة
fitting room	ɣurfat al qiyās (f)	غرفة القياس

to try on	ʒarrab	جرّب
to fit (ab. dress, etc.)	nāsab	ناسب
to fancy (vt)	a'ʒab	أعجب

price	si'r (m)	سعر
price tag	tikit as si'r (m)	تيكت السعر
to cost (vt)	kallaf	كلّف
How much?	bikam?	بكم؟
discount	xaṣm (m)	خصم

inexpensive (adj)	ɣayr ɣāli	غير غال
cheap (adj)	raxīṣ	رخيص
expensive (adj)	ɣāli	غال
It's expensive	haða ɣāli	هذا غال
hire (n)	isti'ʒār (m)	إستئجار
to hire (~ a dinner jacket)	ista'ʒar	إستأجر

credit (trade credit)	i'timān (m)	إئتمان
on credit (adv)	bid dayn	بالدين

84. Money

money	nuqūd (pl)	نقود
currency exchange	taḥwīl 'umla (m)	تحويل عملة
exchange rate	si'r aṣ ṣarf (m)	سعر الصرف
cashpoint	ṣarrāf 'āliy (m)	صرّاف آليّ
coin	qiṭ'a naqdiyya (f)	قطعة نقديّة

dollar	dulār (m)	دولار
euro	yuru (m)	يورو

lira	lira iṭāliyya (f)	ليرة إيطالية
Deutschmark	mark almāniy (m)	مارك ألماني
franc	frank (m)	فرنك
pound sterling	ʒunayh istirlīniy (m)	جنيه استرلينيّ
yen	yīn (m)	ين

debt	dayn (m)	دين
debtor	mudīn (m)	مدين
to lend (money)	sallaf	سلّف
to borrow (vi, vt)	istalaf	إستلف

bank	bank (m)	بنك
account	ḥisāb (m)	حساب
to deposit (vt)	awda'	أودع
to deposit into the account	awda' fil ḥisāb	أودع في الحساب
to withdraw (vt)	saḥab min al ḥisāb	سحب من الحساب

credit card	biṭāqat i'timān (f)	بطاقة إئتمان
cash	nuqūd (pl)	نقود
cheque	ʃīk (m)	شيك
to write a cheque	katab ʃīk	كتب شيكًا
chequebook	daftar ʃīkāt (m)	دفتر شيكات

wallet	maḥfaẓat ʒīb (f)	محفظة جيب
purse	maḥfaẓat fakka (f)	محفظة فكّة
safe	xizāna (f)	خزانة

heir	wāris (m)	وارث
inheritance	wirāθa (f)	وراثة
fortune (wealth)	θarwa (f)	ثروة

lease	'īʒār (m)	إيجار
rent (money)	uʒrat as sakan (f)	أجرة السكن
to rent (sth from sb)	ista'ʒar	إستأجر

price	si'r (m)	سعر
cost	θaman (m)	ثمن
sum	mablaɣ (m)	مبلغ
to spend (vt)	ṣaraf	صرف
expenses	maṣārīf (pl)	مصاريف

| to economize (vi, vt) | waffar | وفّر |
| economical | muwaffir | موفّر |

to pay (vi, vt)	dafaʿ	دفع
payment	dafʿ (m)	دفع
change (give the ~)	al bāqi (m)	الباقي

tax	ḍarība (f)	ضريبة
fine	yarāma (f)	غرامة
to fine (vt)	faraḍ yarāma	فرض غرامة

85. Post. Postal service

post office	maktab al barīd (m)	مكتب البريد
post (letters, etc.)	al barīd (m)	البريد
postman	sāʾi al barīd (m)	ساعي البريد
opening hours	awqāt al ʿamal (pl)	أوقات العمل

letter	risāla (f)	رسالة
registered letter	risāla musaʒʒala (f)	رسالة مسجّلة
postcard	biṭāqa barīdiyya (f)	بطاقة بريديّة
telegram	barqiyya (f)	برقيّة
parcel	ṭard (m)	طرد
money transfer	ḥawāla māliyya (f)	حوالة ماليّة

to receive (vt)	istalam	إستلم
to send (vt)	arsal	أرسل
sending	irsāl (m)	إرسال

address	ʿunwān (m)	عنوان
postcode	raqm al barīd (m)	رقم البريد
sender	mursil (m)	مرسل
receiver	mursal ilayh (m)	مرسل إليه

| name (first name) | ism (m) | إسم |
| surname (last name) | ism al ʿāʾila (m) | إسم العائلة |

postage rate	taʿrīfa (f)	تعريفة
standard (adj)	ʿādiy	عاديّ
economical (adj)	muwaffir	موفّر

weight	wazn (m)	وزن
to weigh (~ letters)	wazan	وزن
envelope	ẓarf (m)	ظرف
postage stamp	ṭābiʿ (m)	طابع
to stamp an envelope	alṣaq ṭābiʿ	ألصق طابعا

Dwelling. House. Home

86. House. Dwelling

house	bayt (m)	بيت
at home (adv)	fil bayt	في البيت
yard	finā' (m)	فناء
fence (iron ~)	sūr (m)	سور
brick (n)	ṭūb (m)	طوب
brick (as adj)	min aṭ ṭūb	من الطوب
stone (n)	haʒar (m)	حجر
stone (as adj)	haʒariy	حجريّ
concrete (n)	xarasāna (f)	خرسانة
concrete (as adj)	xarasāniy	خرسانيّ
new (new-built)	ʒadīd	جديد
old (adj)	qadīm	قديم
decrepit (house)	'āyil lis suqūṭ	آيل للسقوط
modern (adj)	mu'āṣir	معاصر
multistorey (adj)	muta'addid aṭ ṭawābiq	متعدّد الطوابق
tall (~ building)	'āli	عال
floor, storey	ṭābiq (m)	طابق
single-storey (adj)	ðu ṭābiq wāhid	ذو طابق واحد
ground floor	ṭābiq sufliy (m)	طابق سفليّ
top floor	ṭābiq 'ulwiy (m)	طابق علويّ
roof	saqf (m)	سقف
chimney	madxana (f)	مدخنة
roof tiles	qirmīd (m)	قرميد
tiled (adj)	min al qirmīd	من القرميد
loft (attic)	'ullayya (f)	علّية
window	ʃubbāk (m)	شبّاك
glass	zuʒāʒ (m)	زجاج
window ledge	raff ʃubbāk (f)	رف شبّاك
shutters	darf ʃubbāk (m)	درف شبّاك
wall	hā'iṭ (m)	حائط
balcony	ʃurfa (f)	شرفة
downpipe	masūrat at taṣrīf (f)	ماسورة التصريف
upstairs (to be ~)	fawq	فوق
to go upstairs	ṣa'ad	صعد
to come down (the stairs)	nazil	نزل
to move (to new premises)	intaqal	إنتقل

87. House. Entrance. Lift

entrance	madχal (m)	مدخل
stairs (stairway)	sullam (m)	سلّم
steps	daraʒāt (pl)	درجات
banisters	drabizīn (m)	درابزين
lobby (hotel ~)	ṣāla (f)	صالة

postbox	ṣundūq al barīd (m)	صندوق البريد
waste bin	ṣundūq az zubāla (m)	صندوق الزبالة
refuse chute	manfað að ðubāla (m)	منفذ الزبالة

lift	miṣʿad (m)	مصعد
goods lift	miṣʿad aʃʃaḥn (m)	مصعد الشحن
lift cage	kabīna (f)	كابينة
to take the lift	rakib al miṣʿad	ركب المصعد

flat	ʃaqqa (f)	شقّة
residents (~ of a building)	sukkān al 'imāra (pl)	سكّان العمارة
neighbour (masc.)	ʒār (m)	جار
neighbour (fem.)	ʒāra (f)	جارة
neighbours	ʒirān (pl)	جيران

88. House. Electricity

electricity	kahrabā' (m)	كهرباء
light bulb	lamba (f)	لمبة
switch	miftāḥ (m)	مفتاح
fuse (plug fuse)	fāṣima (f)	فاصمة

cable, wire (electric ~)	silk (m)	سلك
wiring	aslāk (pl)	أسلاك
electricity meter	'addād (m)	عدّاد
readings	qirā'a (f)	قراءة

89. House. Doors. Locks

door	bāb (m)	باب
gate (vehicle ~)	bawwāba (f)	بوّابة
handle, doorknob	qabḍat al bāb (f)	قبضة الباب
to unlock (unbolt)	fataḥ	فتح
to open (vt)	fataḥ	فتح
to close (vt)	aγlaq	أغلق

key	miftāḥ (m)	مفتاح
bunch (of keys)	rabṭa (f)	ربطة
to creak (door, etc.)	ṣarr	صرّ
creak	ṣarīr (m)	صرير
hinge (door ~)	mufaṣṣala (f)	مفصّلة
doormat	siʒāda (f)	سجادة
door lock	qifl al bāb (m)	قفل الباب

keyhole	θaqb al bāb (m)	ثقب الباب
crossbar (sliding bar)	tirbās (m)	ترباس
door latch	mizlāӡ (m)	مزلاج
padlock	qifl (m)	قفل

to ring (~ the door bell)	rann	رنّ
ringing (sound)	ranīn (m)	رنين
doorbell	ӡaras (m)	جرس
doorbell button	zirr (m)	زرّ
knock (at the door)	ṭarq, daqq (m)	طرق, دقّ
to knock (vi)	daqq	دقّ

code	kūd (m)	كود
combination lock	kūd (m)	كود
intercom	ӡaras al bāb (m)	جرس الباب
number (on the door)	raqm (m)	رقم
doorplate	lawḥa (f)	لوحة
peephole	al 'ayn as siḥriyya (m)	العين السحريّة

90. Country house

village	qarya (f)	قرية
vegetable garden	bustān xuḍār (m)	بستان خضار
fence	sūr (m)	سور
picket fence	sūr (m)	سور
wicket gate	bawwāba far'iyya (f)	بوّابة فرعيّة

granary	ʃawna (f)	شونة
cellar	sirdāb (m)	سرداب
shed (garden ~)	saqīfa (f)	سقيفة
water well	bi'r (m)	بئر

stove (wood-fired ~)	furn (m)	فرن
to stoke the stove	awqad	أوقد
firewood	ḥaṭab (m)	حطب
log (firewood)	qiṭ'at ḥaṭab (f)	قطعة حطب

veranda	virānda (f)	فيراندة
deck (terrace)	ʃurfa (f)	شرفة
stoop (front steps)	sullam (m)	سلّم
swing (hanging seat)	urӡūḥa (f)	أرجوحة

91. Villa. Mansion

country house	bayt rīfiy (m)	بيت ريفيّ
country-villa	villa (f)	فيلا
wing (~ of a building)	ӡanāḥ (m)	جناح

garden	ḥadīqa (f)	حديقة
park	ḥadīqa (f)	حديقة
conservatory (greenhouse)	dafī'a (f)	دفيئة
to look after (garden, etc.)	ihtamm	إهتمّ

swimming pool	masbaḥ (m)	مسبح
gym (home gym)	qā'at at tamrīnāt (f)	قاعة التمرينات
tennis court	mal'ab tinis (m)	ملعب تنس
home theater (room)	sinima manziliyya (f)	سينما منزليّة
garage	qarāჳ (m)	جراج
private property	milkiyya χāṣṣa (f)	ملكيّة خاصّة
private land	arḍ χāṣṣa (m)	أرض خاصّة
warning (caution)	taḥðīr (m)	تحذير
warning sign	lāfitat taḥðīr (f)	لافتة تحذير
security	ḥirāsa (f)	حراسة
security guard	ḥāris amn (m)	حارس أمن
burglar alarm	ჳihāð inðār (m)	جهاز انذار

92. Castle. Palace

castle	qal'a (f)	قلعة
palace	qaṣr (m)	قصر
fortress	qal'a (f), ḥiṣn (m)	قلعة، حصن
wall (round castle)	sūr (m)	سور
tower	burჳ (m)	برج
keep, donjon	burჳ ra'īsiy (m)	برج رئيسيّ
portcullis	bāb mutaḥarrik (m)	باب متحرّك
subterranean passage	sirdāb (m)	سرداب
moat	χandaq mā'iy (m)	خندق مائيّ
chain	silsila (f)	سلسلة
arrow loop	mazɣal (m)	مزغل
magnificent (adj)	rā'i'	رائع
majestic (adj)	muhīb	مهيب
impregnable (adj)	manī'	منيع
medieval (adj)	min al qurūn al wusṭa	من القرون الوسطى

93. Flat

flat	ʃaqqa (f)	شقّة
room	ɣurfa (f)	غرفة
bedroom	ɣurfat an nawm (f)	غرفة النوم
dining room	ɣurfat il akl (f)	غرفة الأكل
living room	ṣālat al istiqbāl (f)	صالة الإستقبال
study (home office)	maktab (m)	مكتب
entry room	madχal (m)	مدخل
bathroom	ḥammām (m)	حمّام
water closet	ḥammām (m)	حمّام
ceiling	saqf (m)	سقف
floor	arḍ (f)	أرض
corner	zāwiya (f)	زاوية

94. Flat. Cleaning

to clean (vi, vt)	naẓẓaf	نظّف
to put away (to stow)	ʃāl	شال
dust	ɣubār (m)	غبار
dusty (adj)	muɣabbar	مغبّر
to dust (vt)	masaḥ al ɣubār	مسح الغبار
vacuum cleaner	miknasa kahrabā'iyya (f)	مكنسة كهربائيّة
to vacuum (vt)	naẓẓaf bi miknasa kahrabā'iyya	نظّف بمكنسة كهربائيّة

to sweep (vi, vt)	kanas	كنس
sweepings	qumāma (f)	قمامة
order	niẓām (m)	نظام
disorder, mess	'adam an niẓām (m)	عدم النظام

mop	mimsaḥa ṭawīla (f)	ممسحة طويلة
duster	mimsaḥa (f)	ممسحة
short broom	miqaʃʃa (f)	مقشّة
dustpan	ʒārūf (m)	جاروف

95. Furniture. Interior

furniture	aθāθ (m)	أثاث
table	maktab (m)	مكتب
chair	kursiy (m)	كرسيّ
bed	sarīr (m)	سرير
sofa, settee	kanaba (f)	كنبة
armchair	kursiy (m)	كرسيّ

bookcase	xizānat kutub (f)	خزانة كتب
shelf	raff (m)	رفّ

wardrobe	dūlāb (m)	دولاب
coat rack (wall-mounted ~)	ʃammā'a (f)	شمّاعة
coat stand	ʃammā'a (f)	شمّاعة

chest of drawers	dulāb adrāʒ (m)	دولاب أدراج
coffee table	ṭāwilat al qahwa (f)	طاولة القهوة

mirror	mir'āt (f)	مرآة
carpet	siʒāda (f)	سجادة
small carpet	siʒāda (f)	سجادة

fireplace	midfa'a ḥā'iṭiyya (f)	مدفأة حائطيّة
candle	ʃam'a (f)	شمعة
candlestick	ʃam'adān (m)	شمعدان

drapes	satā'ir (pl)	ستائر
wallpaper	waraq ḥī'ṭān (m)	ورق حيطان
blinds (jalousie)	haṣīrat ʃubbāk (f)	حصيرة شبّاك
table lamp	miṣbāḥ aṭ ṭāwila (m)	مصباح الطاولة
wall lamp (sconce)	miṣbāḥ al ḥā'iṭ (f)	مصباح الحائط

standard lamp	miṣbāḥ arḍiy (m)	مصباح أرضيّ
chandelier	naʒafa (f)	نجفة

leg (of a chair, table)	riʒl (f)	رجل
armrest	masnad (m)	مسند
back (backrest)	masnad (m)	مسند
drawer	durʒ (m)	درج

96. Bedding

bedclothes	bayāḍāt as sarīr (pl)	بياضات السرير
pillow	wisāda (f)	وسادة
pillowslip	kīs al wisāda (m)	كيس الوسادة
duvet	baṭṭāniyya (f)	بطّانيّة
sheet	milāya (f)	ملاية
bedspread	ɣiṭā' as sarīr (m)	غطاء السرير

97. Kitchen

kitchen	maṭbaχ (m)	مطبخ
gas	ɣāz (m)	غاز
gas cooker	butuɣāz (m)	بوتوغاز
electric cooker	furn kaharabā'iy (m)	فرن كهربائيّ
oven	furn (m)	فرن
microwave oven	furn al mikruwayv (m)	فرن الميكروويف

refrigerator	θallāʒa (f)	ثلاجة
freezer	frīzir (m)	فريزر
dishwasher	ɣassāla (f)	غسّالة

mincer	farrāmat laḥm (f)	فرّامة لحم
juicer	'aṣṣāra (f)	عصّارة
toaster	maḥmaṣat χubz (f)	محمصة خبز
mixer	χallāṭ (m)	خلّاط

coffee machine	mākinat ṣan' al qahwa (f)	ماكينة صنع القهوة
coffee pot	kanaka (f)	كنكة
coffee grinder	maṭḥanat qahwa (f)	مطحنة قهوة

kettle	barrād (m)	برّاد
teapot	barrād aʃ ʃāy (m)	برّاد الشاي
lid	ɣiṭā' (m)	غطاء
tea strainer	miṣfāt (f)	مصفاة

spoon	mil'aqa (f)	ملعقة
teaspoon	mil'aqat ʃāy (f)	ملعقة شاي
soup spoon	mil'aqa kabīra (f)	ملعقة كبيرة
fork	ʃawka (f)	شوكة
knife	sikkīn (m)	سكّين

tableware (dishes)	ṣuḥūn (pl)	صحون
plate (dinner ~)	ṭabaq (m)	طبق

saucer	ṭabaq finʒān (m)	طبق فنجان
shot glass	ka's (f)	كأس
glass (tumbler)	kubbāya (f)	كبّاية
cup	finʒān (m)	فنجان
sugar bowl	sukkariyya (f)	سكّريّة
salt cellar	mamlaḥa (f)	مملحة
pepper pot	mabhara (f)	مبهرة
butter dish	ṣuḥn zubda (m)	صحن زبدة
stock pot (soup pot)	kassirūlla (f)	كاسرولة
frying pan (skillet)	ṭāsa (f)	طاسة
ladle	miɣrafa (f)	مغرفة
colander	miṣfāt (f)	مصفاة
tray (serving ~)	sīniyya (f)	صينيّة
bottle	zuʒāʒa (f)	زجاجة
jar (glass)	barṭamān (m)	برطمان
tin (can)	tanaka (f)	تنكة
bottle opener	fattāḥa (f)	فتّاحة
tin opener	fattāḥa (f)	فتّاحة
corkscrew	barrīma (f)	بريمة
filter	filtir (m)	فلتر
to filter (vt)	ṣaffa	صفّى
waste (food ~, etc.)	zubāla (f)	زبالة
waste bin (kitchen ~)	ṣundūq az zubāla (m)	صندوق الزبالة

98. Bathroom

bathroom	ḥammām (m)	حمّام
water	mā' (m)	ماء
tap	ḥanafiyya (f)	حنفيّة
hot water	mā' sāxin (m)	ماء ساخن
cold water	mā' bārid (m)	ماء بارد
toothpaste	ma'ʒūn asnān (m)	معجون أسنان
to clean one's teeth	nazzaf al asnān	نظّف الأسنان
toothbrush	furʃat asnān (f)	فرشة أسنان
to shave (vi)	ḥalaq	حلق
shaving foam	raɣwa lil ḥilāqa (f)	رغوة للحلاقة
razor	mūs ḥilāqa (m)	موس حلاقة
to wash (one's hands, etc.)	ɣasal	غسل
to have a bath	istaḥamm	إستحمّ
shower	dūʃ (m)	دوش
to have a shower	axað ad duʃ	أخذ الدش
bath	ḥawd istiḥmām (m)	حوض استحمام
toilet (toilet bowl)	mirḥād (m)	مرحاض
sink (washbasin)	ḥawd (m)	حوض
soap	ṣābūn (m)	صابون

soap dish	ṣabbāna (f)	صبّانة
sponge	līfa (f)	ليفة
shampoo	ʃāmbū (m)	شامبو
towel	fūṭa (f)	فوطة
bathrobe	θawb ḥammām (m)	ثوب حمّام

laundry (laundering)	ɣasīl (m)	غسيل
washing machine	ɣassāla (f)	غسّالة
to do the laundry	ɣasal al malābis	غسل الملابس
washing powder	masḥūq ɣasīl (m)	مسحوق غسيل

99. Household appliances

TV, telly	tilivizyūn (m)	تليفزيون
tape recorder	ʒihāz tasʒīl (m)	جهاز تسجيل
video	ʒihāz tasʒīl vidiyu (m)	جهاز تسجيل فيديو
radio	ʒihāz radiyu (m)	جهاز راديو
player (CD, MP3, etc.)	blayir (m)	بلِيير

video projector	'āriḍ vidiyu (m)	عارض فيديو
home cinema	sinima manziliyya (f)	سينما منزلِيّة
DVD player	di vi di (m)	دي في دي
amplifier	mukabbir aṣ ṣawt (m)	مكبّر الصوت
video game console	'atāri (m)	أتاري

video camera	kamira vidiyu (f)	كاميرا فيديو
camera (photo)	kamira (f)	كاميرا
digital camera	kamira diʒital (f)	كاميرا ديجيتال

vacuum cleaner	miknasa kahrabā'iyya (f)	مكنسة كهربائِيّة
iron (e.g. steam ~)	makwāt (f)	مكواة
ironing board	lawḥat kayy (f)	لوحة كيّ

telephone	hātif (m)	هاتف
mobile phone	hātif maḥmūl (m)	هاتف محمول
typewriter	'āla katiba (f)	آلة كاتبة
sewing machine	'ālat al ɣiyāṭa (f)	آلة الخياطة

microphone	mikrufūn (m)	ميكروفون
headphones	sammā'āt ra'siya (pl)	سمّاعات رأسِيّة
remote control (TV)	rimuwt kuntrūl (m)	ريموت كنترول

CD, compact disc	si di (m)	سي دي
cassette, tape	ʃarīṭ (m)	شريط
vinyl record	usṭuwāna (f)	أسطوانة

100. Repairs. Renovation

renovations	taʒdīdāt (m)	تجديدات
to renovate (vt)	ʒaddad	جدّد
to repair, to fix (vt)	aṣlaḥ	أصلح
to put in order	naẓẓam	نظّم

to redo (do again)	a'ād	أعاد
paint	dihān (m)	دهان
to paint (~ a wall)	dahan	دهن
house painter	dahhān (m)	دهّان
paintbrush	furʃat lit talwīn (f)	فرشة للتلوين
whitewash	maḥlūl mubayyiḍ (m)	محلول مبيّض
to whitewash (vt)	bayyaḍ	بيّض
wallpaper	waraq ḥīʈān (m)	ورق حيطان
to wallpaper (vt)	laṣaq waraq al ḥīʈān	لصق ورق الحيطان
varnish	warnīʃ (m)	ورنيش
to varnish (vt)	ṭala bil warnīʃ	طلى بالورنيش

101. Plumbing

water	mā' (m)	ماء
hot water	mā' sāχin (m)	ماء ساخن
cold water	mā' bārid (m)	ماء بارد
tap	ḥanafiyya (f)	حنفيّة
drop (of water)	qaṭara (f)	قطرة
to drip (vi)	qaṭar	قطر
to leak (ab. pipe)	sarab	سرب
leak (pipe ~)	tasarrub (m)	تسرّب
puddle	birka (f)	بركة
pipe	māsūra (f)	ماسورة
valve (e.g., ball ~)	ṣimām (m)	صمام
to be clogged up	kān masdūdan	كان مسدودًا
tools	adawāt (pl)	أدوات
adjustable spanner	miftāḥ inʒlīziy (m)	مفتاح إنجليزيّ
to unscrew (lid, filter, etc.)	fataḥ	فتح
to screw (tighten)	aḥkam aʃ ʃadd	أحكم الشدّ
to unclog (vt)	sallak	سلّك
plumber	sabbāk (m)	سبّاك
basement	sirdāb (m)	سرداب
sewerage (system)	ʃabakit il maʒāry (f)	شبكة مياه المجاري

102. Fire. Conflagration

fire (accident)	ḥarīq (m)	حريق
flame	ʃu'la (f)	شعلة
spark	ʃarāra (f)	شرارة
smoke (from fire)	duχān (m)	دخان
torch (flaming stick)	ʃu'la (f)	شعلة
campfire	nār muχayyam (m)	نار مخيّم
petrol	banzīn (m)	بنزين
paraffin	kirusīn (m)	كيروسين

flammable (adj)	qābil lil ihtirāq	قابل للإحتراق
explosive (adj)	mutafaʒʒir	متفجّر
NO SMOKING	mamnū' at tadχīn	ممنوع التدخين
safety	amn (m)	أمن
danger	χaṭar (m)	خطر
dangerous (adj)	χaṭīr	خطير
to catch fire	iʃta'al	إشتعل
explosion	infiʒār (m)	إنفجار
to set fire	aʃal an nār	أشعل النار
arsonist	muʃ'il harīq (m)	مشعل حريق
arson	ihrāq (m)	إحراق
to blaze (vi)	talahhab	تلهّب
to burn (be on fire)	ihtaraq	إحترق
to burn down	ihtaraq	إحترق
to call the fire brigade	istad'a qism al harīq	إستدعى قسم الحريق
firefighter, fireman	raʒul iṭfā' (m)	رجل إطفاء
fire engine	sayyārat iṭfā' (f)	سيّارة إطفاء
fire brigade	qism iṭfā' (m)	قسم إطفاء
fire engine ladder	sullam iṭfā' (m)	سلّم إطفاء
fire hose	χarṭūm al mā' (m)	خرطوم الماء
fire extinguisher	miṭfa'at harīq (f)	مطفأة حريق
helmet	χūða (f)	خوذة
siren	ṣaffārat inðār (f)	صفّارة إنذار
to cry (for help)	ṣaraχ	صرخ
to call for help	istaγāθ	إستغاث
rescuer	munqið (m)	منقذ
to rescue (vt)	anqað	أنقذ
to arrive (vi)	waṣal	وصل
to extinguish (vt)	aṭfa'	أطفأ
water	mā' (m)	ماء
sand	raml (m)	رمل
ruins (destruction)	hiṭām (pl)	حطام
to collapse (building, etc.)	inhār	إنهار
to fall down (vi)	inhār	إنهار
to cave in (ceiling, floor)	inhār	إنهار
piece of debris	hiṭma (f)	حطمة
ash	ramād (m)	رماد
to suffocate (die)	iχtanaq	إختنق
to be killed (perish)	halak	هلك

HUMAN ACTIVITIES

Job. Business. Part 1

103. Office. Working in the office

office (company ~)	maktab (m)	مكتب
office (director's ~)	maktab (m)	مكتب
reception desk	istiqbāl (m)	إستقبال
secretary	sikirtīr (m)	سكرتير

director	mudīr (m)	مدير
manager	mudīr (m)	مدير
accountant	muḥāsib (m)	محاسب
employee	muwaẓẓaf (m)	موظف

furniture	aθāθ (m)	أثاث
desk	maktab (m)	مكتب
desk chair	kursiy (m)	كرسيّ
drawer unit	waḥdat adrāʒ (f)	وحدة أدراج
coat stand	ʃammāʻa (f)	شمّاعة

computer	kumbyūtir (m)	كمبيوتر
printer	ṭābiʻa (f)	طابعة
fax machine	faks (m)	فاكس
photocopier	ʼālat nasχ (f)	آلة نسخ

paper	waraq (m)	ورق
office supplies	adawāt al kitāba (pl)	أدوات الكتابة
mouse mat	wisādat faʼra (f)	وسادة فأرة
sheet of paper	waraqa (f)	ورقة
binder	malaff (m)	ملفّ

catalogue	fihris (m)	فهرس
phone directory	dalīl at tilifūn (m)	دليل التليفون
documentation	waθāʼiq (pl)	وثائق
brochure (e.g. 12 pages ~)	naʃra (f)	نشرة
leaflet (promotional ~)	manʃūr (m)	منشور
sample	namūðaʒ (m)	نموذج

training meeting	iʒtimāʻ tadrīb (m)	إجتماع تدريب
meeting (of managers)	iʒtimāʻ (m)	إجتماع
lunch time	fatrat al ɣadāʼ (f)	فترة الغذاء

to make a copy	ṣawwar	صوّر
to make multiple copies	ṣawwar	صوّر
to receive a fax	istalam faks	إستلم فاكس
to send a fax	arsal faks	أرسل فاكس
to call (by phone)	ittaṣal	إتصل

| to answer (vt) | radd | رَدَّ |
| to put through | waṣṣal | وصّل |

to arrange, to set up	ḥaddad	حدّد
to demonstrate (vt)	'araḍ	عرض
to be absent	ɣāb	غاب
absence	ɣiyāb (m)	غياب

104. Business processes. Part 1

occupation	ʃuɣl (m)	شغل
firm	ʃarika (f)	شركة
company	ʃarika (f)	شركة
corporation	mu'assasa tiʒāriyya (f)	مؤسسة تجارية
enterprise	ʃarika (f)	شركة
agency	wikāla (f)	وكالة

agreement (contract)	ittifāqiyya (f)	إتّفاقيّة
contract	'aqd (m)	عقد
deal	ṣafqa (f)	صفقة
order (to place an ~)	ṭalab (m)	طلب
terms (of the contract)	ʃarṭ (m)	شرط

wholesale (adv)	bil ʒumla	بالجملة
wholesale (adj)	al ʒumla	الجملة
wholesale (n)	bay' bil ʒumla (m)	بيع بالجملة
retail (adj)	at taʒzi'a	التجزئة
retail (n)	bay' bit taʒzi'a (m)	بيع بالتجزئة

competitor	munāfis (m)	منافس
competition	munāfasa (f)	منافسة
to compete (vi)	nāfas	نافس

| partner (associate) | ʃarīk (m) | شريك |
| partnership | ʃirāka (f) | شراكة |

crisis	azma (f)	أزمة
bankruptcy	iflās (m)	إفلاس
to go bankrupt	aflas	أفلس
difficulty	ṣu'ūba (f)	صعوبة
problem	muʃkila (f)	مشكلة
catastrophe	kāriθa (f)	كارثة

economy	iqtiṣād (m)	إقتصاد
economic (~ growth)	iqtiṣādiy	إقتصاديّ
economic recession	rukūd iqtiṣādiy (m)	ركود إقتصاديّ

| goal (aim) | hadaf (m) | هدف |
| task | muhimma (f) | مهمّة |

to trade (vi)	tāʒir	تاجر
network (distribution ~)	ʃabaka (f)	شبكة
inventory (stock)	al maxzūn (m)	المخزون
range (assortment)	taʃkīla (f)	تشكيلة

leader (leading company)	qā'id (m)	قائد
large (~ company)	kabīr	كبير
monopoly	iḥtikār (m)	إحتكار

theory	naẓariyya (f)	نظريّة
practice	mumārasa (f)	ممارسة
experience (in my ~)	xibra (f)	خبرة
trend (tendency)	ittiʒāh (m)	إتّجاه
development	tanmiya (f)	تنمية

105. Business processes. Part 2

| profit (foregone ~) | ribḥ (m) | ربح |
| profitable (~ deal) | murbiḥ | مربح |

delegation (group)	wafd (m)	وفد
salary	murattab (m)	مرتّب
to correct (an error)	ṣaḥḥaḥ	صحّح
business trip	riḥlat 'amal (f)	رحلة عمل
commission	laʒna (f)	لجنة

to control (vt)	taḥakkam	تحكّم
conference	mu'tamar (m)	مؤتمر
licence	ruxṣa (f)	رخصة
reliable (~ partner)	mawθūq	موثوق

initiative (undertaking)	mubādara (f)	مبادرة
norm (standard)	mi'yār (m)	معيار
circumstance	ẓarf (m)	ظرف
duty (of an employee)	wāʒib (m)	واجب

organization (company)	munaẓẓama (f)	منظّمة
organization (process)	tanẓīm (m)	تنظيم
organized (adj)	munaẓẓam	منظّم
cancellation	ilɣā' (m)	إلغاء
to cancel (call off)	alɣa	ألغى
report (official ~)	taqrīr (m)	تقرير

patent	bara'at al ixtirā' (f)	براءة الإختراع
to patent (obtain patent)	saʒʒal barā'at al ixtirā'	سجّل براءة الإختراع
to plan (vt)	xaṭṭaṭ	خطّط

bonus (money)	'ilāwa (f)	علاوة
professional (adj)	mihaniy	مهنيّ
procedure	iʒrā' (m)	إجراء

to examine (contract, etc.)	baḥaθ	بحث
calculation	ḥisāb (m)	حساب
reputation	sum'a (f)	سمعة
risk	muxāṭara (f)	مخاطرة

to manage, to run	adār	أدار
information (report)	ma'lūmāt (pl)	معلومات
property	milkiyya (f)	ملكيّة

union	ittiḥād (m)	إتّحاد
life insurance	ta'mīn 'alal ḥayāt (m)	تأمين على الحياة
to insure (vt)	amman	أمّن
insurance	ta'mīn (m)	تأمين
auction (~ sale)	mazād (m)	مزاد
to notify (inform)	ablaɣ	أبلغ
management (process)	idāra (f)	إدارة
service (~ industry)	χidma (f)	خدمة
forum	nadwa (f)	ندوة
to function (vi)	adda waẓīfa	أدّى وظيفته
stage (phase)	marḥala (f)	مرحلة
legal (~ services)	qānūniy	قانونيّ
lawyer (legal advisor)	muḥāmi (m)	محام

106. Production. Works

plant	maṣna' (m)	مصنع
factory	maṣna' (m)	مصنع
workshop	warʃa (f)	ورشة
works, production site	maṣna' (m)	مصنع
industry (manufacturing)	ṣinā'a (f)	صناعة
industrial (adj)	ṣinā'iy	صناعيّ
heavy industry	ṣinā'a θaqīla (f)	صناعة ثقيلة
light industry	ṣinā'a χafīfa (f)	صناعة خفيفة
products	muntaʒāt (pl)	منتجات
to produce (vt)	antaʒ	أنتج
raw materials	mawādd χām (pl)	موادّ خام
foreman (construction ~)	ra'īs al 'ummāl (m)	رئيس العمّال
workers team (crew)	farīq al 'ummāl (m)	فريق العمّال
worker	'āmil (m)	عامل
working day	yawm 'amal (m)	يوم عمل
pause (rest break)	rāḥa (f)	راحة
meeting	iʒtimā' (m)	إجتماع
to discuss (vt)	nāqaʃ	ناقش
plan	χiṭṭa (f)	خطّة
to fulfil the plan	naffað al χuṭṭa	نفّذ الخطّة
rate of output	mu'addal al intāʒ (m)	معدّل الإنتاج
quality	ʒawda (f)	جودة
control (checking)	taftīʃ (m)	تفتيش
quality control	ḍabṭ al ʒawda (m)	ضبط الجودة
workplace safety	salāmat makān al 'amal (f)	سلامة مكان العمل
discipline	indibāṭ (m)	إنضباط
violation (of safety rules, etc.)	muχālafa (f)	مخالفة
to violate (rules)	χālaf	خالف
strike	idrāb (m)	إضراب
striker	mudrib (m)	مضرب

to be on strike	aḍrab	أضرب
trade union	ittiḥād al ʿummāl (m)	إتّحاد العمّال
to invent (machine, etc.)	iχtaraʿ	إخترع
invention	iχtirāʿ (m)	إختراع
research	baḥθ (m)	بحث
to improve (make better)	ḥassan	حسّن
technology	tiknulūʒiya (f)	تكنولوجيا
technical drawing	rasm taqniy (m)	رسم تقنيّ
load, cargo	ʃaḥn (m)	شحن
loader (person)	ḥammāl (m)	حمّال
to load (vehicle, etc.)	ʃaḥan	شحن
loading (process)	taḥmīl (m)	تحميل
to unload (vi, vt)	afraɣ	أفرغ
unloading	ifrāɣ (m)	إفراغ
transport	wasāʾil an naql (pl)	وسائل النقل
transport company	ʃarikat naql (f)	شركة نقل
to transport (vt)	naqal	نقل
wagon	ʿarabat ʃaḥn (f)	عربة شحن
tank (e.g., oil ~)	χazzān (m)	خزّان
lorry	ʃāḥina (f)	شاحنة
machine tool	mākina (f)	ماكنة
mechanism	ʾāliyya (f)	آليّة
industrial waste	muχallafāt ṣināʿiyya (pl)	مخلّفات صناعية
packing (process)	taʿbiʾa (f)	تعبئة
to pack (vt)	ʿabbaʾ	عبّأ

107. Contract. Agreement

contract	ʿaqd (m)	عقد
agreement	ittifāq (m)	إتّفاق
addendum	mulḥaq (m)	ملحق
to sign a contract	waqqaʿ ʿala ʿaqd	وقّع على عقد
signature	tawqīʿ (m)	توقيع
to sign (vt)	waqqaʿ	وقّع
seal (stamp)	χatm (m)	ختم
subject of the contract	mawḍūʿ al ʿaqd (m)	موضوع العقد
clause	band (m)	بند
parties (in contract)	aṭrāf (pl)	أطراف
legal address	ʿunwān qānūniy (m)	عنوان قانوني
to violate the contract	χālaf al ʿaqd	خالف العقد
commitment (obligation)	iltizām (m)	إلتزام
responsibility	masʾūliyya (f)	مسؤوليّة
force majeure	quwwa qāhira (m)	قوّة قاهرة
dispute	χilāf (m)	خلاف
penalties	ʿuqūbāt (pl)	عقوبات

108. Import & Export

import	istīrād (m)	إستيراد
importer	mustawrid (m)	مستورد
to import (vt)	istawrad	إستورد
import (as adj.)	wārid	وارد
export (exportation)	taṣdīr (m)	تصدير
exporter	muṣaddir (m)	مصدّر
to export (vt)	ṣaddar	صدّر
export (as adj.)	sādir	صادر
goods (merchandise)	baḍā'i' (pl)	بضائع
consignment, lot	ʃaḥna (f)	شحنة
weight	wazn (m)	وزن
volume	ḥaʒm (m)	حجم
cubic metre	mitr muka''ab (m)	متر مكعّب
manufacturer	aʃ ʃarika al muṣni'a (f)	الشركة المصنعة
transport company	ʃarikat naql (f)	شركة نقل
container	ḥāwiya (f)	حاوية
border	ḥadd (m)	حدّ
customs	ʒamārik (pl)	جمارك
customs duty	rasm ʒumrukiy (m)	رسم جمركيّ
customs officer	muwazzaf al ʒamārik (m)	موظّف الجمارك
smuggling	tahrīb (m)	تهريب
contraband (smuggled goods)	biḍā'a muharraba (pl)	بضاعة مهرّبة

109. Finances

share, stock	sahm (m)	سهم
bond (certificate)	sanad (m)	سند
promissory note	kimbyāla (f)	كمبيالة
stock exchange	būrṣa (f)	بورصة
stock price	si'r as sahm (m)	سعر السهم
to go down (become cheaper)	raxuṣ	رخص
to go up (become more expensive)	ɣala	غلى
share	naṣīb (m)	نصيب
controlling interest	al maʒmū'a al musaytara (f)	المجموعة المسيطرة
investment	istiθmār (pl)	إستثمار
to invest (vt)	istaθmar	إستثمر
percent	bil mi'a (m)	بالمئة
interest (on investment)	fa'ida (f)	فائدة
profit	ribḥ (m)	ربح
profitable (adj)	murbiḥ	مربح

tax	ḍarība (f)	ضريبة
currency (foreign ~)	ʿumla (f)	عملة
national (adj)	waṭaniy	وطني
exchange (currency ~)	taḥwīl (m)	تحويل
accountant	muḥāsib (m)	محاسب
accounting	maḥasaba (f)	محاسبة
bankruptcy	iflās (m)	إفلاس
collapse, ruin	inhiyār (m)	إنهيار
ruin	iflās (m)	إفلاس
to be ruined (financially)	aflas	أفلس
inflation	tadaxxum māliy (m)	تضخّم مالي
devaluation	taxfīḍ qīmat ʿumla (m)	تخفيض قيمة عملة
capital	ra's māl (m)	رأس مال
income	daxl (m)	دخل
turnover	dawrat ra's al māl (f)	دورة رأس المال
resources	mawārid (pl)	موارد
monetary resources	al mawārid an naqdiyya (pl)	الموارد النقديّة
overheads	nafaqāt ʿāmma (pl)	نفقات عامّة
to reduce (expenses)	xaffaḍ	خفّض

110. Marketing

marketing	taswīq (m)	تسويق
market	sūq (f)	سوق
market segment	qaṭāʿ as sūq (m)	قطاع السوق
product	muntaʒ (m)	منتج
goods (merchandise)	baḍā'iʿ (pl)	بضائع
brand	mārka (f)	ماركة
trademark	mārka tiʒāriyya (f)	ماركة تجاريّة
logotype	ʃiʿār (m)	شعار
logo	ʃiʿār (m)	شعار
demand	ṭalab (m)	طلب
supply	maxzūn (m)	مخزون
need	ḥāʒa (f)	حاجة
consumer	mustahlik (m)	مستهلك
analysis	taḥlīl (m)	تحليل
to analyse (vt)	ḥallal	حلّل
positioning	waḍʿ (m)	وضع
to position (vt)	waḍaʿ	وضع
price	siʿr (m)	سعر
pricing policy	siyāsat al asʿār (f)	سياسة الأسعار
price formation	taʃkīl al asʿār (m)	تشكيل الأسعار

111. Advertising

advertising	iʿlān (m)	إعلان
to advertise (vt)	aʿlan	أعلن

budget	mīzāniyya (f)	ميزانيّة
ad, advertisement	iʻlān (m)	إعلان
TV advertising	iʻlān fit tiliviziyūn (m)	إعلان في التليفزيون
radio advertising	iʻlān fir rādiyu (m)	إعلان في الراديو
outdoor advertising	iʻlān ẓāhiriy (m)	إعلان ظاهريّ

mass medias	wasāʼil al iʻlām (pl)	وسائل الإعلام
periodical (n)	ṣaḥifa dawriyya (f)	صحيفة دورية
image (public appearance)	imiʒ (m)	إيميج

| slogan | ʃiʻār (m) | شعار |
| motto (maxim) | ʃiʻār (m) | شعار |

campaign	ḥamla (f)	حملة
advertising campaign	ḥamla iʻlāniyya (f)	حملة إعلانيّة
target group	maʒmūʻa mustahdafa (f)	مجموعة مستهدفة

business card	biṭāqat al ʻamal (f)	بطاقة العمل
leaflet (promotional ~)	manʃūr (m)	منشور
brochure (e.g. 12 pages ~)	naʃra (f)	نشرة
pamphlet	kutayyib (m)	كتيّب
newsletter	naʃra ixbāriyya (f)	نشرة إخبارية

signboard (store sign, etc.)	lāfita (f)	لافتة
poster	mulṣaq iʻlāniy (m)	ملصق إعلانيّ
hoarding	lawḥat iʻlānāt (f)	لوحة إعلانات

112. Banking

| bank | bank (m) | بنك |
| branch (of a bank) | farʻ (m) | فرع |

| consultant | muwaẓẓaf bank (m) | موظّف بنك |
| manager (director) | mudīr (m) | مدير |

bank account	ḥisāb (m)	حساب
account number	raqm al ḥisāb (m)	رقم الحساب
current account	ḥisāb ʒāri (m)	حساب جار
deposit account	ḥisāb tawfīr (m)	حساب توفير

to open an account	fataḥ ḥisāb	فتح حسابا
to close the account	aɣlaq ḥisāb	أغلق حسابا
to deposit into the account	awdaʻ fil ḥisāb	أودع في الحساب
to withdraw (vt)	saḥab min al ḥisāb	سحب من الحساب

deposit	wadīʻa (f)	وديعة
to make a deposit	awdaʻ	أودع
wire transfer	ḥawāla (f)	حوالة
to wire, to transfer	ḥawwal	حوّل

sum	mablaɣ (m)	مبلغ
How much?	kam?	كم؟
signature	tawqīʻ (m)	توقيع
to sign (vt)	waqqaʻ	وقّع

credit card	biṭāqat i'timān (f)	بطاقة ائتمان
code (PIN code)	kūd (m)	كود
credit card number	raqm biṭāqat i'timān (m)	رقم بطاقة إئتمان
cashpoint	ṣarrāf 'āliy (m)	صراف آلي
cheque	ʃīk (m)	شيك
to write a cheque	katab ʃīk	كتب شيكًا
chequebook	daftar ʃīkāt (m)	دفتر شيكات
loan (bank ~)	qarḍ (m)	قرض
to apply for a loan	qaddam ṭalab lil ḥuṣūl 'ala qarḍ	قدم طلبا للحصول على قرض
to get a loan	ḥaṣal 'ala qarḍ	حصل على قرض
to give a loan	qaddam qarḍ	قدم قرضا
guarantee	ḍamān (m)	ضمان

113. Telephone. Phone conversation

telephone	hātif (m)	هاتف
mobile phone	hātif maḥmūl (m)	هاتف محمول
answerphone	muʒīb al hātif (m)	مجيب الهاتف
to call (by phone)	ittaṣal	إتصل
call, ring	mukālama tilifuniyya (f)	مكالمة تليفونية
to dial a number	ittaṣal bi raqm	إتصل برقم
Hello!	alu!	ألو!
to ask (vt)	sa'al	سأل
to answer (vi, vt)	radd	رد
to hear (vt)	sami'	سمع
well (adv)	ʒayyidan	جيدا
not well (adv)	sayyi'an	سيئًا
noises (interference)	taʃwīʃ (m)	تشويش
receiver	sammā'a (f)	سماعة
to pick up (~ the phone)	rafa' as sammā'a	رفع السماعة
to hang up (~ the phone)	qafal as sammā'a	قفل السماعة
busy (engaged)	maʃɣūl	مشغول
to ring (ab. phone)	rann	رن
telephone book	dalīl at tilifūn (m)	دليل التليفون
local (adj)	maḥalliyya	محلية
local call	mukālama hātifiyya maḥalliyya (f)	مكالمة هاتفية محلية
trunk (e.g. ~ call)	ba'īd al mada	بعيد المدى
trunk call	mukālama ba'īdat al mada (f)	مكالمة بعيدة المدى
international (adj)	duwaliy	دولي
international call	mukālama duwaliyya (f)	مكالمة دولية

114. Mobile telephone

mobile phone	hātif maḥmūl (m)	هاتف محمول
display	ʒihāz ʿarḍ (m)	جهاز عرض
button	zirr (m)	زِر
SIM card	sim kart (m)	سيم كارت
battery	baṭṭāriyya (f)	بطّارِية
to be flat (battery)	xalaṣat	خلصت
charger	ʃāḥin (m)	شاحن
menu	qāʾima (f)	قائمة
settings	awḍāʿ (pl)	أوضاع
tune (melody)	naɣma (f)	نغمة
to select (vt)	ixtār	إختار
calculator	ʾāla ḥāsiba (f)	آلة حاسبة
voice mail	barīd ṣawtiy (m)	بريد صوتِيّ
alarm clock	munabbih (m)	منّبه
contacts	ʒihāt al ittiṣāl (pl)	جهات الإتّصال
SMS (text message)	risāla qaṣīra ɛsɛmɛs (f)	رسالة قصيرة sms
subscriber	muʃtarik (m)	مشترك

115. Stationery

ballpoint pen	qalam ʒāf (m)	قلم جاف
fountain pen	qalam rīʃa (m)	قلم ريشة
pencil	qalam ruṣāṣ (m)	قلم رصاص
highlighter	markir (m)	ماركر
felt-tip pen	qalam xaṭṭāṭ (m)	قلم خطاط
notepad	muðakkira (f)	مذكّرة
diary	ʒadwal al aʿmāl (m)	جدول الأعمال
ruler	masṭara (f)	مسطرة
calculator	ʾāla ḥāsiba (f)	آلة حاسبة
rubber	astīka (f)	استيكة
drawing pin	dabbūs (m)	دبّوس
paper clip	dabbūs waraq (m)	دبّوس ورق
glue	ṣamɣ (m)	صمغ
stapler	dabbāsa (f)	دبّاسة
hole punch	xarrāma (m)	خرّامة
pencil sharpener	mibrāt (f)	مبراة

116. Various kinds of documents

account (report)	taqrīr (m)	تقرير
agreement	ittifāq (m)	إتّفاق

application form	istimārat ṭalab (m)	إستمارة طلب
authentic (adj)	aṣliy	أصليّ
badge (identity tag)	ʃāra (f)	شارة
business card	biṭāqat al ʿamal (f)	بطاقة العمل

certificate (~ of quality)	ʃahāda (f)	شهادة
cheque (e.g. draw a ~)	ʃīk (m)	شيك
bill (in restaurant)	ḥisāb (m)	حساب
constitution	dustūr (m)	دستور

contract (agreement)	ʿaqd (m)	عقد
copy	ṣūra (f)	صورة
copy (of a contract, etc.)	nusχa (f)	نسخة

customs declaration	taṣrīḥ ʒumrukiy (m)	تصريح جمركيّ
document	waθīqa (f)	وثيقة
driving licence	ruχṣat al qiyāda (f)	رخصة قيادة
addendum	mulḥaq (m)	ملحق
form	istimāra (f)	إستمارة

ID card (e.g., warrant card)	biṭāqat al huwiyya (f)	بطاقة الهويّة
inquiry (request)	istifsār (m)	إستفسار
invitation card	biṭāqat daʿwa (f)	بطاقة دعوة
invoice	fātūra (f)	فاتورة

law	qānūn (m)	قانون
letter (mail)	risāla (f)	رسالة
letterhead	tarwīsa (f)	ترويسة
list (of names, etc.)	qāʾima (f)	قائمة
manuscript	maχṭūṭa (f)	مخطوطة
newsletter	naʃra iχbāriyya (f)	نشرة إخبارية
note (short letter)	nūta (f)	نوتة

pass (for worker, visitor)	biṭāqat murūr (f)	بطاقة مرور
passport	ʒawāz as safar (m)	جواز السفر
permit	ruχṣa (f)	رخصة
curriculum vitae, CV	sīra ðātiyya (f)	سيرة ذاتيّة
debt note, IOU	muðakkirat dayn (f)	مذكّرة دين
receipt (for purchase)	ʾīṣāl (m)	إيصال

till receipt	ʾīṣāl (m)	إيصال
report (mil.)	taqrīr (m)	تقرير

to show (ID, etc.)	qaddam	قدّم
to sign (vt)	waqqaʿ	وقّع
signature	tawqīʿ (m)	توقيع
seal (stamp)	χatm (m)	ختم

text	naṣṣ (m)	نصّ
ticket (for entry)	taðkira (f)	تذكرة

to cross out	ʃaṭab	شطب
to fill in (~ a form)	malaʾ	ملأ

waybill (shipping invoice)	bulīṣat ʃaḥn (f)	بوليصة شحن
will (testament)	waṣiyya (f)	وصيّة

117. Kinds of business

accounting services	χidamāt muḥasaba (pl)	خدمات محاسبة
advertising	i'lān (m)	إعلان
advertising agency	wikālat i'lān (f)	وكالة إعلان
air-conditioners	takyīf (m)	تكييف
airline	ʃarikat ṭayarān (f)	شركة طيران
alcoholic beverages	maʃrūbāt kuḥūliyya (pl)	مشروبات كحولية
antiques (antique dealers)	tuḥaf (pl)	تحف
art gallery (contemporary ~)	ma'raḍ fanniy (m)	معرض فنّي
audit services	tadqīq al ḥisābāt (pl)	تدقيق الحسابات
banking industry	al qiṭā' al maṣrafiy (m)	القطاع المصرفي
beauty salon	ṣālūn taʒmīl (m)	صالون تجميل
bookshop	maḥall kutub (m)	محلّ كتب
brewery	maṣna' bīra (m)	مصنع بيرة
business centre	markaz tiʒāriy (m)	مركز تجاري
business school	kulliyyat idārat al a'māl (f)	كلّية إدارة الأعمال
casino	kazinu (m)	كازينو
chemist, pharmacy	ṣaydaliyya (f)	صيدلية
cinema	sinima (f)	سينما
construction	binā' (m)	بناء
consulting	istiʃāra (f)	إستشارة
dental clinic	'iyādat asnān (f)	عيادة أسنان
design	taṣmīm (m)	تصميم
dry cleaners	tanẓīf ʒāff (m)	تنظيف جافّ
employment agency	wikālat tawẓīf (f)	وكالة توظيف
financial services	χidamāt māliyya (pl)	خدمات مالية
food products	mawādd ɣiðā'iyya (pl)	موادّ غذائية
furniture (e.g. house ~)	aθāθ (m)	أثاث
clothing, garment	malābis (pl)	ملابس
hotel	funduq (m)	فندق
ice-cream	muθallaʒāt (pl)	مثلجات
industry (manufacturing)	ṣinā'a (f)	صناعة
insurance	ta'mīn (m)	تأمين
Internet	intirnit (m)	إنترنت
investments (finance)	istiθmārāt (pl)	إستثمارات
jeweller	ṣā'iɣ (m)	صائغ
jewellery	muʒawharāt (pl)	مجوهرات
laundry (shop)	maɣsala (f)	مغسلة
legal adviser	χidamāt qānūniyya (pl)	خدمات قانونية
light industry	ṣinā'a χafīfa (f)	صناعة خفيفة
magazine	maʒalla (f)	مجلّة
mail order selling	bay' bil barīd (m)	بيع بالبريد
medicine	ṭibb (m)	طبّ
museum	matḥaf (m)	متحف
news agency	wikālat anbā' (f)	وكالة أنباء
newspaper	ʒarīda (f)	جريدة

nightclub	malha layliy (m)	ملهى ليليّ
oil (petroleum)	naft (m)	نفط
courier services	xidamāt aʃ ʃahn (pl)	خدمات الشحن
pharmaceutics	ṣaydala (f)	صيدلة
printing (industry)	ṭibāʿa (f)	طباعة
pub	bār (m)	بار
publishing house	dār aṭ ṭibāʿa wan naʃr (f)	دار الطباعة والنشر

radio (~ station)	iðāʿa (f)	إذاعة
real estate	ʿiqārāt (pl)	عقارات
restaurant	maṭʿam (m)	مطعم

security company	ʃarikat amn (f)	شركة أمن
shop	mahall (m)	محلّ
sport	riyāḍa (f)	رياضة
stock exchange	būrṣa (f)	بورصة
supermarket	subirmarkit (m)	سوبرماركت
swimming pool (public ~)	masbah (m)	مسبح

tailor shop	ṣālūn (m)	صالون
television	tilivizyūn (m)	تليفزيون
theatre	masrah (m)	مسرح
trade (commerce)	tiʒāra (f)	تجارة
transport companies	wasāʾil an naql (pl)	وسائل النقل
travel	siyāha (f)	سياحة

undertakers	bayt al ʒanāzāt (m)	بيت الجنازات
veterinary surgeon	ṭabīb bayṭariy (m)	طبيب بيطريّ
warehouse	mustawdaʿ (m)	مستودع
waste collection	ʒamʿ an nufāyāt (m)	جمع النفايات

Job. Business. Part 2

118. Show. Exhibition

exhibition, show	ma'raḍ (m)	معرض
trade show	ma'raḍ tiӡāriy (m)	معرض تجاريّ
participation	iʃtirāk (m)	إشتراك
to participate (vi)	iʃtarak	إشترك
participant (exhibitor)	muʃtarik (m)	مشترك
director	mudīr (m)	مدير
organizers' office	maktab al munaẓẓimīn (m)	مكتب المنظّمين
organizer	munaẓẓim (m)	منظّم
to organize (vt)	naẓẓam	نظّم
participation form	istimārat al iʃtirāk (f)	إستمارة الإشتراك
to fill in (vt)	mala'	ملأ
details	tafāṣīl (pl)	تفاصيل
information	isti'lāmāt (pl)	إستعلامات
price (cost, rate)	si'r (m)	سعر
including	bima fīh	بما فيه
to include (vt)	taḍamman	تضمّن
to pay (vi, vt)	dafa'	دفع
registration fee	rusūm at tasӡīl (pl)	رسوم التسجيل
entrance	madχal (m)	مدخل
pavilion, hall	ӡanāḥ (m)	جناح
to register (vt)	saӡӡal	سجّل
badge (identity tag)	ʃāra (f)	شارة
stand	kuʃk (m)	كشك
to reserve, to book	ḥaӡaz	حجز
display case	vatrīna (f)	فترينة
spotlight	miṣbāḥ (m)	مصباح
design	taṣmīm (m)	تصميم
to place (put, set)	waḍa'	وضع
distributor	muwazzi' (m)	موزّع
supplier	muwarrid (m)	موّرد
country	balad (m)	بلد
foreign (adj)	aӡnabiy	أجنبيّ
product	muntaӡ (m)	منتج
association	ӡam'iyya (f)	جمعيّة
conference hall	qā'at al mu'tamarāt (f)	قاعة المؤتمرات
congress	mu'tamar (m)	مؤتمر

contest (competition)	musābaqa (f)	مسابقة
visitor (attendee)	zā'ir (m)	زائر
to visit (attend)	ḥaḍar	حضر
customer	zubūn (m)	زبون

119. Mass Media

newspaper	ӡarīda (f)	جريدة
magazine	maӡalla (f)	مجلّة
press (printed media)	ṣiḥāfa (f)	صحافة
radio	iðā'a (f)	إذاعة
radio station	maḥaṭṭat iðā'a (f)	محطّة إذاعة
television	tilivizyūn (m)	تليفزيون

presenter, host	mu'addim (m)	مقدّم
newsreader	muðī' (m)	مذيع
commentator	mu'alliq (m)	معلّق

journalist	ṣuḥufiy (m)	صحفيّ
correspondent (reporter)	murāsil (m)	مراسل
press photographer	muṣawwir ṣuḥufiy (m)	مصوّر صحفيّ
reporter	ṣuḥufiy (m)	صحفيّ

editor	muḥarrir (m)	محرّر
editor-in-chief	ra'īs taḥrīr (m)	رئيس تحرير
to subscribe (to …)	iʃtarak	إشترك
subscription	iʃtirāk (m)	إشتراك
subscriber	muʃtarik (m)	مشترك
to read (vi, vt)	qara'	قرأ
reader	qāri' (m)	قارئ

circulation (of a newspaper)	tadāwul (m)	تداول
monthly (adj)	ʃahriy	شهريّ
weekly (adj)	usbū'iy	أسبوعيّ
issue (edition)	'adad (m)	عدد
new (~ issue)	ӡadīd	جديد

headline	'unwān (m)	عنوان
short article	maqāla qaṣīra (f)	مقالة قصيرة
column (regular article)	'amūd (m)	عمود
article	maqāla (f)	مقالة
page	ṣafḥa (f)	صفحة

reportage, report	taqrīr (m)	تقرير
event (happening)	ḥadaθ (m)	حدث
sensation (news)	ḍaӡӡa (f)	ضجّة
scandal	faḍīḥa (f)	فضيحة
scandalous (adj)	fāḍiḥ	فاضح
great (~ scandal)	ʃahīr	شهير

programme (e.g. cooking ~)	barnāmaӡ (m)	برنامج
interview	muqābala (f)	مقابلة
live broadcast	iðā'a mubāʃira (f)	إذاعة مباشرة
channel	qanāt (f)	قناة

120. Agriculture

agriculture	zirā'a (f)	زراعة
peasant (masc.)	fallāḥ (m)	فلاح
peasant (fem.)	fallāḥa (f)	فلاحة
farmer	muzāri' (m)	مزارع
tractor	ӡarrār (m)	جرّار
combine, harvester	ḥaṣṣāda (f)	حصّادة
plough	miḥrāθ (m)	محراث
to plough (vi, vt)	ḥaraθ	حرث
ploughland	ḥaql maḥrūθ (m)	حقل محروث
furrow (in field)	talam (m)	تلم
to sow (vi, vt)	baðar	بذر
seeder	baðð āra (f)	بذّارة
sowing (process)	zar' (m)	زرع
scythe	miḥaʃʃ (m)	محشّ
to mow, to scythe	ḥaʃʃ	حشّ
spade (tool)	karīk (m)	مجرفة
to till (vt)	ḥafar	حفر
hoe	mi'zaqa (f)	معزقة
to hoe, to weed	ista'ṣal nabātāt	إستأصل نباتات
weed (plant)	ḥaʃīʃa (m)	حشيشة
watering can	miraʃʃa al miyāh (f)	مرشّة المياه
to water (plants)	saqa	سقى
watering (act)	saqy (m)	سقي
pitchfork	maðrāt (f)	مذراة
rake	midamma (f)	مدمّة
fertiliser	samād (m)	سماد
to fertilise (vt)	sammad	سمّد
manure (fertiliser)	zibd (m)	زبل
field	ḥaql (m)	حقل
meadow	marӡ (m)	مرج
vegetable garden	bustān xuḍār (m)	بستان خضار
orchard (e.g. apple ~)	bustān (m)	بستان
to graze (vt)	ra'a	رعى
herdsman	rā'i (m)	راع
pasture	mar'a (m)	مرعى
cattle breeding	tarbiyat al mawāʃi (f)	تربية المواشي
sheep farming	tarbiyat aɣnām (f)	تربية أغنام
plantation	mazra'a (f)	مزرعة
row (garden bed ~s)	ḥawḍ (m)	حوض
hothouse	daffa (f)	دفيئة

| drought (lack of rain) | ʒafāf (m) | جفاف |
| dry (~ summer) | ʒāff | جافّ |

grain	ḥubūb (pl)	حبوب
cereal crops	maḥāṣīl al ḥubūb (pl)	محاصيل الحبوب
to harvest, to gather	ḥaṣad	حصد

miller (person)	ṭaḥḥān (m)	طحّان
mill (e.g. gristmill)	ṭāḥūna (f)	طاحونة
to grind (grain)	ṭaḥan al ḥubūb	طحن الحبوب
flour	daqīq (m)	دقيق
straw	qaʃʃ (m)	قشّ

121. Building. Building process

building site	arḍ binā' (f)	أرض بناء
to build (vt)	bana	بنى
building worker	'āmil binā' (m)	عامل بناء

project	maʃrū' (m)	مشروع
architect	muhandis mi'māriy (m)	مهندس معماريّ
worker	'āmil (m)	عامل

foundations (of a building)	asās (m)	أساس
roof	saqf (m)	سقف
foundation pile	watad al asās (f)	وتد الأساس
wall	ḥā'iṭ (m)	حائط

| reinforcing bars | ḥadīd taslīḥ (m) | حديد تسليح |
| scaffolding | saqāla (f) | سقالة |

concrete	xarasāna (f)	خرسانة
granite	granīt (m)	جرانيت
stone	ḥaʒar (m)	حجر
brick	ṭūb (m)	طوب

sand	raml (m)	رمل
cement	ismant (m)	إسمنت
plaster (for walls)	qiṣāra (m)	قصارة
to plaster (vt)	ṭala bil ʒiṣṣ	طلى بالجصّ
paint	dihān (m)	دهان

| to paint (~ a wall) | dahhan | دهّن |
| barrel | barmīl (m) | برميل |

crane	rāfi'a (f)	رافعة
to lift, to hoist (vt)	rafa'	رفع
to lower (vt)	anzal	أنزل

bulldozer	ʒarrāfa (f)	جرّافة
excavator	ḥaffāra (f)	حفّارة
scoop, bucket	dalw (m)	دلو
to dig (excavate)	ḥafar	حفر
hard hat	xūða (f)	خوذة

122. Science. Research. Scientists

science	'ilm (m)	علم
scientific (adj)	'ilmiy	علميّ
scientist	'ālim (m)	عالم
theory	naẓariyya (f)	نظريّة

axiom	badīhiyya (f)	بديهيّة
analysis	taḥlīl (m)	تحليل
to analyse (vt)	ḥallal	حلّل
argument (strong ~)	burhān (m)	برهان
substance (matter)	mādda (f)	مادّة

hypothesis	farḍiyya (f)	فرضيّة
dilemma	mu'ḍila (f)	معضلة
dissertation	risāla 'ilmiyya (f)	رسالة علميّة
dogma	'aqīda (f)	عقيدة

doctrine	maðhab (m)	مذهب
research	baḥθ (m)	بحث
to research (vt)	baḥaθ	بحث
tests (laboratory ~)	iχtibārāt (pl)	إختبارات
laboratory	muχtabar (m)	مختبر

method	manhaȝ (m)	منهج
molecule	ȝuzayi' (m)	جزيء
monitoring	riqāba (f)	رقابة
discovery (act, event)	iktiʃāf (m)	إكتشاف

postulate	musallama (f)	مسلّمة
principle	mabda' (m)	مبدأ
forecast	tanabbu' (m)	تنبّؤ
to forecast (vt)	tanabba'	تنبّأ

synthesis	tarkīb (m)	تركيب
trend (tendency)	ittiȝāh (m)	إتّجاه
theorem	naẓariyya (f)	نظريّة

teachings	ta'ālīm (pl)	تعاليم
fact	ḥaqīqa (f)	حقيقة
expedition	ba'θa (f)	بعثة
experiment	taȝriba (f)	تجربة

academician	akadīmiy (m)	أكاديميّ
bachelor (e.g. ~ of Arts)	bakalūriyūs (m)	بكالوريوس
doctor (PhD)	duktūr (m)	دكتور
Associate Professor	ustāð muʃārik (m)	أستاذ مشارك
Master (e.g. ~ of Arts)	maȝistīr (m)	ماجستير
professor	brufissūr (m)	بروفيسور

Professions and occupations

job	'amal (m)	عمل
staff (work force)	kawādir (pl)	كوادر
personnel	ṭāqim al 'āmilīn (m)	طاقم العاملين
career	masār mihniy (m)	مسار مهنيّ
prospects (chances)	'āfāq (pl)	آفاق
skills (mastery)	mahārāt (pl)	مهارات
selection (screening)	iχtiyār (m)	إختيار
employment agency	wikālat tawẓīf (f)	وكالة توظيف
curriculum vitae, CV	sīra ðātiyya (f)	سيرة ذاتيّة
job interview	mu'ābalat 'amal (f)	مقابلة عمل
vacancy	waẓīfa χāliya (f)	وظيفة خالية
salary, pay	murattab (m)	مرتّب
fixed salary	rātib θābit (m)	راتب ثابت
pay, compensation	uʒra (f)	أجرة
position (job)	manṣib (m)	منصب
duty (of an employee)	wāʒib (m)	واجب
range of duties	maʒmūʿa min al wāʒibāt (f)	مجموعة من الواجبات
busy (I'm ~)	maʃɣūl	مشغول
to fire (dismiss)	aqāl	أقال
dismissal	iqāla (m)	إقالة
unemployment	biṭāla (f)	بطالة
unemployed (n)	'āṭil (m)	عاطل
retirement	ma'āʃ (m)	معاش
to retire (from job)	uḥīl 'alal ma'āʃ	أحيل على المعاش

director	muðīr (m)	مدير
manager (director)	muðīr (m)	مدير
boss	muðīr (m), ra'īs (m)	مدير, رئيس
superior	ra'īs (m)	رئيس
superiors	ru'asā' (pl)	رؤساء
president	ra'īs (m)	رئيس
chairman	ra'īs (m)	رئيس
deputy (substitute)	nā'ib (m)	نائب
assistant	musā'id (m)	مساعد

| secretary | sikirtīr (m) | سكرتير |
| personal assistant | sikritīr χāṣṣ (m) | سكرتير خاص |

businessman	raʒul aʿmāl (m)	رجل أعمال
entrepreneur	rāʾid aʿmāl (m)	رائد أعمال
founder	muʾassis (m)	مؤسّس
to found (vt)	assas	أسّس

founding member	muʾassis (m)	مؤسّس
partner	ʃarīk (m)	شريك
shareholder	musāhim (m)	مساهم

millionaire	milyunīr (m)	مليونير
billionaire	milyardīr (m)	ملياردير
owner, proprietor	ṣāḥib (m)	صاحب
landowner	ṣāḥib al arḍ (m)	صاحب الأرض

client	ʿamīl (m)	عميل
regular client	ʿamīl dāʾim (m)	عميل دائم
buyer (customer)	muʃtari (m)	مشتر
visitor	zāʾir (m)	زائر

professional (n)	muḥtarif (m)	محترف
expert	χabīr (m)	خبير
specialist	mutaχaṣṣiṣ (m)	متخصّص

| banker | ṣāḥib maṣraf (m) | صاحب مصرف |
| broker | simsār (m) | سمسار |

cashier	ṣarrāf (m)	صرّاف
accountant	muḥāsib (m)	محاسب
security guard	ḥāris amn (m)	حارس أمن

investor	mustaθmir (m)	مستثمر
debtor	mudīn (m)	مدين
creditor	dāʾin (m)	دائن
borrower	muqtariḍ (m)	مقترض

| importer | mustawrid (m) | مستورد |
| exporter | muṣaddir (m) | مصدّر |

manufacturer	aʃ ʃarika al muṣniʿa (f)	الشركة المصنعة
distributor	muwazziʿ (m)	موزّع
middleman	wasīṭ (m)	وسيط

consultant	mustaʃār (m)	مستشار
sales representative	mandūb mabiʿāt (m)	مندوب مبيعات
agent	wakīl (m)	وكيل
insurance agent	wakīl at taʾmīn (m)	وكيل التأمين

125. Service professions

| cook | ṭabbāχ (m) | طبّاخ |
| chef (kitchen chef) | ʃāf (m) | شاف |

baker	χabbāz (m)	خبّاز
barman	bārman (m)	بارمان
waiter	nādil (m)	نادل
waitress	nādila (f)	نادلة
lawyer, barrister	muḥāmi (m)	محام
lawyer (legal expert)	muḥāmi (m)	محام
notary public	muwaθθaq (m)	موئق
electrician	kahrabā'iy (m)	كهربائيّ
plumber	sabbāk (m)	سبّاك
carpenter	naʒʒār (m)	نجّار
masseur	mudallik (m)	مدلّك
masseuse	mudallika (f)	مدلّكة
doctor	ṭabīb (m)	طبيب
taxi driver	sā'iq taksi (m)	سائق تاكسي
driver	sā'iq (m)	سائق
delivery man	sā'i (m)	ساع
chambermaid	'āmilat tanẓīf ɣuraf (f)	عاملة تنظيف غرف
security guard	ḥāris amn (m)	حارس أمن
flight attendant (fem.)	muḍīfat ṭayarān (f)	مضيفة طيران
schoolteacher	mudarris madrasa (m)	مدرّس مدرسة
librarian	amīn maktaba (m)	أمين مكتبة
translator	mutarʒim (m)	مترجم
interpreter	mutarʒim fawriy (m)	مترجم فوريّ
guide	murʃid (m)	مرشد
hairdresser	ḥallāq (m)	حلّاق
postman	sā'i al barīd (m)	ساعي البريد
salesman (store staff)	bā'iʿ (m)	بائع
gardener	bustāniy (m)	بستانيّ
domestic servant	χādim (m)	خادم
maid (female servant)	χādima (f)	خادمة
cleaner (cleaning lady)	'āmilat tanẓīf (f)	عاملة تنظيف

126. Military professions and ranks

private	ʒundiy (m)	جنديّ
sergeant	raqīb (m)	رقيب
lieutenant	mulāzim (m)	ملازم
captain	naqīb (m)	نقيب
major	rā'id (m)	رائد
colonel	'aqīd (m)	عقيد
general	ʒinirāl (m)	جنرال
marshal	mārʃāl (m)	مارشال
admiral	amirāl (m)	أميرال
military (n)	'askariy (m)	عسكريّ
soldier	ʒundiy (m)	جنديّ

| officer | ḍābiṭ (m) | ضابط |
| commander | qā'id (m) | قائد |

border guard	ḥāris ḥudūd (m)	حارس حدود
radio operator	'āmil lāsilkiy (m)	عامل لاسلكيّ
scout (searcher)	mustakʃif (m)	مستكشف
pioneer (sapper)	muhandis 'askariy (m)	مهندس عسكريّ
marksman	rāmi (m)	رام
navigator	mallāḥ (m)	ملّاح

127. Officials. Priests

| king | malik (m) | ملك |
| queen | malika (f) | ملكة |

| prince | amīr (m) | أمير |
| princess | amīra (f) | أميرة |

| czar | qayṣar (m) | قيصر |
| czarina | qayṣara (f) | قيصرة |

president	raʔīs (m)	رئيس
Secretary (minister)	wazīr (m)	وزير
prime minister	raʔīs wuzarā' (m)	رئيس وزراء
senator	'uḍw maʒlis aʃ ʃuyūχ (m)	عضو مجلس الشيوخ

diplomat	diblumāsiy (m)	دبلوماسيّ
consul	qunṣul (m)	قنصل
ambassador	safīr (m)	سفير
counselor (diplomatic officer)	mustaʃār (m)	مستشار

official, functionary (civil servant)	muwaẓẓaf (m)	موظّف
prefect	raʔīs idārat al ḥayy (m)	رئيس إدارة الحيّ
mayor	raʔīs al baladiyya (m)	رئيس البلديّة

| judge | qāḍi (m) | قاض |
| prosecutor | mudda'i (m) | مدّع |

missionary	mubaʃʃir (m)	مبشّر
monk	rāhib (m)	راهب
abbot	raʔīs ad dayr (m)	رئيس الدير
rabbi	ḥāχām (m)	حاخام

vizier	wazīr (m)	وزير
shah	ʃāh (m)	شاه
sheikh	ʃɛyχ (m)	شيخ

128. Agricultural professions

| beekeeper | naḥḥāl (m) | نحّال |
| shepherd | rā'i (m) | راع |

agronomist	muhandis zirā'iy (m)	مهندس زراعيّ
cattle breeder	murabbi al mawāʃi (m)	مربّي المواشي
veterinary surgeon	ṭabīb bayṭariy (m)	طبيب بيطري

farmer	muzāriʻ (m)	مزارع
winemaker	ṣāniʻ an nabīð (m)	صانع النبيذ
zoologist	χabīr fi ʻilm al ḥayawān (m)	خبير في علم الحيوان
cowboy	rāʻi al baqar (m)	راعي البقر

129. Art professions

| actor | mumaθθil (m) | ممثّل |
| actress | mumaθθila (f) | ممثّلة |

| singer (masc.) | muɣanni (m) | مغنّ |
| singer (fem.) | muɣanniya (f) | مغنّية |

| dancer (masc.) | rāqiṣ (m) | راقص |
| dancer (fem.) | rāqiṣa (f) | راقصة |

| performer (masc.) | fannān (m) | فنّان |
| performer (fem.) | fannāna (f) | فنّانة |

musician	ʻāzif (m)	عازف
pianist	ʻāzif biyānu (m)	عازف بيانو
guitar player	ʻāzif gitār (m)	عازف جيتار

conductor (orchestra ~)	qā'id urkistra (m)	قائد أركسترا
composer	mulaḥḥin (m)	ملحّن
impresario	mudīr firqa (m)	مدير فرقة

film director	muχriʒ (m)	مخرج
producer	muntiʒ (m)	منتج
scriptwriter	kātib sināriyu (m)	كاتب سيناريو
critic	nāqid (m)	ناقد

writer	kātib (m)	كاتب
poet	ʃāʻir (m)	شاعر
sculptor	naḥḥāt (m)	نحّات
artist (painter)	rassām (m)	رسّام

juggler	bahlawān (m)	بهلوان
clown	muharriʒ (m)	مهرّج
acrobat	bahlawān (m)	بهلوان
magician	sāḥir (m)	ساحر

130. Various professions

doctor	ṭabīb (m)	طبيب
nurse	mumarriḍa (f)	ممرّضة
psychiatrist	ṭabīb nafsiy (m)	طبيب نفسيّ
dentist	ṭabīb al asnān (m)	طبيب الأسنان

surgeon	ʒarrāḥ (m)	جرّاح
astronaut	rāʾid faḍāʾ (m)	رائد فضاء
astronomer	ʿālim falak (m)	عالم فلك
pilot	ṭayyār (m)	طيّار

driver (of a taxi, etc.)	sāʾiq (m)	سائق
train driver	sāʾiq (m)	سائق
mechanic	mikanīkiy (m)	ميكانيكيّ

miner	ʿāmil manʒam (m)	عامل منجم
worker	ʿāmil (m)	عامل
locksmith	qaffāl (m)	قفّال
joiner (carpenter)	naʒʒār (m)	نجّار
turner (lathe operator)	xarrāṭ (m)	خرّاط
building worker	ʿāmil bināʾ (m)	عامل بناء
welder	laḥḥām (m)	لحّام

professor (title)	brufissūr (m)	بروفيسور
architect	muhandis miʿmāriy (m)	مهندس معماريّ
historian	muʾarrix (m)	مؤرّخ
scientist	ʿālim (m)	عالم
physicist	fizyāʾiy (m)	فيزيائيّ
chemist (scientist)	kimyāʾiy (m)	كيميائيّ

archaeologist	ʿālim ʾāθār (m)	عالم آثار
geologist	ʒiulūʒiy (m)	جيولوجيّ
researcher (scientist)	bāḥiθ (m)	باحث

| babysitter | murabbiyat aṭfāl (f) | مربّية الأطفال |
| teacher, educator | muʿallim (m) | معلّم |

editor	muḥarrir (m)	محرّر
editor-in-chief	raʾīs taḥrīr (m)	رئيس تحرير
correspondent	murāsil (m)	مراسل
typist (fem.)	kātiba ʿalal ʾāla al kātiba (f)	كاتبة على الآلة الكاتبة

designer	muṣammim (m)	مصمّم
computer expert	mutaxaṣṣiṣ bil kumbyūtir (m)	متخصّص بالكمبيوتر
programmer	mubarmiʒ (m)	مبرمج
engineer (designer)	muhandis (m)	مهندس

sailor	baḥḥār (m)	بحّار
seaman	baḥḥār (m)	بحّار
rescuer	munqið (m)	منقذ

firefighter	raʒul iṭfāʾ (m)	رجل إطفاء
police officer	ʃurṭiy (m)	شرطيّ
watchman	ḥāris (m)	حارس
detective	muḥaqqiq (m)	محقّق

customs officer	muwazzaf al ʒamārik (m)	موظّف الجمارك
bodyguard	ḥāris ʃaxṣiy (m)	حارس شخصيّ
prison officer	ḥāris siʒn (m)	حارس سجن
inspector	mufattiʃ (m)	مفتّش
sportsman	riyāḍiy (m)	رياضيّ
trainer, coach	mudarrib (m)	مدرّب

butcher	ʒazzār (m)	جزّار
cobbler (shoe repairer)	iskāfiy (m)	إسكافيّ
merchant	tāʒir (m)	تاجر
loader (person)	ḥammāl (m)	حمّال

| fashion designer | muṣammim azyā' (m) | مصمّم أزياء |
| model (fem.) | mudīl (f) | موديل |

131. Occupations. Social status

| schoolboy | tilmīð (m) | تلميذ |
| student (college ~) | ṭālib (m) | طالب |

philosopher	faylasūf (m)	فيلسوف
economist	iqtiṣādiy (m)	إقتصاديّ
inventor	muxtariʿ (m)	مخترع

unemployed (n)	ʿāṭil (m)	عاطل
retiree, pensioner	mutaqāʿid (m)	متقاعد
spy, secret agent	ʒāsūs (m)	جاسوس

prisoner	saʒīn (m)	سجين
striker	muḍrib (m)	مضرب
bureaucrat	buruqrāṭiy (m)	بيروقراطيّ
traveller (globetrotter)	raḥḥāla (m)	رحّالة

gay, homosexual (n)	miθliy ʒinsiyyan (m)	مثليّ جنسيًا
hacker	hākir (m)	هاكر
hippie	hippi (m)	هيبي

bandit	qāṭiʿ ṭarīq (m)	قاطع طريق
hit man, killer	qātil ma'ʒūr (m)	قاتل مأجور
drug addict	mudmin muxaddirāt (m)	مدمن مخدّرات
drug dealer	tāʒir muxaddirāt (m)	تاجر مخدّرات
prostitute (fem.)	ʿāhira (f)	عاهرة
pimp	qawwād (m)	قوّاد

sorcerer	sāḥir (m)	ساحر
sorceress (evil ~)	sāḥira (f)	ساحرة
pirate	qurṣān (m)	قرصان
slave	ʿabd (m)	عبد
samurai	samurāy (m)	ساموراي
savage (primitive)	mutawaḥḥiʃ (m)	متوحّش

Sports

Kinds of sports. Sportspersons

sportsman	riyāḍiy (m)	رياضيّ
kind of sport	nawʿ min ar riyāḍa (m)	نوع من الرياضة
basketball	kurat as salla (f)	كرة السلّة
basketball player	lāʿib kūrat as salla (m)	لاعب كرة السلّة
baseball	kurat al qāʿida (f)	كرة القاعدة
baseball player	lāʿib kurat al qāʿida (m)	لاعب كرة القاعدة
football	kurat al qadam (f)	كرة القدم
football player	lāʿib kurat al qadam (m)	لاعب كرة القدم
goalkeeper	ḥāris al marma (m)	حارس المرمى
ice hockey	huki (m)	هوكي
ice hockey player	lāʿib huki (m)	لاعب هوكي
volleyball	al kura aṭ ṭāʾira (m)	الكرة الطائرة
volleyball player	lāʿib al kura aṭ ṭāʾira (m)	لاعب الكرة الطائرة
boxing	mulākama (f)	ملاكمة
boxer	mulākim (m)	ملاكم
wrestling	muṣāraʿa (f)	مصارعة
wrestler	muṣāriʿ (m)	مصارع
karate	karatī (m)	كاراتيه
karate fighter	lāʿib karatī (m)	لاعب كاراتيه
judo	ʒudu (m)	جودو
judo athlete	lāʿib ʒudu (m)	لاعب جودو
tennis	tinis (m)	تنس
tennis player	lāʿib tinnis (m)	لاعب تنس
swimming	sibāḥa (f)	سباحة
swimmer	sabbāḥ (m)	سبّاح
fencing	musāyafa (f)	مسايفة
fencer	mubāriz (m)	مبارز
chess	ʃaṭranʒ (m)	شطرنج
chess player	lāʿib ʃaṭranʒ (m)	لاعب شطرنج
alpinism	tasalluq al ʒibāl (m)	تسلّق الجبال
alpinist	mutasalliq al ʒibāl (m)	متسلّق الجبال
running	ʒary (m)	جري

runner	'addā' (m)	عدّاء
athletics	al'āb al qiwa (pl)	ألعاب القوى
athlete	lā'ib riyāḍiy (m)	لاعب رياضيّ
horse riding	riyāḍat al furūsiyya (f)	رياضة الفروسيّة
horse rider	fāris (m)	فارس
figure skating	tazalluʒ fanniy 'alal ʒalīd (m)	تزلّج فنّيّ على الجليد
figure skater (masc.)	mutazalliʒ fanniy (m)	متزلّج فنّيّ
figure skater (fem.)	mutazalliʒa fanniyya (f)	متزلّجة فنّيّة
powerlifting	raf' al aθqāl (m)	رفع الأثقال
powerlifter	rāfi' al aθqāl (m)	رافع الأثقال
car racing	sibāq as sayyārāt (m)	سباق السيّارات
racer (driver)	sā'iq sibāq (m)	سائق سباق
cycling	sibāq ad darrāʒāt (m)	سباق الدرّاجات
cyclist	lā'ib ad darrāʒāt (m)	لاعب الدرّاجات
long jump	al qafz aṭ ṭawīl (m)	القفز الطويل
pole vaulting	al qafz biz zāna (m)	القفز بالزانة
jumper	qāfiz (m)	قافز

133. Kinds of sports. Miscellaneous

American football	kurat al qadam (f)	كرة القدم
badminton	kurat ar rīʃa (f)	كرة الريشة
biathlon	al biatlūn (m)	البياثلون
billiards	bilyārdu (m)	بلياردو
bobsleigh	zallāʒa ʒama'iyya (f)	زلّاجة جماعيّة
bodybuilding	kamāl aʒsām (m)	كمال أجسام
water polo	kurat al mā' (f)	كرة الماء
handball	kurat al yad (f)	كرة اليد
golf	gūlf (m)	جولف
rowing	taʒðīf (m)	تجذيف
scuba diving	al ɣaws taḥt al mā' (m)	الغوص تحت الماء
cross-country skiing	riyāḍat al iski (f)	رياضة الإسكي
table tennis (ping-pong)	kurat aṭ ṭāwila (f)	كرة الطاولة
sailing	riyāḍa ibḥār al marākib (f)	رياضة إبحار المراكب
rally	sibāq as sayyārāt (m)	سباق السيّارات
rugby	raɣbi (m)	رغبي
snowboarding	tazalluʒ 'laθ θulūʒ (m)	تزلّج على الثلوج
archery	rimāya (f)	رماية

134. Gym

barbell	ḥadīda (f)	حديدة
dumbbells	dambilz (m)	دمبلز

training machine	ʒihāz tadrīb (m)	جهاز تدريب
exercise bicycle	darrāʒat tadrīb (f)	دراجة تدريب
treadmill	ʒihāz al maʃy (m)	جهاز المشي

horizontal bar	'uqla (f)	عقلة
parallel bars	al mutawāzi (m)	المتوازي
vault (vaulting horse)	hisān al maqābid (m)	حصان المقابض
mat (exercise ~)	hasīra (f)	حصيرة

skipping rope	habl an natt (m)	حبل النطّ
aerobics	at tamrīnāt al hiwā'iyya (pl)	التمرينات الهوائية
yoga	yūga (f)	يوجا

135. Ice hockey

ice hockey	huki (m)	هوكي
ice hockey player	lā'ib huki (m)	لاعب هوكي
to play ice hockey	la'ib al hūki	لعب الهوكي
ice	ʒalīd (m)	جليد

puck	qurs al huky (m)	قرص الهوكي
ice hockey stick	midrab al huki (m)	مضرب الهوكي
ice skates	zallāʒāt (pl)	زلاجات

| board (ice hockey rink ~) | ʒānib (m) | جانب |
| shot | ramya (f) | رمية |

goaltender	hāris al marma (m)	حارس المرمى
goal (score)	hadaf (m)	هدف
to score a goal	asāb al hadaf	أصاب الهدف

period	ʃawt (m)	شوط
second period	aʃ ʃawt aθ θāni (m)	الشوط الثاني
substitutes bench	dikkat al ihtiāty (f)	دكة الإحتياطي

136. Football

football	kurat al qadam (f)	كرة القدم
football player	lā'ib kurat al qadam (m)	لاعب كرة القدم
to play football	la'ib kurat al qadam	لعب كرة القدم

major league	ad dawriy al kibīr (m)	الدوريّ الكبير
football club	nādy kurat al qadam (m)	نادي كرة القدم
coach	mudarrib (m)	مدرّب
owner, proprietor	sāhib (m)	صاحب

team	farīq (m)	فريق
team captain	kabtan al farīq (m)	كابتن الفريق
player	lā'ib (m)	لاعب
substitute	lā'ib ihtiyātiy (m)	لاعب إحتياطيّ
forward	lā'ib huʒūm (m)	لاعب هجوم
centre forward	wasat al huʒūm (m)	وسط الهجوم

scorer	haddāf (m)	هدّاف
defender, back	mudāfiʿ (m)	مدافع
midfielder, halfback	lāʿib wasaṭ (m)	لاعب وسط

match	mubārāt (f)	مباراة
to meet (vi, vt)	qābal	قابل
final	mubarāt nihāʾiyya (f)	مباراة نهائيّة
semi-final	dawr an niṣf an nihāʾiy (m)	دور النصف النهائيّ
championship	buṭūla (f)	بطولة

period, half	ʃawṭ (m)	شوط
first period	aʃ ʃawṭ al awwal (m)	الشوط الأوّل
half-time	istirāḥa ma bayn aʃ ʃawṭayn (f)	إستراحة ما بين الشوطين

goal	marma (m)	مرمى
goalkeeper	ḥāris al marma (m)	حارس المرمى
goalpost	ʿāriḍa (f)	عارضة
crossbar	ʿāriḍa (f)	عارضة
net	ʃabaka (f)	شبكة
to concede a goal	samaḥ bi iṣābat al hadaf	سمح بإصابة الهدف

ball	kura (f)	كرة
pass	tamrīra (f)	تمريرة
kick	ḍarba (f)	ضربة
to kick (~ the ball)	ḍarab	ضرب
free kick (direct ~)	ḍarba ḥurra (f)	ضربة حرّة
corner kick	ḍarba zāwiya (f)	ضربة زاوية

attack	huʒūm (m)	هجوم
counterattack	haʒma muḍādda (f)	هجمة مضادّة
combination	tarkīb (m)	تركيب

referee	ḥakam (m)	حكم
to blow the whistle	ṣaffar	صفّر
whistle (sound)	ṣaffāra (f)	صفّارة
foul, misconduct	muxālafa (f)	مخالفة
to commit a foul	xālaf	خالف
to send off	ṭarad min al malʿab	طرد من الملعب

yellow card	al kārt al aṣfar (m)	الكارت الأصفر
red card	al kart al aḥmar (m)	الكارت الأحمر
disqualification	ḥirmān (m)	حرمان
to disqualify (vt)	ḥaram	حرم

penalty kick	ḍarbat ʒazāʾ (f)	ضربة جزاء
wall	ḥāʾiṭ (m)	حائط
to score (vi, vt)	aṣāb al hadaf	أصاب الهدف
goal (score)	hadaf (m)	هدف
to score a goal	aṣāb al hadaf	أصاب الهدف

substitution	tabdīl (m)	تبديل
to replace (a player)	baddal	بدّل
rules	qawāʿid (pl)	قواعد
tactics	taktīk (m)	تكتيك
stadium	malʿab (m)	ملعب
terrace	mudarraʒ (m)	مدرّج

| fan, supporter | muʃaʒʒiʿ (m) | مشجّع |
| to shout (vi) | ṣaraχ | صرخ |

| scoreboard | lawḥat an natīʒa (f) | لوحة النتيجة |
| score | natīʒa (f) | نتيجة |

defeat	hazīma (f)	هزيمة
to lose (not win)	χasir	خسر
draw	taʿādul (m)	تعادل
to draw (vi)	taʿādal	تعادل

victory	fawz (m)	فوز
to win (vi, vt)	fāz	فاز
champion	baṭal (m)	بطل
best (adj)	aḥsan	أحسن
to congratulate (vt)	hanna'	هنّأ

commentator	muʿalliq (m)	معلّق
to commentate (vt)	ʿallaq	علّق
broadcast	iðāʿa (f)	إذاعة

137. Alpine skiing

skis	zallāʒāt (pl)	زلّاجات
to ski (vi)	tazallaʒ	تزلّج
mountain-ski resort	muntaʒaʿ ʒabaliy lit tazalluʒ (m)	منتجع جبليّ للتزلّج
ski lift	miṣʿad (m)	مصعد

ski poles	ʿaṣayān at tazalluʒ (pl)	عصيان التزلّج
slope	munḥadar (m)	منحدر
slalom	slālum (m)	سلالوم

138. Tennis. Golf

golf	gūlf (m)	جولف
golf club	nādi gūlf (m)	نادي جولف
golfer	lāʿib gūlf (m)	لاعب جولف

hole	taʒwīf (m)	تجويف
club	miḍrab (m)	مضرب
golf trolley	ʿaraba lil gūlf (f)	عربة للجولف

| tennis | tinis (m) | تنس |
| tennis court | malʿab tinis (m) | ملعب تنس |

| serve | munāwala (f) | مناولة |
| to serve (vt) | nāwil | ناول |

racket	miḍrab (m)	مضرب
net	ʃabaka (f)	شبكة
ball	kura (f)	كرة

139. Chess

chess	ʃaṭranʒ (m)	شطرنج
chessmen	qiṭaʿ aʃ ʃaṭranʒ (pl)	قطع الشطرنج
chess player	lāʿib ʃaṭranʒ (m)	لاعب شطرنج
chessboard	lawḥat aʃ ʃaṭranʒ (f)	لوحة الشطرنج
chessman	qiṭʿa (f)	قطعة
White (white pieces)	qiṭaʿ bayḍāʾ (pl)	قطع بيضاء
Black (black pieces)	qiṭaʿ sawdāʾ (pl)	قطع سوداء
pawn	baydaq (m)	بيدق
bishop	fīl (m)	فيل
knight	ḥiṣān (m)	حصان
rook	qalʿa (f)	قلعة
queen	malika (f)	ملكة
king	malik (m)	ملك
move	xaṭwa (f)	خطوة
to move (vi, vt)	ḥarrak	حرّك
to sacrifice (vt)	ḍaḥḥa	ضحّى
castling	at tabyīt (m)	التبييت
check	kaʃ (m)	كش
checkmate	kaʃ māt (m)	كش مات
chess tournament	buṭūlat ʃaṭranʒ (f)	بطولة شطرنج
Grand Master	ustāð kabīr (m)	أستاذ كبير
combination	tarkīb (m)	تركيب
game (in chess)	dawr (m)	دور
draughts	dāma (f)	ضامة

140. Boxing

boxing	mulākama (f)	ملاكمة
fight (bout)	mulākama (f)	ملاكمة
boxing match	mubārāt mulākama (f)	مباراة ملاكمة
round (in boxing)	ʒawla (f)	جولة
ring	ḥalba (f)	حلبة
gong	nāqūs (m)	ناقوس
punch	ḍarba (f)	ضربة
knockdown	ḍarba ḥāsima (f)	ضربة حاسمة
knockout	ḍarba qāḍiya (f)	ضربة قاضية
to knock out	ḍarab ḍarba qāḍiya	ضرب ضربة قاضية
boxing glove	quffāz al mulākama (m)	قفاز الملاكمة
referee	ḥakam (m)	حكم
lightweight	al wazn al xafīf (m)	الوزن الخفيف
middleweight	al wazn al mutawassiṭ (m)	الوزن المتوسط
heavyweight	al wazn aθ θaqīl (m)	الوزن الثقيل

141. Sports. Miscellaneous

Olympic Games	alʿāb ulumbiyya (pl)	ألعاب أولمبيّة
winner	fā'iz (m)	فائز
to be winning	fāz	فاز
to win (vi)	fāz	فاز
leader	zaʿīm (m)	زعيم
to lead (vi)	taqaddam	تقدّم
first place	al martaba al ūla (f)	المرتبة الأولى
second place	al martaba aθ θāniya (f)	المرتبة الثانية
third place	al martaba aθ θāliθa (f)	المرتبة الثالثة
medal	midāliyya (f)	ميداليّة
trophy	ӡā'iza (f)	جائزة
prize cup (trophy)	ka's (m)	كأس
prize (in game)	ӡā'iza (f)	جائزة
main prize	akbar ӡā'iza (f)	أكبر جائزة
record	raqm qiyāsiy (m)	رقم قياسيّ
to set a record	fāz bi raqm qiyāsiy	فاز برقم قياسيّ
final	mubarāt nihā'iyya (f)	مباراة نهائيّة
final (adj)	nihā'iy	نهائيّ
champion	baṭal (m)	بطل
championship	buṭūla (f)	بطولة
stadium	malʿab (m)	ملعب
terrace	mudarraӡ (m)	مدرّج
fan, supporter	muʃaӡӡiʿ (m)	مشجّع
opponent, rival	ʿaduww (m)	عدوّ
start (start line)	χaṭṭ al bidāya (m)	خطّ البداية
finish line	χaṭṭ an nihāya (m)	خطّ النهاية
defeat	hazīma (f)	هزيمة
to lose (not win)	χasir	خسر
referee	ḥakam (m)	حكم
jury (judges)	hay'at al ḥukm (f)	هيئة الحكم
score	natīӡa (f)	نتيجة
draw	taʿādul (m)	تعادل
to draw (vi)	taʿādal	تعادل
point	nuqṭa (f)	نقطة
result (final score)	natīӡa nihā'iyya (f)	نتيجة نهائية
period	ʃawṭ (m)	شوط
half-time	istirāḥa ma bayn aʃ ʃawṭayn (f)	إستراحة ما بين الشوطين
doping	munaʃʃiṭāt (pl)	منشّطات
to penalise (vt)	ʿāqab	عاقب
to disqualify (vt)	ḥaram	حرم
apparatus	maʿadd riyāḍiy (f)	معدّ رياضيّ
javelin	rumḥ (m)	رمح

shot (metal ball)	ʒulla (f)	جلّة
ball (snooker, etc.)	kura (f)	كرة
aim (target)	hadaf (m)	هدف
target	hadaf (m)	هدف
to shoot (vi)	aṭlaq an nār	أطلق النار
accurate (~ shot)	maḍbūṭ	مضبوط
trainer, coach	mudarrib (m)	مدرّب
to train (sb)	darrab	درّب
to train (vi)	tadarrab	تدرّب
training	tadrīb (m)	تدريب
gym	markaz li liyāqa badaniyya (m)	مركز للياقة بدنيّة
exercise (physical)	tamrīn (m)	تمرين
warm-up (athlete ~)	tasχīn (m)	تسخين

Education

school	madrasa (f)	مدرسة
headmaster	mudīr madrasa (m)	مدير مدرسة
student (m)	tilmīð (m)	تلميذ
student (f)	tilmīða (f)	تلميذة
schoolboy	tilmīð (m)	تلميذ
schoolgirl	tilmīða (f)	تلميذة
to teach (sb)	'allam	علّم
to learn (language, etc.)	ta'allam	تعلّم
to learn by heart	ḥafaẓ	حفظ
to learn (~ to count, etc.)	ta'allam	تعلّم
to be at school	daras	درس
to go to school	ðahab ilal madrasa	ذهب إلى المدرسة
alphabet	alifbā' (m)	الفباء
subject (at school)	mādda (f)	مادّة
classroom	faṣl (m)	فصل
lesson	dars (m)	درس
playtime, break	istirāḥa (f)	إستراحة
school bell	ʒaras al madrasa (m)	جرس المدرسة
school desk	taxta lil madrasa (m)	تخّتة للمدرسة
blackboard	sabbūra (f)	سبّورة
mark	daraʒa (f)	درجة
good mark	daraʒa ʒayyida (f)	درجة جيّدة
bad mark	daraʒa ɣayr ʒayyida (f)	درجة غير جيّدة
to give a mark	a'ṭa daraʒa	أعطى درجة
mistake, error	xaṭa' (m)	خطأ
to make mistakes	axṭa'	أخطأ
to correct (an error)	ṣaḥḥaḥ	صحّح
crib	waraqat ɣaʃʃ (f)	ورقة غشّ
homework	wāʒib manziliy (m)	واجب منزليّ
exercise (in education)	tamrīn (m)	تمرين
to be present	ḥaḍar	حضر
to be absent	ɣāb	غاب
to miss school	taɣayyab 'an al madrasa	تغيّب عن المدرسة
to punish (vt)	'āqab	عاقب
punishment	'uqūba (f), 'iqāb (m)	عقوبة, عقاب
conduct (behaviour)	sulūk (m)	سلوك

school report	at taqrīr al madrasiy (m)	التقرير المدرسيّ
pencil	qalam ruṣāṣ (m)	قلم رصاص
rubber	astīka (f)	استيكة
chalk	ṭabāʃīr (m)	طباشير
pencil case	maqlama (f)	مقلمة

schoolbag	ʃanṭat al madrasa (f)	شنطة المدرسة
pen	qalam (m)	قلم
exercise book	daftar (m)	دفتر
textbook	kitāb taʕlīm (m)	كتاب تعليم
compasses	barȝal (m)	برجل

| to make technical drawings | rasam rasm taqniy | رسم رسمًا تقنيًا |
| technical drawing | rasm taqniy (m) | رسم تقنيّ |

poem	qaṣīda (f)	قصيدة
by heart (adv)	ʕan ẓahr qalb	عن ظهر قلب
to learn by heart	ḥafaẓ	حفظ

school holidays	ʕuṭla madrasiyya (f)	عطلة مدرسيّة
to be on holiday	ʕindahu ʕuṭla	عنده عطلة
to spend holidays	qaḍa al ʕuṭla	قضى العطلة

test (at school)	imtiḥān (m)	إمتحان
essay (composition)	inʃā' (m)	إنشاء
dictation	imlā' (m)	إملاء
exam (examination)	imtiḥān (m)	إمتحان
to do an exam	marr al imtiḥān	مرّ الإمتحان
experiment (e.g., chemistry ~)	taȝriba (f)	تجربة

143. College. University

academy	akadīmiyya (f)	أكاديميّة
university	ȝāmiʕa (f)	جامعة
faculty (e.g., ~ of Medicine)	kulliyya (f)	كلّيّة

student (masc.)	ṭālib (m)	طالب
student (fem.)	ṭāliba (f)	طالبة
lecturer (teacher)	muḥāḍir (m)	محاضر

| lecture hall, room | mudarraȝ (m) | مدرّج |
| graduate | mutaxarriȝ (m) | متخرّج |

| diploma | diblūma (f) | دبلومة |
| dissertation | risāla ʕilmiyya (f) | رسالة علميّة |

| study (report) | dirāsa (f) | دراسة |
| laboratory | muxtabar (m) | مختبر |

lecture	muḥāḍara (f)	محاضرة
coursemate	zamīl fiṣ ṣaff (m)	زميل في الصفّ
scholarship, bursary	minḥa dirāsiyya (f)	منحة دراسيّة
academic degree	daraȝa ʕilmiyya (f)	درجة علميّة

144. Sciences. Disciplines

mathematics	riyāḍīyyāt (pl)	رياضيّات
algebra	al ʒabr (m)	الجبر
geometry	handasa (f)	هندسة
astronomy	'ilm al falak (m)	علم الفلك
biology	'ilm al aḥyā' (m)	علم الأحياء
geography	ʒuɣrāfiya (f)	جغرافيا
geology	ʒiulūʒiya (f)	جيولوجيا
history	tarīχ (m)	تاريخ
medicine	ṭibb (m)	طبّ
pedagogy	'ilm at tarbiya (f)	علم التربية
law	qānūn (m)	قانون
physics	fizyā' (f)	فيزياء
chemistry	kimyā' (f)	كيمياء
philosophy	falsafa (f)	فلسفة
psychology	'ilm an nafs (m)	علم النفس

145. Writing system. Orthography

grammar	an naḥw waṣ ṣarf (m)	النحو والصرف
vocabulary	mufradāt al luɣa (pl)	مفردات اللغة
phonetics	ṣawtīyyāt (pl)	صوتيّات
noun	ism (m)	إسم
adjective	ṣifa (f)	صفة
verb	fi'l (m)	فعل
adverb	ẓarf (m)	ظرف
pronoun	ḍamīr (m)	ضمير
interjection	ḥarf nidā' (m)	حرف نداء
preposition	ḥarf al ʒarr (m)	حرف الجرّ
root	ʒiðr al kalima (m)	جذر الكلمة
ending	nihāya (f)	نهاية
prefix	sābiqa (f)	سابقة
syllable	maqṭa' lafʒiy (m)	مقطع لفظيّ
suffix	lāḥiqa (f)	لاحقة
stress mark	nabra (f)	نبرة
apostrophe	'alāmat ḥaðf (f)	علامة حذف
full stop	nuqṭa (f)	نقطة
comma	fāṣila (f)	فاصلة
semicolon	nuqṭa wa fāṣila (f)	نقطة وفاصلة
colon	nuqṭatān ra'siyyatān (du)	نقطتان رأسيتان
ellipsis	θalāθ nuqaṭ (pl)	ثلاث نقط
question mark	'alāmat istifhām (f)	علامة إستفهام
exclamation mark	'alāmat ta'aʒʒub (f)	علامة تعجّب

inverted commas	ʿalāmāt al iqtibās (pl)	علامات الإقتباس
in inverted commas	bayn ʿalāmatay al iqtibās	بين علامتي الإقتباس
parenthesis	qawsān (du)	قوسان
in parenthesis	bayn al qawsayn	بين القوسين

hyphen	ʿalāmat waṣl (f)	علامة وصل
dash	ʃurṭa (f)	شرطة
space (between words)	farāɣ (m)	فراغ

| letter | ḥarf (m) | حرف |
| capital letter | ḥarf kabīr (m) | حرف كبير |

| vowel (n) | ḥarf ṣawtiy (m) | حرف صوتيّ |
| consonant (n) | ḥarf sākin (m) | حرف ساكن |

sentence	ʒumla (f)	جملة
subject	fāʿil (m)	فاعل
predicate	musnad (m)	مسند

line	saṭr (m)	سطر
on a new line	min bidāyat as saṭr	من بداية السطر
paragraph	fiqra (f)	فقرة

word	kalima (f)	كلمة
group of words	maʒmūʿa min al kalimāt (pl)	مجموعة من الكلمات
expression	ʿibāra (f)	عبارة
synonym	murādif (m)	مرادف
antonym	mutaḍādd luɣawiy (m)	متضادّ

rule	qāʿida (f)	قاعدة
exception	istiθnāʾ (m)	إستثناء
correct (adj)	ṣaḥīḥ	صحيح

conjugation	ṣarf (m)	صرف
declension	taṣrīf al asmāʾ (m)	تصريف الأسماء
nominal case	ḥāla ismiyya (f)	حالة إسميّة
question	suʾāl (m)	سؤال
to underline (vt)	waḍaʿ xaṭṭ taḥt	وضع خطّا تحت
dotted line	xaṭṭ munaqqaṭ (m)	خط منقط

146. Foreign languages

language	luɣa (f)	لغة
foreign (adj)	aʒnabiy	أجنبيّ
foreign language	luɣa aʒnabiyya (f)	لغة أجنبيّة
to study (vt)	daras	درس
to learn (language, etc.)	taʿallam	تعلّم

to read (vi, vt)	qaraʾ	قرأ
to speak (vi, vt)	takallam	تكلّم
to understand (vt)	fahim	فهم
to write (vt)	katab	كتب
fast (adv)	bi surʿa	بسرعة
slowly (adv)	bi buṭʾ	ببطء

fluently (adv)	bi ṭalāqa	بطلاقة
rules	qawāʻid (pl)	قواعد
grammar	an nahw waṣ ṣarf (m)	النحو والصرف
vocabulary	mufradāt al luɣa (pl)	مفردات اللغة
phonetics	ṣawtīyyāt (pl)	صوتيّات

textbook	kitāb taʻlīm (m)	كتاب تعليم
dictionary	qāmūs (m)	قاموس
teach-yourself book	kitāb taʻlīm ðātiy (m)	كتاب تعليم ذاتيّ
phrasebook	kitāb lil ʻibārāt aʃ ʃāʼiʻa (m)	كتاب للعبارت الشائعة

cassette, tape	ʃarīṭ (m)	شريط
videotape	ʃarīṭ vidiyu (m)	شريط فيديو
CD, compact disc	si di (m)	سي دي
DVD	di vi di (m)	دي في دي

alphabet	alifbāʼ (m)	الفباء
to spell (vt)	tahaʒʒa	تهجّى
pronunciation	nuṭq (m)	نطق

accent	lukna (f)	لكنة
with an accent	bi lukna	بلكنة
without an accent	bi dūn lukna	بدون لكنة

| word | kalima (f) | كلمة |
| meaning | maʻna (m) | معنى |

course (e.g. a French ~)	dawra (f)	دورة
to sign up	saʒʒal ismahu	سجّل إسمه
teacher	mudarris (m)	مدرس

translation (process)	tarʒama (f)	ترجمة
translation (text, etc.)	tarʒama (f)	ترجمة
translator	mutarʒim (m)	مترجم
interpreter	mutarʒim fawriy (m)	مترجم فوريّ

| polyglot | ʻalīm bi ʻiddat luɣāt (m) | عليم بعدّة لغات |
| memory | ðākira (f) | ذاكرة |

147. Fairy tale characters

Father Christmas	baba nuwīl (m)	بابا نويل
Cinderella	sindrīla	سيندريلا
mermaid	ḥūriyyat al bahr (f)	حوريّة البحر
Neptune	nibtūn (m)	نبتون

magician, wizard	sāḥir (m)	ساحر
fairy	sāḥira (f)	ساحرة
magic (adj)	siḥriy	سحريّ
magic wand	ʻaṣa siḥriyya (f)	عصا سحريّة

fairy tale	ḥikāya xayāliyya (f)	حكاية خياليّة
miracle	muʻʒiza (f)	معجزة
dwarf	qazam (m)	قزم

to turn into …	taḥawwal ila …	...تحوّل إلى
ghost	ʃabaḥ (m)	شبح
phantom	ʃabaḥ (m)	شبح
monster	waḥʃ (m)	وحش
dragon	tinnīn (m)	تنّين
giant	ʿimlāq (m)	عملاق

148. Zodiac Signs

Aries	burʒ al ḥamal (m)	برج الحمل
Taurus	burʒ aθ θawr (m)	برج الثور
Gemini	burʒ al ʒawzāʾ (m)	برج الجوزاء
Cancer	burʒ as saraṭān (m)	برج السرطان
Leo	burʒ al asad (m)	برج الأسد
Virgo	burʒ al ʿaðrāʾ (m)	برج العذراء
Libra	burʒ al mīzān (m)	برج الميزان
Scorpio	burʒ al ʿaqrab (m)	برج العقرب
Sagittarius	burʒ al qaws (m)	برج القوس
Capricorn	burʒ al ʒaday (m)	برج الجدي
Aquarius	burʒ ad dalw (m)	برج الدلو
Pisces	burʒ al ḥūt (m)	برج الحوت
character	ṭabʿ (m)	طبع
character traits	aṣ ṣifāt aʃ ʃaxṣiyya (pl)	الصفات الشخصيّة
behaviour	sulūk (m)	سلوك
to tell fortunes	tanabbaʾ	تنبّأ
fortune-teller	ʿarrāfa (f)	عرّافة
horoscope	tawaqquʿāt al abrāʒ (pl)	توقّعات الأبراج

Arts

theatre	masraḥ (m)	مسرح
opera	ubra (f)	أوبرا
operetta	ubirīt (f)	أوبريت
ballet	balīh (m)	باليه

theatre poster	mulṣaq (m)	ملصق
theatre company	firqa (f)	فرقة
tour	ʒawlat fannānīn (f)	جولة فنانين
to be on tour	taʒawwal	تجوّل
to rehearse (vi, vt)	aʒra bruvāt	أجرى بروفات
rehearsal	brūva (f)	بروفة
repertoire	barnāmaʒ al masraḥ (m)	برنامج المسرح

performance	adā' fanniy (m)	أداء فنّيّ
theatrical show	'arḍ masraḥiy (m)	عرض مسرحيّ
play	masraḥiyya (f)	مسرحيّة

ticket	taðkira (f)	تذكرة
booking office	ʃubbāk at taðākir (m)	شبّاك التذاكر
lobby, foyer	ṣāla (f)	صالة
coat check (cloakroom)	ɣurfat al ma'āṭif (f)	غرفة المعاطف
cloakroom ticket	biṭāqat 'īdā' al ma'āṭif (f)	بطاقة إيداع المعاطف
binoculars	minẓār (m)	منظار
usher	ḥāʒib (m)	حاجب

stalls (orchestra seats)	karāsi al urkistra (pl)	كراسي الأوركسترا
balcony	balakūna (f)	بلكونة
dress circle	ʃurfa (f)	شرفة
box	lūʒ (m)	لوج
row	ṣaff (m)	صفّ
seat	maq'ad (m)	مقعد

audience	ʒumhūr (m)	جمهور
spectator	muʃāhid (m)	مشاهد
to clap (vi, vt)	ṣaffaq	صفّق
applause	taṣfīq (m)	تصفيق
ovation	taṣfīq ḥārr (m)	تصفيق حارّ

stage	xaʃabat al masraḥ (f)	خشبة المسرح
curtain	sitāra (f)	ستارة
scenery	dikūr (m)	ديكور
backstage	kawalīs (pl)	كواليس

scene (e.g. the last ~)	maʃhad (m)	مشهد
act	faṣl (m)	فصل
interval	istirāḥa (f)	إستراحة

150. Cinema

| actor | mumaθθil (m) | ممثّل |
| actress | mumaθθila (f) | ممثّلة |

cinema (industry)	sinima (f)	سينما
film	film sinimā'iy (m)	فيلم سينمائيّ
episode	ʒuz' min al film (m)	جزء من الفيلم

detective film	film bulīsiy (m)	فيلم بوليسيّ
action film	film ḥaraka (m)	فيلم حركة
adventure film	film muɣāmarāt (m)	فيلم مغامرات
science fiction film	film ɣayāl 'ilmiy (m)	فيلم خيال علميّ
horror film	film ru'b (m)	فيلم رعب

comedy film	film kumīdiya (f)	فيلم كوميديا
melodrama	miludrāma (m)	ميلودراما
drama	drāma (f)	دراما

fictional film	film fanniy (m)	فيلم فنّيّ
documentary	film waθā'iqiy (m)	فيلم وثائقيّ
cartoon	film kartūn (m)	فيلم كرتون
silent films	sinima ṣāmita (f)	سينما صامتة

role (part)	dawr (m)	دور
leading role	dawr ra'īsi (m)	دور رئيسي
to play (vi, vt)	maθθal	مثّل

film star	naʒm sinimā'iy (m)	نجم سينمائيّ
well-known (adj)	ma'rūf	معروف
famous (adj)	maʃhūr	مشهور
popular (adj)	maḥbūb	محبوب

script (screenplay)	sināriyu (m)	سيناريو
scriptwriter	kātib sināriyu (m)	كاتب سيناريو
film director	muɣriʒ (m)	مخرج
producer	muntiʒ (m)	منتج
assistant	musā'id (m)	مساعد
cameraman	muṣawwir (m)	مصوّر
stuntman	mu'addi maʃahid ɣaṭīra (m)	مؤدّي مشاهد خطيرة
double (body double)	mumaθθil badīl (m)	ممثّل بديل

to shoot a film	ṣawwar film	صوّر فيلمًا
audition, screen test	taʒribat adā' (f)	تجربة أداء
shooting	taṣwīr (m)	تصوير
film crew	ṭāqim al film (m)	طاقم الفيلم
film set	mintaqat at taṣwīr (f)	منطقة التصوير
camera	kamira sinimā'iyya (f)	كاميرا سينمائيّة

cinema	sinima (f)	سينما
screen (e.g. big ~)	ʃāʃa (f)	شاشة
to show a film	'araḍ film	عرض فيلمًا

| soundtrack | musīqa taṣwīriyya (f) | موسيقى تصويريّة |
| special effects | mu'aθθirāt ɣāṣṣa (pl) | مؤثّرات خاصّة |

subtitles	tarӡamat al ḥiwār (f)	ترجمة الحوار
credits	ʃārat an nihāya (f)	شارة النهاية
translation	tarӡama (f)	ترجمة

151. Painting

art	fann (m)	فنّ
fine arts	funūn ӡamīla (pl)	فنون جميلة
art gallery	maʿraḍ fanniy (m)	معرض فنّيّ
art exhibition	maʿraḍ fanniy (m)	معرض فنّيّ

painting (art)	taṣwīr (m)	تصوير
graphic art	rusūmiyyāt (pl)	رسوميّات
abstract art	fann taӡrīdiy (m)	فنّ تجريديّ
impressionism	al intibāʿiyya (f)	الإنطباعيّة

picture (painting)	lawḥa (f)	لوحة
drawing	rasm (m)	رسم
poster	mulṣaq iʿlāniy (m)	ملصق إعلانيّ

illustration (picture)	rasm tawḍīḥiy (m)	رسم توضيحيّ
miniature	ṣūra muṣaɣɣara (f)	صورة مصغّرة
copy (of painting, etc.)	nusχa (f)	نسخة
reproduction	nusχa ṭibq al aṣl (f)	نسخة طبق الأصل

mosaic	fusayfisāʾ (f)	فسيفساء
stained glass window	zuӡāӡ muʿaʃʃaq (m)	زجاج معشّق
fresco	taṣwīr ӡiṣṣiy (m)	تصوير جصّيّ
engraving	naqʃ (m)	نقش

bust (sculpture)	timθāl niṣfiy (m)	تمثال نصفيّ
sculpture	naḥt (m)	نحت
statue	timθāl (m)	تمثال
plaster of Paris	ӡībs (m)	جيبس
plaster (as adj)	min al ӡībs	من الجيبس

portrait	burtrī (m)	بورتريه
self-portrait	burtrīh ðātiy (m)	بورتريه ذاتيّ
landscape painting	lawḥat manẓar ṭabīʿiy (f)	لوحة منظر طبيعيّ
still life	ṭabīʿa ṣāmita (f)	طبيعة صامتة
caricature	ṣūra karikaturiyya (f)	صورة كاريكاتوريّة
sketch	rasm tamhīdiy (m)	رسم تمهيديّ

paint	lawn (m)	لون
watercolor paint	alwān māʾiyya (m)	ألوان مائية
oil (paint)	zayt (m)	زيت
pencil	qalam ruṣāṣ (m)	قلم رصاص
Indian ink	ḥibr hindiy (m)	حبر هنديّ
charcoal	faḥm (m)	فحم

to draw (vi, vt)	rasam	رسم
to paint (vi, vt)	rasam	رسم
to pose (vi)	qaʿad	قعد
artist's model (masc.)	mudil ḥay (m)	موديل حيّ

artist's model (fem.)	mudil ḥay (m)	موديل حيّ
artist (painter)	rassām (m)	رسّام
work of art	'amal fanniy (m)	عمل فنّيّ
masterpiece	tuḥfa fanniyya (f)	تحفة فنّيّة
studio (artist's workroom)	warʃa (f)	ورشة

canvas (cloth)	kanava (f)	كانفا
easel	musnad ar rasm (m)	مسند الرسم
palette	lawḥat al alwān (f)	لوحة الألوان

frame (picture ~, etc.)	iṭār (m)	إطار
restoration	tarmīm (m)	ترميم
to restore (vt)	rammam	رمّم

152. Literature & Poetry

literature	adab (m)	أدب
author (writer)	mu'allif (m)	مؤلّف
pseudonym	ism musta'ār (m)	إسم مستعار

book	kitāb (m)	كتاب
volume	muʒallad (m)	مجلّد
table of contents	fihris (m)	فهرس
page	ṣafḥa (f)	صفحة
main character	aʃ ʃaχṣiyya ar raʔīsiyya (f)	الشخصيّة الرئيسيّة
autograph	tawqīʕ al mu'allif (m)	توقيع المؤلّف

short story	qiṣṣa qaṣīra (f)	قصّة قصيرة
story (novella)	qiṣṣa (f)	قصّة
novel	riwāya (f)	رواية
work (writing)	mu'allif (m)	مؤلّف
fable	ḥikāya (f)	حكاية
detective novel	riwāya bulīsiyya (f)	رواية بوليسيّة

poem (verse)	qaṣīda (f)	قصيدة
poetry	ʃi'r (m)	شعر
poem (epic, ballad)	qaṣīda (f)	قصيدة
poet	ʃā'ir (m)	شاعر

fiction	adab ʒamīl (m)	أدب جميل
science fiction	χayāl 'ilmiy (m)	خيال علميّ
adventures	adab al muɣāmarāt (m)	أدب المغامرات
educational literature	adab tarbawiy (m)	أدب تربويّ
children's literature	adab al aṭfāl (m)	أدب الأطفال

153. Circus

circus	sirk (m)	سيرك
travelling circus	sirk mutanaqqil (m)	سيرك متنقّل
programme	barnāmaʒ (m)	برنامج
performance	adā' fanniy (m)	أداء فنّيّ
act (circus ~)	dawr (m)	دور

circus ring	ḥalbat as sirk (f)	حلبة السيرك
pantomime (act)	'arḍ 'īmā'y (m)	عرض إيمائي
clown	muharriʒ (m)	مهرّج
acrobat	bahlawān (m)	بهلوان
acrobatics	al'āb bahlawāniyya (f)	ألعاب بهلوانيّة
gymnast	lā'ib ʒumbāz (m)	لاعب جنباز
acrobatic gymnastics	ʒumbāz (m)	جنباز
somersault	ʃaqlaba (f)	شقلبة
strongman	lā'ib riyāḍiy (m)	لاعب رياضيّ
tamer (e.g., lion ~)	murawwiḍ (m)	مروّض
rider (circus horse ~)	fāris (m)	فارس
assistant	musā'id (m)	مساعد
stunt	al'āb bahlawāniyya (f)	ألعاب بهلوانيّة
magic trick	xid'a siḥriyya (f)	خدعة سحريّة
conjurer, magician	sāḥir (m)	ساحر
juggler	bahlawān (m)	بهلوان
to juggle (vi, vt)	la'ib bi kurāt 'adīda	لعب بكرات عديدة
animal trainer	mudarrib ḥayawānāt (m)	مدرّب حيوانات
animal training	tadrīb al ḥayawānāt (m)	تدريب الحيوانات
to train (animals)	darrab	درّب

154. Music. Pop music

music	musīqa (f)	موسيقى
musician	'āzif (m)	عازف
musical instrument	'āla musiqiyya (f)	آلة موسيقيّة
to play ...	'azaf ...	عزف...
guitar	gitār (m)	جيتار
violin	kamān (m)	كمان
cello	tʃīlu (m)	تشيلو
double bass	kamān aʒhar (m)	كمان أجهر
harp	qiθār (m)	قيثار
piano	biānu (m)	بيانو
grand piano	biānu kibīr (m)	بيانو كبير
organ	arɣan (m)	أرغن
wind instruments	'ālāt nafxiyya (pl)	آلات نفخيّة
oboe	ubwa (m)	أوبوا
saxophone	saksufūn (m)	ساكسوفون
clarinet	klarnīt (m)	كلارنيت
flute	flut (m)	فلوت
trumpet	būq (m)	بوق
accordion	ukurdiūn (m)	أكورديون
drum	ṭabla (f)	طبلة
duo	θunā'iy (m)	ثنائيّ
trio	θulāθy (m)	ثلاثيّ

quartet	rubāʿiy (m)	رباعيّ
choir	χūrus (m)	خورس
orchestra	urkistra (f)	أوركسترا
pop music	musīqa al bub (f)	موسيقى البوب
rock music	musīqa ar rūk (f)	موسيقى الروك
rock group	firqat ar rūk (f)	فرقة الروك
jazz	ʒāz (m)	جاز
idol	maʿbūd (m)	معبود
admirer, fan	muʿʒab (m)	معجب
concert	ḥafla mūsiqiyya (f)	حفلة موسيقيّة
symphony	simfūniyya (f)	سمفونيّة
composition	qiṭʿa mūsiqiyya (f)	قطعة موسيقيّة
to compose (write)	allaf	ألّف
singing (n)	γināʾ (m)	غناء
song	uγniyya (f)	أغنيّة
tune (melody)	laḥn (m)	لحن
rhythm	ʾīqāʿ (m)	إيقاع
blues	musīqa al blūz (f)	موسيقى البلوز
sheet music	nutāt (pl)	نوتات
baton	ʿaṣa al mayistru (m)	عصا المايسترو
bow	qaws (m)	قوس
string	watar (m)	وتر
case (e.g. guitar ~)	ʃanṭa (f)	شنطة

Rest. Entertainment. Travel

155. Trip. Travel

tourism, travel	siyāḥa (f)	سياحة
tourist	sā'iḥ (m)	سائح
trip, voyage	riḥla (f)	رحلة
adventure	muɣāmara (f)	مغامرة
trip, journey	riḥla (f)	رحلة
holiday	ʿuṭla (f)	عطلة
to be on holiday	ʿindahu ʿuṭla	عنده عطلة
rest	istirāḥa (f)	إستراحة
train	qiṭār (m)	قطار
by train	bil qiṭār	بالقطار
aeroplane	ṭā'ira (f)	طائرة
by aeroplane	biṭ ṭā'ira	بالطائرة
by car	bis sayyāra	بالسيّارة
by ship	bis safīna	بالسفينة
luggage	aʃ ʃunaṭ (pl)	الشنط
suitcase	ḥaqībat safar (f)	حقيبة سفر
luggage trolley	ʿarabat ʃunaṭ (f)	عربة شنط
passport	ʒawāz as safar (m)	جواز السفر
visa	taʃīra (f)	تأشيرة
ticket	taðkira (f)	تذكرة
air ticket	taðkirat ṭā'ira (f)	تذكرة طائرة
guidebook	dalīl (m)	دليل
map (tourist ~)	xarīṭa (f)	خريطة
area (rural ~)	mintaqa (f)	منطقة
place, site	makān (m)	مكان
exotica (n)	ɣarāba (f)	غرابة
exotic (adj)	ɣarīb	غريب
amazing (adj)	mudhiʃ	مدهش
group	maʒmūʿa (f)	مجموعة
excursion, sightseeing tour	ʒawla (f)	جولة
guide (person)	murʃid (m)	مرشد

156. Hotel

hotel	funduq (m)	فندق
motel	mutīl (m)	موتيل
three-star (~ hotel)	θalāθat nuʒūm	ثلاثة نجوم

five-star	xamsat nuʒūm	خمسة نجوم
to stay (in a hotel, etc.)	nazal	نزل
room	ɣurfa (f)	غرفة
single room	ɣurfa li ʃaxṣ wāḥid (f)	غرفة لشخص واحد
double room	ɣurfa li ʃaxṣayn (f)	غرفة لشخصين
to book a room	ḥaʒaz ɣurfa	حجز غرفة
half board	waʒbitān fil yawm (du)	وجبتان في اليوم
full board	θalāθ waʒabāt fil yawm	ثلاث وجبات في اليوم
with bath	bi ḥawḍ al istiḥmām	بحوض الإستحمام
with shower	bid duʃ	بالدوش
satellite television	tilivizyūn faḍā'iy (m)	تلفزيون فضائيّ
air-conditioner	takyīf (m)	تكييف
towel	fūṭa (f)	فوطة
key	miftāḥ (m)	مفتاح
administrator	mudīr (m)	مدير
chambermaid	'āmilat tanẓīf ɣuraf (f)	عاملة تنظيف غرف
porter	ḥammāl (m)	حمّال
doorman	bawwāb (m)	بوّاب
restaurant	maṭ'am (m)	مطعم
pub, bar	bār (m)	بار
breakfast	fuṭūr (m)	فطور
dinner	'aʃā' (m)	عشاء
buffet	bufīh (m)	بوفيه
lobby	radha (f)	ردهة
lift	miṣ'ad (m)	مصعد
DO NOT DISTURB	ar raʒā' 'adam al iz'āʒ	الرجاء عدم الإزعاج
NO SMOKING	mamnū' at tadxīn	ممنوع التدخين

157. Books. Reading

book	kitāb (m)	كتاب
author	mu'allif (m)	مؤلّف
writer	kātib (m)	كاتب
to write (~ a book)	allaf	ألّف
reader	qāri' (m)	قارئ
to read (vi, vt)	qara'	قرأ
reading (activity)	qirā'a (f)	قراءة
silently (to oneself)	sirran	سرًّا
aloud (adv)	bi ṣawt 'āli	بصوت عال
to publish (vt)	naʃar	نشر
publishing (process)	naʃr (m)	نشر
publisher	nāʃir (m)	ناشر
publishing house	dār aṭ ṭibā'a wan naʃr (f)	دار الطباعة والنشر
to come out (be released)	ṣadar	صدر

release (of a book)	ṣudūr (m)	صدور
print run	'adad an nusaχ (m)	عدد النسخ
bookshop	maḥall kutub (m)	محلّ كتب
library	maktaba (f)	مكتبة
story (novella)	qiṣṣa (f)	قصّة
short story	qiṣṣa qaṣīra (f)	قصّة قصيرة
novel	riwāya (f)	رواية
detective novel	riwāya bulīsiyya (f)	رواية بوليسيّة
memoirs	muðakkirāt (pl)	مذكّرات
legend	usṭūra (f)	أسطورة
myth	χurāfa (f)	خرافة
poetry, poems	ʃiʿr (m)	شعر
autobiography	sīrat ḥayāt (f)	سيرة حياة
selected works	muχtārāt (pl)	مختارات
science fiction	χayāl 'ilmiy (m)	خيال علميّ
title	'unwān (m)	عنوان
introduction	muqaddima (f)	مقدّمة
title page	ṣafḥat al 'unwān (f)	صفحة العنوان
chapter	faṣl (m)	فصل
extract	qiṭʿa (f)	قطعة
episode	maʃhad (m)	مشهد
plot (storyline)	mawdūʿ (m)	موضوع
contents	muḥtawayāt (pl)	محتويات
table of contents	fihris (m)	فهرس
main character	aʃ ʃaχṣiyya ar raʾīsiyya (f)	الشخصيّة الرئيسيّة
volume	muʒallad (m)	مجلّد
cover	ɣilāf (m)	غلاف
binding	taʒlīd (m)	تجليد
bookmark	ʃarīṭ (m)	شريط
page	ṣafḥa (f)	صفحة
to page through	qallab aṣ ṣafaḥāt	قلّب الصفحات
margins	hāmiʃ (m)	هامش
annotation (marginal note, etc.)	mulāḥaza (f)	ملاحظة
footnote	mulāḥaza (f)	ملاحظة
text	naṣṣ (m)	نصّ
type, fount	nawʿ al χaṭṭ (m)	نوع الخطّ
misprint, typo	χaṭaʾ maṭbaʿiy (m)	خطأ مطبعيّ
translation	tarʒama (f)	ترجمة
to translate (vt)	tarʒam	ترجم
original (n)	aṣliy (m)	أصليّ
famous (adj)	maʃhūr	مشهور
unknown (not famous)	ɣayr maʿrūf	غير معروف
interesting (adj)	mumtiʿ	ممتع

bestseller	akθar mabī'an (m)	أكثر مبيعًا
dictionary	qāmūs (m)	قاموس
textbook	kitāb ta'līm (m)	كتاب تعليم
encyclopedia	mawsū'a (f)	موسوعة

158. Hunting. Fishing

hunting	ṣayd (m)	صيد
to hunt (vi, vt)	iṣṭād	إصطاد
hunter	ṣayyād (m)	صيّاد
to shoot (vi)	aṭlaq an nār	أطلق النار
rifle	bunduqiyya (f)	بندقيّة
bullet (shell)	ruṣāṣa (f)	رصاصة
shot (lead balls)	raʃʃ (m)	رشّ
steel trap	maṣyada (f)	مصيدة
snare (for birds, etc.)	faχχ (m)	فخّ
to fall into the steel trap	waqa' fi faχχ	وقع في فخّ
to lay a steel trap	naṣab faχχ	نصب فخّا
poacher	sāriq aṣ ṣayd (m)	سارق الصيد
game (in hunting)	ṣayd (m)	صيد
hound dog	kalb ṣayd (m)	كلب صيد
safari	safāri (m)	سفاري
mounted animal	ḥayawān muḥannaṭ (m)	حيوان محنّط
fisherman	ṣayyād as samak (m)	صيّاد السمك
fishing (angling)	ṣayd as samak (m)	صيد السمك
to fish (vi)	iṣṭād as samak	إصطاد السمك
fishing rod	ṣannāra (f)	صنّارة
fishing line	χayṭ (m)	خيط
hook	ʃaṣṣ aṣ ṣayd (m)	شصّ الصيد
float	'awwāma (f)	عوّامة
bait	ṭu'm (m)	طعم
to cast a line	ṭaraḥ aṣ ṣinnāra	طرح الصنّارة
to bite (ab. fish)	'aḍḍ	عضّ
catch (of fish)	as samak al muṣṭād (m)	السمك المصطاد
ice-hole	fatḥa fil ʒalīd (f)	فتحة في الجليد
fishing net	ʃabakat aṣ ṣayd (f)	شبكة الصيد
boat	markab (m)	مركب
to net (to fish with a net)	iṣṭād biʃ ʃabaka	إصطاد بالشبكة
to cast[throw] the net	rama ʃabaka	رمى شبكة
to haul the net in	aχraʒ ʃabaka	أخرج شبكة
to fall into the net	waqa' fi ʃabaka	وقع في شبكة
whaler (person)	ṣayyād al ḥūt (m)	صيّاد الحوت
whaleboat	safīnat ṣayd al ḥītān (f)	سفينة صيد الحيتان
harpoon	ḥarba (f)	حربة

159. Games. Billiards

billiards	bilyārdu (m)	بليباردو
billiard room, hall	qā'at bilyārdu (m)	قاعة بلياردو
ball (snooker, etc.)	kura (f)	كرة
to pocket a ball	aṣqaṭ kura	أصقط كرة
cue	'aṣa bilyardu (f)	عصا بلياردو
pocket	ʒayb bilyārdu (m)	جيب بلياردو

160. Games. Playing cards

diamonds	ad dināriy (m)	الديناريّ
spades	al bastūniy (m)	البستونيّ
hearts	al kūba (f)	الكوية
clubs	as sibātiy (m)	السباتيّ
ace	'ās (m)	آس
king	malik (m)	ملك
queen	malika (f)	ملكة
jack, knave	walad (m)	ولد
playing card	waraqa (f)	ورقة
cards	waraq (m)	ورق
trump	waraqa rābiḥa (f)	ورقة رابحة
pack of cards	dasta waraq al la'b (f)	دستة ورق اللعب
point	nuqṭa (f)	نقطة
to deal (vi, vt)	farraq	فرّق
to shuffle (cards)	xallaṭ	خلط
lead, turn (n)	dawr (m)	دور
cardsharp	muḥtāl fil qimār (m)	محتال في القمار

161. Casino. Roulette

casino	kazinu (m)	كازينو
roulette (game)	rulīt (m)	روليت
bet	rihān (m)	رهان
to place bets	waḍa' ar rihān	وضع الرهان
red	aḥmar (m)	أحمر
black	aswad (m)	أسود
to bet on red	wada' ar rihān 'alal aḥmar	وضع الرهان على الأحمر
to bet on black	wada' ar rihān 'alal aswad	وضع الرهان على الأسود
croupier (dealer)	muwaẓẓaf nādi al qimār (m)	موظف نادي القمار
to spin the wheel	dawwar al 'aʒala	دوّر العجلة
rules (~ of the game)	qawā'id (pl)	قواعد
chip	fīʃa (f)	فيشة
to win (vi, vt)	kasab	كسب
win (winnings)	ribḥ (m)	ربح

| to lose (~ 100 dollars) | χasir | خسر |
| loss (losses) | χisāra (f) | خسارة |

player	lā'ib (m)	لاعب
blackjack (card game)	blɛkdʒɛk (m)	بلاك جاك
craps (dice game)	lu'bat an nard (f)	لعبة النرد
dice (a pair of ~)	zahr an nard (m)	زهر النرد
fruit machine	'ālat qumār (f)	آلة قمار

162. Rest. Games. Miscellaneous

to stroll (vi, vt)	tanazzah	تنزّه
stroll (leisurely walk)	tanazzuh (m)	تنزّه
car ride	ʒawla bis sayyāra (f)	جولة بالسيّارة
adventure	muɣāmara (f)	مغامرة
picnic	nuzha (f)	نزهة

game (chess, etc.)	lu'ba (f)	لعبة
player	lā'ib (m)	لاعب
game (one ~ of chess)	dawr (m)	دور

collector (e.g. philatelist)	ʒāmi' (m)	جامع
to collect (stamps, etc.)	ʒama'	جمع
collection	maʒmū'a (f)	مجموعة

crossword puzzle	kalimāt mutaqāṭi'a (pl)	كلمات متقاطعة
racecourse (hippodrome)	ḥalbat sibāq al χuyūl (f)	حلبة سباق الخيول
disco (discotheque)	disku (m)	ديسكو

| sauna | sāuna (f) | ساونا |
| lottery | yanaṣīb (m) | يانصيب |

camping trip	riḥlat taχyīm (f)	رحلة تخييم
camp	muχayyam (m)	مخيّم
tent (for camping)	χayma (f)	خيمة
compass	būṣila (f)	بوصلة
camper	muχayyim (m)	مخيّم

to watch (film, etc.)	ʃāhid	شاهد
viewer	muʃāhid (m)	مشاهد
TV show (TV program)	barnāmaʒ tiliviziyūniy (m)	برنامج تليفزيونيّ

163. Photography

| camera (photo) | kamira (f) | كاميرا |
| photo, picture | ṣūra (f) | صورة |

photographer	muṣawwir (m)	مصوّر
photo studio	istūdiyu taṣwīr (m)	إستوديو تصوير
photo album	albūm aṣ ṣuwar (m)	ألبوم الصور
camera lens	'adasa (f)	عدسة
telephoto lens	'adasa tiliskūpiyya (f)	عدسة تلسكوبيّة

| filter | filtir (m) | فلتر |
| lens | 'adasa (f) | عدسة |

optics (high-quality ~)	aʒhiza baṣariyya (pl)	أجهزة بصريّة
diaphragm (aperture)	bu'ra (f)	بؤرة
exposure time (shutter speed)	muddat at ta'rīḍ (f)	مدة التعريض
viewfinder	al 'ayn al fāḥiṣa (f)	العين الفاحصة

digital camera	kamira raqmiyya (f)	كاميرا رقميّة
tripod	ḥāmil θulāθiy (m)	حامل ثلاثيّ
flash	flāʃ (m)	فلاش

to photograph (vt)	ṣawwar	صوّر
to take pictures	ṣawwar	صوّر
to have one's picture taken	taṣawwar	تصوّر

focus	bu'rat al 'adasa (f)	بؤرة العدسة
to focus	rakkaz	ركّز
sharp, in focus (adj)	wāḍiḥ	واضح
sharpness	wuḍūḥ (m)	وضوح

| contrast | tabāyun (m) | تباين |
| contrast (as adj) | mutabāyin | متباين |

picture (photo)	ṣūra (f)	صورة
negative (n)	ṣūra sāliba (f)	صورة سالبة
film (a roll of ~)	film (m)	فيلم
frame (still)	iṭār (m)	إطار
to print (photos)	ṭaba'	طبع

164. Beach. Swimming

beach	ʃāṭi' (m)	شاطئ
sand	raml (m)	رمل
deserted (beach)	mahʒūr	مهجور

suntan	sumrat al baʃara (f)	سمرة البشرة
to get a tan	taʃammas	تشمّس
tanned (adj)	asmar	أسمر
sunscreen	krīm wāqi aʃ ʃams (m)	كريم واقي الشمس

bikini	bikini (m)	بكيني
swimsuit, bikini	libās sibāḥa (m)	لباس سباحة
swim trunks	libās sibāḥa riʒāliy (m)	لباس سباحة رجاليّ

swimming pool	masbaḥ (m)	مسبح
to swim (vi)	sabaḥ	سبح
shower	dūʃ (m)	دوش
to change (one's clothes)	ɣayyar libāsuh	غيّر لباسه
towel	fūṭa (f)	فوطة

| boat | markab (m) | مركب |
| motorboat | lanʃ (m) | لنش |

water ski	tazalluʒ 'alal mā' (m)	تزلج على الماء
pedalo	'aʒala mā'iyya (f)	عجلة مائية
surfing	rukūb al amwāʒ (m)	ركوب الأمواج
surfer	rākib al amwāʒ (m)	راكب الأمواج
scuba set	ʒihāz at tanaffus (m)	جهاز التنفس
flippers (swim fins)	za'ānif as sibāḥa (pl)	زعانف السباحة
mask (diving ~)	kimāma (f)	كمامة
diver	ɣawwāṣ (m)	غوّاص
to dive (vi)	ɣāṣ	غاص
underwater (adv)	taḥt al mā'	تحت الماء
beach umbrella	ʃamsiyya (f)	شمسيّة
beach chair (sun lounger)	kursiy blāʒ (m)	كرسيّ بلاج
sunglasses	naẓẓārat ʃams (f)	نظارة شمس
air mattress	martaba hawā'iyya (f)	مرتبة هوائيّة
to play (amuse oneself)	la'ib	لعب
to go for a swim	sabaḥ	سبح
beach ball	kura (f)	كرة
to inflate (vt)	nafaχ	نفخ
inflatable, air (adj)	qābil lin nafχ	قابل للنفخ
wave	mawʒa (f)	موجة
buoy (line of ~s)	ʃamandūra (f)	شمندورة
to drown (ab. person)	ɣariq	غرق
to save, to rescue	anqað	أنقذ
life jacket	sutrat naʒāt (f)	سترة نجاة
to observe, to watch	rāqab	راقب
lifeguard	ḥāris ʃāṭi' (m)	حارس شاطئ

TECHNICAL EQUIPMENT. TRANSPORT

Technical equipment

165. Computer

computer	kumbyūtir (m)	كمبيوتر
notebook, laptop	kumbyūtir maḥmūl (m)	كمبيوتر محمول
to turn on	ʃayyal	شغّل
to turn off	aylaq	أغلق
keyboard	lawḥat al mafātīḥ (f)	لوحة المفاتيح
key	miftāḥ (m)	مفتاح
mouse	fa'ra (f)	فأرة
mouse mat	wisādat fa'ra (f)	وسادة فأرة
button	zirr (m)	زرّ
cursor	mu'aʃʃir (m)	مؤشر
monitor	ʃāʃa (f)	شاشة
screen	ʃāʃa (f)	شاشة
hard disk	qurṣ ṣalib (m)	قرص صلب
hard disk capacity	si'at taxzīn (f)	سعة تخزين
memory	ðākira (f)	ذاكرة
random access memory	ðākirat al wuṣūl al 'aʃwā'iy (f)	ذاكرة الوصول العشوائيّ
file	malaff (m)	ملفّ
folder	ḥāfiẓa (m)	حافظة
to open (vt)	fataḥ	فتح
to close (vt)	aylaq	أغلق
to save (vt)	ḥafaẓ	حفظ
to delete (vt)	masaḥ	مسح
to copy (vt)	nasax	نسخ
to sort (vt)	ṣannaf	صنّف
to transfer (copy)	naqal	نقل
programme	barnāmaʒ (m)	برنامج
software	barāmiʒ kumbyūtir (pl)	برامج كمبيوتر
programmer	mubarmiʒ (m)	مبرمج
to program (vt)	barmaʒ	برمج
hacker	hākir (m)	هاكر
password	kalimat as sirr (f)	كلمة السرّ
virus	virūs (m)	فيروس
to find, to detect	waʒad	وجد
byte	bayt (m)	بايت

megabyte	miʒabāyt (m)	ميجابايت
data	bayānāt (pl)	بيانات
database	qaʿidat bayānāt (f)	قاعدة بيانات

cable (USB, etc.)	kābil (m)	كابل
to disconnect (vt)	faṣal	فصل
to connect (sth to sth)	waṣṣal	وصّل

166. Internet. E-mail

Internet	intirnit (m)	إنترنت
browser	mutaṣaffiḥ (m)	متصفح
search engine	muḥarrik baḥθ (m)	محرّك بحث
provider	ʃarikat al intirnīt (f)	شركة الإنترنيت

webmaster	mudīr al mawqiʿ (m)	مدير الموقع
website	mawqiʿ iliktrūniy (m)	موقع إلكتروني
web page	ṣafḥat wīb (f)	صفحة ويب

| address (e-mail ~) | ʿunwān (m) | عنوان |
| address book | daftar al ʿanāwīn (m) | دفتر العناوين |

postbox	ṣundūq al barīd (m)	صندوق البريد
post	barīd (m)	بريد
full (adj)	mumtaliʾ	ممتلىء

message	risāla iliktrūniyya (f)	رسالة إلكترونيّة
incoming messages	rasaʾil wārida (pl)	رسائل واردة
outgoing messages	rasaʾil ṣādira (pl)	رسائل صادرة
sender	mursil (m)	مرسل
to send (vt)	arsal	أرسل
sending (of mail)	irsāl (m)	إرسال
receiver	mursal ilayh (m)	مرسل إليه
to receive (vt)	istalam	إستلم

| correspondence | murāsala (f) | مراسلة |
| to correspond (vi) | tarāsal | تراسل |

file	malaff (m)	ملفّ
to download (vt)	ḥammal	حمّل
to create (vt)	anʃaʾ	أنشأ
to delete (vt)	masaḥ	مسح
deleted (adj)	mamsūḥ	ممسوح

connection (ADSL, etc.)	ittiṣāl (m)	إتّصال
speed	surʿa (f)	سرعة
modem	mudim (m)	مودم
access	wuṣūl (m)	وصول
port (e.g. input ~)	maxraʒ (m)	مخرج

connection (make a ~)	ittiṣāl (m)	إتّصال
to connect to ... (vi)	ittaṣal	إتّصل
to select (vt)	ixtār	إختار
to search (for ...)	baḥaθ	بحث

167. Electricity

electricity	kahrabā' (m)	كهرباء
electric, electrical (adj)	kahrabā'iy	كهربائيّ
electric power station	maḥaṭṭa kahrabā'iyya (f)	محطّة كهربائيّة
energy	ṭāqa (f)	طاقة
electric power	ṭāqa kahrabā'iyya (f)	طاقة كهربائيّة

light bulb	lamba (f)	لمبة
torch	kaʃʃāf an nūr (m)	كشّاف النور
street light	'amūd an nūr (m)	عمود النور

light	nūr (m)	نور
to turn on	fataḥ, ʃaɣɣal	فتح، شغّل
to turn off	ṭaffa	طفّى
to turn off the light	ṭaffa n nūr	طفّى النور

to burn out (vi)	intafa'	إنطفأ
short circuit	da'ira kahrabā'iyya qaṣīra (f)	دائرة كهربائية قصيرة
broken wire	silk maqṭūʿ (m)	سلك مقطوع
contact (electrical ~)	talāmus (m)	تلامس

light switch	miftāḥ an nūr (m)	مفتاح النور
socket outlet	barizat al kahrabā' (f)	بريزة الكهرباء
plug	fīʃat al kahrabā' (f)	فيشة الكهرباء
extension lead	silk tawṣīl (m)	سلك توصيل

fuse	fāṣima (f)	فاصمة
cable, wire	silk (m)	سلك
wiring	aslāk (pl)	أسلاك

| ampere | ambīr (m) | أمبير |
| amperage | ʃiddat at tayyār al kahrabā'iy (f) | شدّة التيّار الكهربائيّ |

| volt | vūlt (m) | فولت |
| voltage | ʒuhd kahrabā'iy (m) | جهد كهربائيّ |

| electrical device | ʒihāz kahrabā'iy (m) | جهاز كهربائيّ |
| indicator | mu'aʃʃir (m) | مؤشّر |

electrician	kahrabā'iy (m)	كهربائيّ
to solder (vt)	laḥam	لحم
soldering iron	adāt laḥm (f)	أداة لحم
electric current	tayyār kahrabā'iy (m)	تيّار كهربائيّ

168. Tools

tool, instrument	adāt (f)	أداة
tools	adawāt (pl)	أدوات
equipment (factory ~)	mu'addāt (pl)	معدّات

| hammer | miṭraqa (f) | مطرقة |
| screwdriver | mifakk (m) | مفكّ |

axe	fa's (m)	فأس
saw	minʃār (m)	منشار
to saw (vt)	naʃar	نشر
plane (tool)	masḥāʒ (m)	مسحج
to plane (vt)	saḥaʒ	سحج
soldering iron	adāt laḥm (f)	أداة لحم
to solder (vt)	laḥam	لحم

file (tool)	mibrad (m)	مبرد
carpenter pincers	kammāʃa (f)	كمّاشة
combination pliers	zardiyya (f)	زرديّة
chisel	izmīl (m)	إزميل

drill bit	luqmat θaqb (m)	لقمة ثقب
electric drill	miθqab (m)	مثقب
to drill (vi, vt)	θaqab	ثقب

knife	sikkīn (m)	سكّين
pocket knife	sikkīn ʒayb (m)	سكّين جيب
blade	ʃafra (f)	شفرة

sharp (blade, etc.)	ḥādd	حادّ
dull, blunt (adj)	θālim	ثالم
to get blunt (dull)	taθallam	تثلّم
to sharpen (vt)	ʃaḥað	شحذ

bolt	mismār qalāwūz (m)	مسمار قلاووظ
nut	ṣamūla (f)	صامولة
thread (of a screw)	naẓm (m)	نظم
wood screw	qalāwūz (m)	قلاووظ

| nail | mismār (m) | مسمار |
| nailhead | ra's al mismār (m) | رأس المسمار |

ruler (for measuring)	masṭara (f)	مسطرة
tape measure	ʃarīṭ al qiyās (m)	شريط القياس
spirit level	mīzān al mā' (m)	ميزان الماء
magnifying glass	'adasa mukabbira (f)	عدسة مكبّرة

measuring instrument	ʒihāz qiyās (m)	جهاز قياس
to measure (vt)	qās	قاس
scale (temperature ~, etc.)	miqyās (m)	مقياس
readings	qirā'a (f)	قراءة

| compressor | ḍāɣiṭ al ɣāz (m) | ضاغط الغاز |
| microscope | mikruskūb (m) | ميكروسكوب |

pump (e.g. water ~)	ṭulumba (f)	طلمبة
robot	rūbut (m)	روبوت
laser	layzir (m)	ليزر

spanner	miftāḥ aṣ ṣawāmīl (m)	مفتاح الصواميل
adhesive tape	lazq (m)	لزق
glue	ṣamɣ (m)	صمغ
sandpaper	waraq ṣanfara (m)	ورق صنفرة
spring	sūsta (f)	سوستة

magnet	miɣnaṭīs (m)	مغنطيس
gloves	quffāz (m)	قفّاز

rope	ḥabl (m)	حبل
cord	ḥabl (m)	حبل
wire (e.g. telephone ~)	silk (m)	سلك
cable	kābil (m)	كابل

sledgehammer	mirzaba (f)	مرزبة
prybar	ʿatala (f)	عتلة
ladder	sullam (m)	سلّم
stepladder	sullam (m)	سلّم

to screw (tighten)	ahkam aʃʃadd	أحكم الشدّ
to unscrew (lid, filter, etc.)	fataḥ	فتح
to tighten (e.g. with a clamp)	kamaʃ	كمش
to glue, to stick	alṣaq	ألصق
to cut (vt)	qaṭaʿ	قطع

malfunction (fault)	taʿaṭṭul (m)	تعطّل
repair (mending)	iṣlāḥ (m)	إصلاح
to repair, to fix (vt)	aṣlaḥ	أصلح
to adjust (machine, etc.)	ḍabaṭ	ضبط

to check (to examine)	iɣtabar	إختبر
checking	faḥṣ (m)	فحص
readings	qirāʾa (f)	قراءة

reliable, solid (machine)	matīn	متين
complex (adj)	murakkab	مركّب

to rust (get rusted)	ṣadiʾ	صدئ
rusty (adj)	ṣadīʾ	صديء
rust	ṣadaʾ (m)	صدأ

Transport

aeroplane	ṭā'ira (f)	طائرة
air ticket	taðkirat ṭā'ira (f)	تذكرة طائرة
airline	ʃarikat ṭayarān (f)	شركة طيران
airport	maṭār (m)	مطار
supersonic (adj)	χāriq liṣ ṣawt	خارق للصوت

captain	qā'id aṭ ṭā'ira (m)	قائد الطائرة
crew	ṭāqim (m)	طاقم
pilot	ṭayyār (m)	طيّار
stewardess	muɖīfat ṭayarān (f)	مضيفة طيران
navigator	mallāḥ (m)	مّلاح

wings	aʒniḥa (pl)	أجنحة
tail	ðayl (m)	ذيل
cockpit	kabīna (f)	كابينة
engine	mutūr (m)	موتور
undercarriage (landing gear)	'aʒalāt al hubūṭ (pl)	عجلات الهبوط
turbine	turbīna (f)	تربينة

propeller	mirwaḥa (f)	مروحة
black box	musaʒʒil aṭ ṭayarān (m)	مسجّل الطيران
yoke (control column)	'aʒalat qiyāda (f)	عجلة قيادة
fuel	wuqūd (m)	وقود

safety card	biṭāqat as salāma (f)	بطاقة السلامة
oxygen mask	qinā' uksiʒīn (m)	قناع أوكسيجين
uniform	libās muwaḥḥad (m)	لباس موحّد

| lifejacket | sutrat naʒāt (f) | سترة نجاة |
| parachute | miẓallat hubūṭ (f) | مظلّة هبوط |

takeoff	iqlā' (m)	إقلاع
to take off (vi)	aqla'at	أقلعت
runway	madraʒ aṭ ṭā'irāt (m)	مدرج الطائرات

| visibility | ru'ya (f) | رؤية |
| flight (act of flying) | ṭayarān (m) | طيران |

| altitude | irtifā' (m) | إرتفاع |
| air pocket | ʒayb hawā'iy (m) | جيب هوائيّ |

seat	maq'ad (m)	مقعد
headphones	sammā'āt ra'siya (pl)	سمّاعات رأسيّة
folding tray (tray table)	ṣīniyya qābila liṭ ṭayy (f)	صينية قابلة للطيّ
airplane window	ʃubbāk aṭ ṭā'ira (m)	شبّاك الطائرة
aisle	mamarr (m)	ممرّ

170. Train

train	qiṭār (m)	قطار
commuter train	qiṭār (m)	قطار
express train	qiṭār sarī' (m)	قطار سريع
diesel locomotive	qāṭirat dīzil (f)	قاطرة ديزل
steam locomotive	qāṭira buxāriyya (f)	قاطرة بخارية

| coach, carriage | 'araba (f) | عربة |
| buffet car | 'arabat al maṭ'am (f) | عربة المطعم |

rails	quḍubān (pl)	قضبان
railway	sikka ḥadīdiyya (f)	سكة حديدية
sleeper (track support)	'āriḍa (f)	عارضة

platform (railway ~)	raṣīf (m)	رصيف
platform (~ 1, 2, etc.)	xaṭṭ (m)	خط
semaphore	simafūr (m)	سيمافور
station	maḥaṭṭa (f)	محطة

train driver	sā'iq (m)	سائق
porter (of luggage)	ḥammāl (m)	حمّال
carriage attendant	mas'ūl 'arabat al qiṭār (m)	مسؤول عربة القطار
passenger	rākib (m)	راكب
ticket inspector	kamsariy (m)	كمسري

| corridor (in train) | mamarr (m) | ممرّ |
| emergency brake | farāmil aṭ ṭawāri' (pl) | فرامل الطوارئ |

compartment	yurfa (f)	غرفة
berth	sarīr (m)	سرير
upper berth	sarīr 'ulwiy (m)	سرير علوي
lower berth	sarīr sufliy (m)	سرير سفلي
bed linen, bedding	ayṭiyat as sarīr (pl)	أغطية السرير

ticket	taðkira (f)	تذكرة
timetable	ʒadwal (m)	جدول
information display	lawḥat ma'lūmāt (f)	لوحة معلومات

| to leave, to depart | yādar | غادر |
| departure (of a train) | muyādara (f) | مغادرة |

| to arrive (ab. train) | waṣal | وصل |
| arrival | wuṣūl (m) | وصول |

to arrive by train	waṣal bil qiṭār	وصل بالقطار
to get on the train	rakib al qiṭār	ركب القطار
to get off the train	nazil min al qiṭār	نزل من القطار

train crash	ḥiṭām qiṭār (m)	حطام قطار
to derail (vi)	xaraʒ 'an xaṭṭ sayrih	خرج عن خط سيره
steam locomotive	qāṭira buxāriyya (f)	قاطرة بخارية
stoker, fireman	'aṭaʃʒiy (m)	عطشجي
firebox	furn al muḥarrik (m)	فرن المحرّك
coal	faḥm (m)	فحم

171. Ship

ship	safīna (f)	سفينة
vessel	safīna (f)	سفينة
steamship	bāxira (f)	باخرة
riverboat	bāxira nahriyya (f)	باخرة نهرِيّة
cruise ship	bāxira siyaḥiyya (f)	باخرة سياحِيّة
cruiser	ṭarrād (m)	طرّاد
yacht	yaxt (m)	يخت
tugboat	qāṭira (f)	قاطرة
barge	ṣandal (m)	صندل
ferry	ʻabbāra (f)	عبّارة
sailing ship	safīna ʃirāʻiyya (m)	سفينة شراعِيّة
brigantine	markab ʃirāʻiy (m)	مركب شراعيّ
ice breaker	muḥaṭṭimat ʒalīd (f)	محطّمة جليد
submarine	ɣawwāṣa (f)	غوّاصة
boat (flat-bottomed ~)	markab (m)	مركب
dinghy (lifeboat)	zawraq (m)	زورق
lifeboat	qārib naʒāt (m)	قارب نجاة
motorboat	lanʃ (m)	لنش
captain	qubṭān (m)	قبطان
seaman	baḥḥār (m)	بحّار
sailor	baḥḥār (m)	بحّار
crew	ṭāqim (m)	طاقم
boatswain	raʼīs al baḥḥāra (m)	رئيس البحّارة
ship's boy	ṣabiy as safīna (m)	صبي السفينة
cook	ṭabbāx (m)	طبّاخ
ship's doctor	ṭabīb as safīna (m)	طبيب السفينة
deck	saṭḥ as safīna (m)	سطح السفينة
mast	sāriya (f)	سارية
sail	ʃirāʻ (m)	شراع
hold	ʻambar (m)	عنبر
bow (prow)	muqaddama (m)	مقدّمة
stern	muʼaxirat as safīna (f)	مؤخّرة السفينة
oar	miʒðāf (m)	مجذاف
screw propeller	mirwaḥa (f)	مروحة
cabin	kabīna (f)	كابينة
wardroom	ɣurfat al istirāḥa (f)	غرفة الإستراحة
engine room	qism al ʼālāt (m)	قسم الآلات
bridge	burʒ al qiyāda (m)	برج القيادة
radio room	ɣurfat al lāsilkiy (f)	غرفة اللاسلكيّ
wave (radio)	mawʒa (f)	موجة
logbook	siʒil as safīna (m)	سجل السفينة
spyglass	minẓār (m)	منظار
bell	ʒaras (m)	جرس

flag	'alam (m)	علم
hawser (mooring ~)	ḥabl (m)	حبل
knot (bowline, etc.)	'uqda (f)	عقدة

deckrails	drabizīn (m)	درابزين
gangway	sullam (m)	سلّم

anchor	mirsāt (f)	مرساة
to weigh anchor	rafa' mirsāt	رفع مرساة
to drop anchor	rasa	رسا
anchor chain	silsilat mirsāt (f)	سلسلة مرساة

port (harbour)	mīnā' (m)	ميناء
quay, wharf	marsa (m)	مرسى
to berth (moor)	rasa	رسا
to cast off	aqla'	أقلع

trip, voyage	riḥla (f)	رحلة
cruise (sea trip)	riḥla baḥriyya (f)	رحلة بحرية
course (route)	masār (m)	مسار
route (itinerary)	ṭarīq (m)	طريق

fairway (safe water channel)	maʒra milāḥiy (m)	مجرى ملاحيّ
shallows	miyāh ḍaḥla (f)	مياه ضحلة
to run aground	ʒanaḥ	جنح

storm	'āṣifa (f)	عاصفة
signal	iʃāra (f)	إشارة
to sink (vi)	ɣariq	غرق
Man overboard!	saqaṭ raʒul min as safīna!	سقط رجل من السفينة!
SOS (distress signal)	nidā' iɣāθa (m)	نداء إغاثة
ring buoy	ṭawq naʒāt (m)	طوق نجاة

172. Airport

airport	maṭār (m)	مطار
aeroplane	ṭā'ira (f)	طائرة
airline	ʃarikat ṭayarān (f)	شركة طيران
air traffic controller	marāqib al ḥaraka al ʒawwiyya (pl)	مراقب الحركة الجوية

departure	muɣādara (f)	مغادرة
arrival	wuṣūl (m)	وصول
to arrive (by plane)	waṣal	وصل

departure time	waqt al muɣādara (m)	وقت المغادرة
arrival time	waqt al wuṣūl (m)	وقت الوصول

to be delayed	ta'aχχar	تأخّر
flight delay	ta'aχχur ar riḥla (m)	تأخّر الرحلة

information board	lawḥat al ma'lūmāt (f)	لوحة المعلومات
information	isti'lāmāt (pl)	إستعلامات
to announce (vt)	a'lan	أعلن

flight (e.g. next ~)	riḥla (f)	رحلة
customs	ӡamārik (pl)	جمارك
customs officer	muwaẓẓaf al ӡamārik (m)	موظّف الجمارك

customs declaration	taṣrīḥ ӡumrukiy (m)	تصريح جمركيّ
to fill in (vt)	mala'	ملأ
to fill in the declaration	mala' at taṣrīḥ	ملأ التصريح
passport control	taftīʃ al ӡawāzāt (m)	تفتيش الجوازات

luggage	aʃʃunaṭ (pl)	الشنط
hand luggage	ʃunaṭ al yad (pl)	شنط اليد
luggage trolley	'arabat ʃunaṭ (f)	عربة شنط

landing	hubūṭ (m)	هبوط
landing strip	mamarr al hubūṭ (m)	ممرّ الهبوط
to land (vi)	habaṭ	هبط
airstair (passenger stair)	sullam aṭ ṭā'ira (m)	سلّم الطائرة

check-in	tasӡīl (m)	تسجيل
check-in counter	makān at tasӡīl (m)	مكان التسجيل
to check-in (vi)	saӡӡal	سجّل
boarding card	biṭāqat ṣu'ūd (f)	بطاقة صعود
departure gate	bawwābat al muɣādara (f)	بوّابة المغادرة

transit	tranzīt (m)	ترانزيت
to wait (vt)	intazar	إنتظر
departure lounge	qā'at al muɣādara (f)	قاعة المغادرة
to see off	wadda'	ودّع
to say goodbye	wadda'	ودّع

173. Bicycle. Motorcycle

bicycle	darrāӡa (f)	درّاجة
scooter	skutir (m)	سكوتر
motorbike	darrāӡa nāriyya (f)	درّاجة ناريّة

to go by bicycle	rakib ad darrāӡa	ركب الدرّاجة
handlebars	miqwad (m)	مقود
pedal	dawwāsa (f)	دوّاسة
brakes	farāmil (pl)	فرامل
bicycle seat (saddle)	maq'ad (m)	مقعد

pump	ṭulumba (f)	طلمبة
pannier rack	raff al amti'a (m)	رفّ الأمتعة
front lamp	miṣbāḥ (m)	مصباح
helmet	χūða (f)	خوذة

wheel	'aӡala (f)	عجلة
mudguard	rafraf (m)	رفرف
rim	iṭār (m)	إطار
spoke	barmaq al 'aӡala (m)	برمق العجلة

Cars

car	sayyāra (f)	سيّارة
sports car	sayyāra riyāḍiyya (f)	سيّارة رياضيّة
limousine	limuzīn (m)	ليموزين
off-road vehicle	sayyārat ṭuruq wa'ra (f)	سيّارة طرق وعرة
drophead coupé (convertible)	kabriulīh (m)	كابريوليه
minibus	mikrubāṣ (m)	ميكروباص
ambulance	is'āf (m)	إسعاف
snowplough	ӡarrāfat θalӡ (f)	جرّافة ثلج
lorry	ʃāḥina (f)	شاحنة
road tanker	nāqilat bitrūl (f)	ناقلة بترول
van (small truck)	'arabat naql (f)	عربة نقل
tractor unit	ӡarrār (m)	جرّار
trailer	maqṭūra (f)	مقطورة
comfortable (adj)	murīḥ	مريح
used (adj)	musta'mal	مستعمل

bonnet	kabbūt (m)	كبّوت
wing	rafraf (m)	رفرف
roof	saqf (m)	سقف
windscreen	zuӡāӡ amāmiy (m)	زجاج أماميّ
rear-view mirror	mir'āt dāxiliyya (f)	مرآة داخليّة
windscreen washer	munaẓẓif az zuӡāӡ (m)	منظّف الزجاج
windscreen wipers	massāḥāt (pl)	مسّاحات
side window	zuӡāӡ ӡānibiy (m)	زجاج جانبيّ
electric window	mākina zuӡāӡ (f)	ماكينة زجاج
aerial	hawā'iy (m)	هوائيّ
sunroof	nāfiðat as saqf (f)	نافذة السقف
bumper	miṣadd as sayyāra (m)	مصدّ السيارة
boot	ṣundūq as sayyāra (m)	صندوق السيّارة
roof luggage rack	raff saqf as sayyāra (m)	رفّ سقف السيّارة
door	bāb (m)	باب
door handle	ukrat al bāb (f)	أوكرة الباب
door lock	qifl al bāb (m)	قفل الباب
number plate	lawḥat raqm as sayyāra (f)	لوحة رقم السيارة
silencer	kātim aṣ ṣawt (m)	كاتم الصوت

petrol tank	χazzān al banzīn (m)	خزّان البنزين
exhaust pipe	umbūb al 'ādim (m)	أنبوب العادم
accelerator	γāz (m)	غاز
pedal	dawwāsa (f)	دوّاسة
accelerator pedal	dawwāsat al wuqūd (f)	دوّاسة الوقود
brake	farāmil (pl)	فرامل
brake pedal	dawwāsat al farāmil (m)	دوّاسة الفرامل
to brake (use the brake)	farmal	فرمل
handbrake	farmalat al yad (f)	فرملة اليد
clutch	ta'ʃīq (m)	تعشيق
clutch pedal	dawwāsat at ta'ʃīq (f)	دوّاسة التعشيق
clutch disc	qurṣ at ta'ʃīq (m)	قرص التعشيق
shock absorber	mumtaṣṣ liṣ ṣadamāt (m)	ممتصّ الصدمات
wheel	'aʒala (f)	عجلة
spare tyre	'aʒala iḥtiyāṭiyya (f)	عجلة احتياطيّة
tyre	iṭār (m)	إطار
wheel cover (hubcap)	γitā' miḥwar al 'aʒala (m)	غطاء محور العجلة
driving wheels	'aʒalāt al qiyāda (pl)	عجلات القيادة
front-wheel drive (as adj)	daf' amāmiy (m)	دفع أماميّ
rear-wheel drive (as adj)	daf' χalfiy (m)	دفع خلفيّ
all-wheel drive (as adj)	daf' rubā'iy (m)	دفع رباعيّ
gearbox	ṣundūq at turūs (m)	صندوق التروس
automatic (adj)	utumatīkiy	أوتوماتيكيّ
mechanical (adj)	yadawiy	يدويّ
gear lever	nāqil as sur'a (m)	ناقل السرعة
headlamp	al miṣbāḥ al amāmiy (m)	المصباح الأماميّ
headlights	al maṣābīḥ al amāmiyya (pl)	المصابيح الأماميّة
dipped headlights	al anwār al munχafiḍa (pl)	الأنوار المنخفضة
full headlights	al anwār al 'āliya (m)	الأنوار العالية
brake light	ḍū' al farāmil (m)	ضوء الفرامل
sidelights	aḍwā' ʒānibiyya (pl)	أضواء جانبيّة
hazard lights	aḍwā' at taḥŏīr (pl)	أضواء التحذير
fog lights	aḍwā' aḍ ḍabāb (pl)	أضواء الضباب
turn indicator	iʃārat al in'iṭāf (f)	إشارة الإنعطاف
reversing light	miṣbāḥ ar ruʒū' lil χalf (m)	مصباح الرجوع للخلف

176. Cars. Passenger compartment

car interior	ṣālūn as sayyāra (m)	صالون السيّارة
leather (as adj)	min al ʒild	من الجلد
velour (as adj)	min al muχmal	من المخمل
upholstery	tanʒīd (m)	تنجيد
instrument (gage)	ʒihāz (m)	جهاز
dashboard	lawḥat at taḥakkum (f)	لوحة التحكم

speedometer	'addād sur'a (m)	عدّاد سرعة
needle (pointer)	mu'aʃʃir (m)	مؤشّر
mileometer	'addād al masāfāt (m)	عدّاد المسافات
indicator (sensor)	'addād (m)	عدّاد
level	mustawa (m)	مستوى
warning light	lammbat inðār (f)	لمبة إنذار
steering wheel	miqwad (m)	مقود
horn	zāmūr (m)	زامور
button	zirr (m)	زرّ
switch	nāqil, miftāḥ (m)	ناقل, مفتاح
seat	maq'ad (m)	مقعد
backrest	misnad aẓ ẓahr (m)	مسند الظهر
headrest	masnad ar ra's (m)	مسند الرأس
seat belt	ḥizām al amn (m)	حزام الأمن
to fasten the belt	rabaṭ al ḥizām	ربط الحزام
adjustment (of seats)	ḍabṭ (m)	ضبط
airbag	wisāda hawā'iyya (f)	وسادة هوائيّة
air-conditioner	takyīf (m)	تكييف
radio	iðā'a (f)	إذاعة
CD player	muʃaɣɣil sidi (m)	مشغّل سي دي
to turn on	fataḥ, ʃaɣɣal	فتح, شغّل
aerial	hawā'iy (m)	هوائيّ
glove box	durʒ (m)	درج
ashtray	ṭaqṭūqa (f)	طقطوقة

177. Cars. Engine

engine	muḥarrik (m)	محرّك
motor	mutūr (m)	موتور
diesel (as adj)	dīzil	ديزل
petrol (as adj)	'alal banzīn	على البنزين
engine volume	si'at al muḥarrik (f)	سعة المحرّك
power	qudra (f)	قدرة
horsepower	ḥiṣān (m)	حصان
piston	mikbas (m)	مكبس
cylinder	usṭuwāna (f)	أسطوانة
valve	ṣimām (m)	صمام
injector	ʒihāz baxxāx (f)	جهاز بخّاخ
generator (alternator)	muwallid (m)	مولّد
carburettor	karburātir (m)	كاربراتير
motor oil	zayt al muḥarrik (m)	زيت المحرّك
radiator	mubarrid al muḥarrik (m)	مبرّد المحرّك
coolant	mādda mubarrida (f)	مادّة مبرّدة
cooling fan	mirwaḥa (f)	مروحة
battery (accumulator)	baṭṭāriyya (f)	بطاريّة
starter	miftāḥ at taʃɣīl (m)	مفتاح التشغيل

ignition	niẓām taʃɣīl (m)	نظام تشغيل
sparking plug	ʃamʿat al iḥtirāq (f)	شمعة الاحتراق
terminal (battery ~)	ṭaraf tawṣīl (m)	طرف توصيل
positive terminal	ṭaraf mūʒab (m)	طرف موجب
negative terminal	ṭaraf sālib (m)	طرف سالب
fuse	fāṣima (f)	فاصمة
air filter	miṣfāt al hawā' (f)	مصفاة الهواء
oil filter	miṣfāt az zayt (f)	مصفاة الزيت
fuel filter	miṣfāt al banzīn (f)	مصفاة البنزين

178. Cars. Crash. Repair

car crash	ḥādiθ sayyāra (f)	حادث سيارة
traffic accident	ḥādiθ murūriy (m)	حادث مروري
to crash (into the wall, etc.)	iṣṭadam	إصطدم
to get smashed up	taḥaṭṭam	تحطم
damage	χasāra (f)	خسارة
intact (unscathed)	salīm	سليم
to break down (vi)	taʿaṭṭal	تعطّل
towrope	ḥabl as saḥb (m)	حبل السحب
puncture	θuqb (m)	ثقب
to have a puncture	faʃʃ	فشّ
to pump up	nafaχ	نفخ
pressure	dayṭ (m)	ضغط
to check (to examine)	iχtabar	إختبر
repair	iṣlāḥ (m)	إصلاح
garage (auto service shop)	warʃat iṣlāḥ as sayyārāt (f)	ورشة إصلاح السيّارات
spare part	qiṭʿat ɣiyār (f)	قطعة غيار
part	qiṭʿa (f)	قطعة
bolt (with nut)	mismār qalāwūz (m)	مسمار قلاووظ
screw (fastener)	burɣiy (m)	برغي
nut	ṣamūla (f)	صامولة
washer	ḥalqa (f)	حلقة
bearing (e.g. ball ~)	maḥmal (m)	محمل
tube	umbūba (f)	أنبوبة
gasket (head ~)	ʿazaqa (f)	عزقة
cable, wire	silk (m)	سلك
jack	rāfiʿat sayyāra (f)	رافعة سيّارة
spanner	miftāḥ aṣ ṣawāmīl (m)	مفتاح الصواميل
hammer	miṭraqa (f)	مطرقة
pump	ṭulumba (f)	طلمبة
screwdriver	mifakk (m)	مفكّ
fire extinguisher	miṭfa'at ḥarīq (f)	مطفأة حريق
warning triangle	muθallaθ taḥðīr (m)	مثلّث تحذير
to stall (vi)	tawaqqaf	توقّف

stall (n)	tawaqquf (m)	توقّف
to be broken	kān maksūran	كان مكسورًا
to overheat (vi)	saxan bi ∫idda	سخن بشدّة
to be clogged up	kān masdūdan	كان مسدودًا
to freeze up (pipes, etc.)	taʒammad	تجمّد
to burst (vi, ab. tube)	infaʒar	إنفجر
pressure	daɣt (m)	ضغط
level	mustawa (m)	مستوى
slack (~ belt)	da'īf	ضعيف
dent	ba'ʒa (f)	بعجة
knocking noise (engine)	daqq (m)	دقّ
crack	∫aqq (m)	شقّ
scratch	xad∫ (m)	خدش

179. Cars. Road

road	ṭarīq (m)	طريق
motorway	ṭarīq sarī' (m)	طريق سريع
highway	ṭarīq sarī' (m)	طريق سريع
direction (way)	ittiʒāh (m)	إتّجاه
distance	masāfa (f)	مسافة
bridge	ʒisr (m)	جسر
car park	mawqif as sayyārāt (m)	موقف السيّارات
square	maydān (m)	ميدان
road junction	taqāṭu' ṭuruq (m)	تقاطع طرق
tunnel	nafaq (m)	نفق
petrol station	maḥaṭṭat banzīn (f)	محطّة بنزين
car park	mawqif as sayyārāt (m)	موقف السيّارات
petrol pump	midaxxat banzīn (f)	مضخّة بنزين
auto repair shop	war∫at iṣlāḥ as sayyārāt (f)	ورشة إصلاح السيّارات
to fill up	mala' bil wuqūd	ملأ بالوقود
fuel	wuqūd (m)	وقود
jerrycan	ʒirikan (m)	جركن
asphalt, tarmac	asfalt (m)	أسفلت
road markings	'alāmāt aṭ ṭarīq (pl)	علامات الطريق
kerb	ḥāffat ar raṣīf (f)	حافّة الرصيف
crash barrier	sūr (m)	سور
ditch	qanāt (f)	قناة
roadside (shoulder)	ḥāffat aṭ ṭarīq (f)	حافّة الطريق
lamppost	'amūd nūr (m)	عمود نور
to drive (a car)	sāq	ساق
to turn (e.g., ~ left)	in'aṭaf	إنعطف
to make a U-turn	istadār lil xalf	إستدار للخلف
reverse (~ gear)	ḥaraka ilal warā' (f)	حركة إلى الوراء
to honk (vi)	zammar	زمّر
honk (sound)	ṣawt az zāmūr (m)	صوت الزامور

to get stuck (in the mud, etc.)	waḥil	وحل
to spin the wheels	dawwar al ʿaʒala	دوِّر العجلة
to cut, to turn off (vt)	awqaf	أوقف
speed	surʿa (f)	سرعة
to exceed the speed limit	taʒāwaz as surʿa al quṣwa	تجاوز السرعة القصوى
to give a ticket	faraḍ ɣarāma	فرض غرامة
traffic lights	iʃārāt al murūr (pl)	إشارات المرور
driving licence	ruxṣat al qiyāda (f)	رخصة قيادة
level crossing	maʿbar (m)	معبر
crossroads	taqāṭuʿ (m)	تقاطع
zebra crossing	maʿbar al muʃāt (m)	معبر المشاة
bend, curve	munʿatif (m)	منعطف
pedestrian precinct	makān muxaṣṣaṣ lil muʃāt (f)	مكان مخصّص للمشاة

180. Signs

Highway Code	qawāʿid al murūr (pl)	قواعد المرور
road sign (traffic sign)	ʿalāma (f)	علامة
overtaking	taʒāwuz (m)	تجاوز
curve	munʿatif (m)	منعطف
U-turn	dawarān lil xalf (m)	دوران للخلف
roundabout	dawarān murūriy (m)	دوران مروري
No entry	mamnūʿ ad duxūl	ممنوع الدخول
All vehicles prohibited	mamnūʿ murūr as sayyārāt	ممنوع مرور السيارات
No overtaking	mamnūʿ at taʒāwuz	ممنوع التجاوز
No parking	mamnūʿ al wuqūf	ممنوع الوقوف
No stopping	mamnūʿ al wuqūf	ممنوع الوقوف
dangerous curve	munʿataf xaṭir (m)	منعطف خطر
steep descent	munḥadar xaṭar (m)	منحدر خطر
one-way traffic	ṭarīq ittiʒāh wāḥid (m)	طريق إتجاه واحد
zebra crossing	maʿbar al muʃāt (m)	معبر المشاة
slippery road	ṭarīq zaliq (m)	طريق زلق
GIVE WAY	iʃārat waḍʿiyyat tark al awlawiyya	إشارة وضعيّة ترك الأولويّة

PEOPLE. LIFE EVENTS

181. Holidays. Event

celebration, holiday	ʿīd (m)	عيد
national day	ʿīd waṭaniy (m)	عيد وطنيّ
public holiday	yawm al ʿuṭla ar rasmiyya (m)	يوم العطلة الرسمية
to commemorate (vt)	iḥtafal	إحتفل
event (happening)	ḥadaθ (m)	حدث
event (organized activity)	munasaba (f)	مناسبة
banquet (party)	walīma (f)	وليمة
reception (formal party)	ḥaflat istiqbāl (f)	حفلة إستقبال
feast	walīma (f)	وليمة
anniversary	ðikra sanawiyya (f)	ذكرى سنويّة
jubilee	yubīl (m)	يوبيل
to celebrate (vt)	iḥtafal	إحتفل
New Year	ra's as sana (m)	رأس السنة
Happy New Year!	kull sana wa anta ṭayyib!	كلّ سنة وأنت طيّب!
Father Christmas	baba nuwīl (m)	بابا نويل
Christmas	ʿīd al mīlād (m)	عيد الميلاد
Merry Christmas!	ʿīd mīlād saʿīd!	عيد ميلاد سعيد!
Christmas tree	ʃaʒarat ra's as sana (f)	شجرة رأس السنة
fireworks (fireworks show)	alʿāb nāriyya (pl)	ألعاب ناريّة
wedding	zifāf (m)	زفاف
groom	ʿarīs (m)	عريس
bride	ʿarūsa (f)	عروسة
to invite (vt)	daʿa	دعا
invitation card	biṭāqat daʿwa (f)	بطاقة دعوة
guest	ḍayf (m)	ضيف
to visit (~ your parents, etc.)	zār	زار
to meet the guests	istaqbal aḍ ḍuyūf	إستقبل الضيوف
gift, present	hadiyya (f)	هديّة
to give (sth as present)	qaddam	قدّم
to receive gifts	istalam al hadāya	إستلم الهدايا
bouquet (of flowers)	bāqat zuhūr (f)	باقة زهور
congratulations	tahniʾa (f)	تهنئة
to congratulate (vt)	hannaʾ	هنّأ
greetings card	biṭāqat tahniʾa (f)	بطاقة تهنئة
to send a postcard	arsal biṭāqat tahniʾa	أرسل بطاقة تهنئة
to get a postcard	istalam biṭāqat tahniʾa	إستلم بطاقة تهنئة

toast	naxb (m)	نخب
to offer (a drink, etc.)	dayyaf	ضيّف
champagne	ʃambāniya (f)	شمبانيا
to enjoy oneself	istamtaʿ	إستمتع
merriment (gaiety)	faraḥ (m)	فرح
joy (emotion)	saʿāda (f)	سعادة
dance	rāqiṣa (f)	رقصة
to dance (vi, vt)	raqaṣ	رقص
waltz	vāls (m)	فالس
tango	tāngu (m)	تانجو

182. Funerals. Burial

cemetery	maqbara (f)	مقبرة
grave, tomb	qabr (m)	قبر
cross	ṣalīb (m)	صليب
gravestone	ʃāhid al qabr (m)	شاهد القبر
fence	sūr (m)	سور
chapel	kanīsa sayīra (f)	كنيسة صغيرة
death	mawt (m)	موت
to die (vi)	māt	مات
the deceased	al mutawaffi (m)	المتوفّي
mourning	ḥidād (m)	حداد
to bury (vt)	dafan	دفن
undertakers	bayt al ʒanāzāt (m)	بيت الجنازات
funeral	ʒanāza (f)	جنازة
wreath	iklīl (m)	إكليل
coffin	tābūt (m)	تابوت
hearse	sayyārat naql al mawta (f)	سيّارة نقل الموتى
shroud	kafan (m)	كفن
funeral procession	ʒanāza (f)	جنازة
funerary urn	qārūra li ḥifz ramād al mawta (f)	قارورة لحفظ رماد الموتى
crematorium	maḥraqat ʒuθaθ al mawta (f)	محرقة جثث الموتى
obituary	naʿiy (m)	نعيّ
to cry (weep)	baka	بكى
to sob (vi)	naḥab	نحب

183. War. Soldiers

platoon	faṣīla (f)	فصيلة
company	sariyya (f)	سريّة
regiment	fawʒ (m)	فوج
army	ʒayʃ (m)	جيش

161

division	firqa (f)	فرقة
section, squad	waḥda (f)	وحدة
host (army)	ʒayʃ (m)	جيش

| soldier | ʒundiy (m) | جنديّ |
| officer | ḍābiṭ (m) | ضابط |

private	ʒundiy (m)	جنديّ
sergeant	raqīb (m)	رقيب
lieutenant	mulāzim (m)	ملازم
captain	naqīb (m)	نقيب
major	rā'id (m)	رائد
colonel	ʿaqīd (m)	عقيد
general	ʒinirāl (m)	جنرال

sailor	baḥḥār (m)	بحّار
captain	qubṭān (m)	قبطان
boatswain	raʾīs al baḥḥāra (m)	رئيس البحّارة
artilleryman	madfaʿiy (m)	مدفعيّ
paratrooper	ʒundiy al maẓallāt (m)	جنديّ المظلّات
pilot	ṭayyār (m)	طيّار
navigator	mallāḥ (m)	ملّاح
mechanic	mikanīkiy (m)	ميكانيكيّ

pioneer (sapper)	muhandis ʿaskariy (m)	مهندس عسكريّ
parachutist	miẓalliy (m)	مظلّيّ
reconnaissance scout	mustakʃif (m)	مستكشف
sniper	qannāṣ (m)	قنّاص

patrol (group)	dawriyya (f)	دوريّة
to patrol (vt)	qām bi dawriyya	قام بدوريّة
sentry, guard	ḥāris (m)	حارس
warrior	muḥārib (m)	محارب
patriot	waṭaniy (m)	وطنيّ
hero	baṭal (m)	بطل
heroine	baṭala (f)	بطلة

traitor	χā'in (m)	خائن
to betray (vt)	χān	خان
deserter	hārib min al ʒayʃ (m)	هارب من الجيش
to desert (vi)	harab min al ʒayʃ	هرب من الجيش

mercenary	ma'ʒūr (m)	مأجور
recruit	ʒundiy ʒadīd (m)	جنديّ جديد
volunteer	mutaṭawwiʿ (m)	متطوّع

dead (n)	qatīl (m)	قتيل
wounded (n)	ʒarīḥ (m)	جريح
prisoner of war	asīr (m)	أسير

184. War. Military actions. Part 1

| war | ḥarb (f) | حرب |
| to be at war | ḥārab | حارب |

civil war	ḥarb ahliyya (f)	حرب أهليّة
treacherously (adv)	γadran	غدرًا
declaration of war	i'lān ḥarb (m)	إعلان حرب
to declare (~ war)	a'lan	أعلن
aggression	'udwān (m)	عدوان
to attack (invade)	haʒam	هجم
to invade (vt)	iḥtall	إحتلّ
invader	muḥtall (m)	محتلّ
conqueror	fātiḥ (m)	فاتح
defence	difā' (m)	دفاع
to defend (a country, etc.)	dāfa'	دافع
to defend (against ...)	dāfa' 'an nafsih	دافع عن نفسه
enemy	'aduww (m)	عدوّ
foe, adversary	χaṣm (m)	خصم
enemy (as adj)	'aduww	عدوّ
strategy	istratiʒiyya (f)	إستراتيجيّة
tactics	taktīk (m)	تكتيك
order	amr (m)	أمر
command (order)	amr (m)	أمر
to order (vt)	amar	أمر
mission	muhimma (f)	مهمّة
secret (adj)	sirriy	سرّي
battle	ma'raka (f)	معركة
combat	qitāl (m)	قتال
attack	huʒūm (m)	هجوم
charge (assault)	inqiḍāḍ (m)	إنقضاض
to storm (vt)	inqaḍḍ	إنقضّ
siege (to be under ~)	ḥiṣār (m)	حصار
offensive (n)	huʒūm (m)	هجوم
to go on the offensive	haʒam	هجم
retreat	insiḥāb (m)	إنسحاب
to retreat (vi)	insaḥab	إنسحب
encirclement	iḥāṭa (f)	إحاطة
to encircle (vt)	aḥāṭ	أحاط
bombing (by aircraft)	qaṣf (m)	قصف
to drop a bomb	asqaṭ qumbula	أسقط قنبلة
to bomb (vt)	qaṣaf	قصف
explosion	infiʒār (m)	إنفجار
shot	ṭalaqa (f)	طلقة
to fire (~ a shot)	aṭlaq an nār	أطلق النار
firing (burst of ~)	iṭlāq an nār (m)	إطلاق النار
to aim (to point a weapon)	ṣawwab	صوّب
to point (a gun)	ṣawwab	صوّب

to hit (the target)	aṣāb al hadaf	أصاب الهدف
to sink (~ a ship)	aɣraq	أغرق
hole (in a ship)	θuqb (m)	ثقب
to founder, to sink (vi)	ɣariq	غرق

front (war ~)	ʒabha (f)	جبهة
evacuation	iχlā' aṭ ṭawāri' (m)	إخلاء الطوارئ
to evacuate (vt)	aχla	أخلى

trench	χandaq (m)	خندق
barbed wire	aslāk ʃā'ika (pl)	أسلاك شائكة
barrier (anti tank ~)	ḥāʒiz (m)	حاجز
watchtower	burʒ muraqaba (m)	برج مراقبة

military hospital	mustaʃfa 'askariy (m)	مستشفى عسكريّ
to wound (vt)	ʒaraḥ	جرح
wound	ʒurḥ (m)	جرح
wounded (n)	ʒarīḥ (m)	جريح
to be wounded	uṣīb bil ʒirāḥ	أصيب بالجراح
serious (wound)	χaṭīr	خطير

185. War. Military actions. Part 2

captivity	asr (m)	أسر
to take captive	asar	أسر
to be held captive	kān asīran	كان أسيرًا
to be taken captive	waqa' fil asr	وقع في الأسر

concentration camp	mu'askar i'tiqāl (m)	معسكر إعتقال
prisoner of war	asīr (m)	أسير
to escape (vi)	harab	هرب

to betray (vt)	χān	خان
betrayer	χā'in (m)	خائن
betrayal	χiyāna (f)	خيانة

| to execute (by firing squad) | a'dam ramyan bir raṣāṣ | أعدم رميًا بالرصاص |
| execution (by firing squad) | i'dām ramyan bir raṣāṣ (m) | إعدام رميًا بالرصاص |

equipment (military gear)	al 'itād al 'askariy (m)	العتاد العسكريّ
shoulder board	katāfa (f)	كتافة
gas mask	qinā' al ɣāz (m)	قناع الغاز

field radio	ʒihāz lāsilkiy (m)	جهاز لاسلكيّ
cipher, code	ʃifra (f)	شفرة
secrecy	sirriyya (f)	سرّية
password	kalimat al murūr (f)	كلمة مرور

land mine	laɣm (m)	لغم
to mine (road, etc.)	laɣɣam	لغّم
minefield	ḥaql alɣām (m)	حقل ألغام

| air-raid warning | inðār ʒawwiy (m) | إنذار جوّيّ |
| alarm (alert signal) | inðār (m) | إنذار |

| signal | iʃāra (f) | إشارة |
| signal flare | iʃāra muḍī'a (f) | إشارة مضيئة |

headquarters	maqarr (m)	مقرّ
reconnaissance	kaʃʃāfat al istiṭlāʿ (f)	كشّافة الإستطلاع
situation	waḍʿ (m)	وضع
report	taqrīr (m)	تقرير
ambush	kamīn (m)	كمين
reinforcement (army)	imdādāt ʿaskariyya (pl)	إمدادات عسكريّة

target	hadaf (m)	هدف
training area	ḥaql taʒārib (m)	حقل تجارب
military exercise	munāwarāt ʿaskariyya (pl)	مناورات عسكريّة

panic	ðuʿr (m)	ذعر
devastation	damār (m)	دمار
destruction, ruins	ḥiṭām (pl)	حطام
to destroy (vt)	dammar	دمّر

to survive (vi, vt)	naʒa	نجا
to disarm (vt)	ʒarrad min as silāḥ	جرّد من السلاح
to handle (~ a gun)	istaʿmal	إستعمل

| Attention! | intibāh! | إنتباه! |
| At ease! | istariḥ! | إسترح! |

feat, act of courage	maʼθara (f)	مأثرة
oath (vow)	qasam (m)	قسم
to swear (an oath)	aqsam	أقسم

decoration (medal, etc.)	wisām (m)	وسام
to award (give a medal to)	manaḥ	منح
medal	midāliyya (f)	ميداليّة
order (e.g. ~ of Merit)	wisām ʿaskariy (m)	وسام عسكريّ

victory	intiṣār - fawz (m)	إنتصار, فوز
defeat	hazīma (f)	هزيمة
armistice	hudna (f)	هدنة

standard (battle flag)	rāyat al maʿraka (f)	راية المعركة
glory (honour, fame)	maʒd (m)	مجد
parade	istiʿrāḍ ʿaskariy (m)	إستعراض عسكريّ
to march (on parade)	sār	سار

186. Weapons

weapons	asliḥa (pl)	أسلحة
firearms	asliḥa nāriyya (pl)	أسلحة ناريّة
cold weapons (knives, etc.)	asliḥa bayḍā' (pl)	أسلحة بيضاء

chemical weapons	asliḥa kīmyā'iyya (pl)	أسلحة كيميائيّة
nuclear (adj)	nawawiy	نوويّ
nuclear weapons	asliḥa nawawiyya (pl)	أسلحة نوويّة
bomb	qumbula (f)	قنبلة

atomic bomb	qumbula nawawiyya (f)	قنبلة نوويّة
pistol (gun)	musaddas (m)	مسدّس
rifle	bunduqiyya (f)	بندقيّة
submachine gun	bunduqiyya huʒūmiyya (f)	بندقيّة هجوميّة
machine gun	raʃʃāʃ (m)	رشّاش
muzzle	fūha (f)	فوهة
barrel	sabṭāna (f)	سبطانة
calibre	ʿiyār (m)	عيار
trigger	zinād (m)	زناد
sight (aiming device)	muṣawwib (m)	مصوّب
magazine	maχzan (m)	مخزن
butt (shoulder stock)	ʿaqab al bunduqiyya (m)	عقب البندقيّة
hand grenade	qumbula yadawiyya (f)	قنبلة يدويّة
explosive	mawādd mutafaʒʒira (pl)	موادُّ متفجّرة
bullet	ruṣāṣa (f)	رصاصة
cartridge	χarṭūʃa (f)	خرطوشة
charge	haʃwa (f)	حشوة
ammunition	ðaχāʾir (pl)	ذخائر
bomber (aircraft)	qāðifat qanābil (f)	قاذفة قنابل
fighter	ṭāʾira muqātila (f)	طائرة مقاتلة
helicopter	hiliukūbtir (m)	هليكوبتر
anti-aircraft gun	madfaθ muḍādd liṭ ṭaʾirāṭ (m)	مدفع مضادّ للطائرات
tank	dabbāba (f)	دبّابة
tank gun	madfaʿ ad dabbāba (m)	مدفع الدبّابة
artillery	madfaʿiyya (f)	مدفعيّة
gun (cannon, howitzer)	madfaʿ (m)	مدفع
to lay (a gun)	ṣawwab	صوّب
shell (projectile)	qaðīfa (f)	قذيفة
mortar bomb	qumbula hāwun (f)	قنبلة هاون
mortar	hāwun (m)	هاون
splinter (shell fragment)	ʃaẓiyya (f)	شظيّة
submarine	ɣawwāṣa (f)	غوّاصة
torpedo	ṭurbīd (m)	طوربيد
missile	ṣārūχ (m)	صاروخ
to load (gun)	haʃa	حشا
to shoot (vi)	aṭlaq an nār	أطلق النار
to point at (the cannon)	ṣawwab	صوّب
bayonet	harba (f)	حربة
rapier	ʃīʃ (m)	شيش
sabre (e.g. cavalry ~)	sayf munhani (m)	سيف منحن
spear (weapon)	rumh (m)	رمح
bow	qaws (m)	قوس
arrow	sahm (m)	سهم
musket	muskīt (m)	مسكيت
crossbow	qaws mustaʿraḍ (m)	قوس مستعرض

187. Ancient people

primitive (prehistoric)	bidā'iy	بدائيّ
prehistoric (adj)	ma qabl at tarīχ	ما قبل التاريخ
ancient (~ civilization)	qadīm	قديم
Stone Age	al 'aṣr al ḥaʒariy (m)	العصر الحجريّ
Bronze Age	al 'aṣr al brunziy (m)	العصر البرونزيّ
Ice Age	al 'aṣr al ʒalīdiy (m)	العصر الجليديّ
tribe	qabīla (f)	قبيلة
cannibal	'ākil laḥm al baʃar (m)	آكل لحم البشر
hunter	ṣayyād (m)	صيّاد
to hunt (vi, vt)	iṣṭād	إصطاد
mammoth	mamūθ (m)	ماموث
cave	kahf (m)	كهف
fire	nār (f)	نار
campfire	nār muχayyam (m)	نار مخيّم
cave painting	rasm fil kahf (m)	رسم في الكهف
tool (e.g. stone axe)	adāt (f)	أداة
spear	rumḥ (m)	رمح
stone axe	fa's haʒariy (m)	فأس حجريّ
to be at war	ḥārab	حارب
to domesticate (vt)	daʒʒan	دجّن
idol	ṣanam (m)	صنم
to worship (vt)	'abad	عبد
superstition	χurāfa (f)	خرافة
rite	mansak (m)	منسك
evolution	taṭawwur (m)	تطوّر
development	numuww (m)	نموّ
disappearance (extinction)	iχtifā' (m)	إختفاء
to adapt oneself	takayyaf	تكيّف
archaeology	'ilm al 'āθār (m)	علم الآثار
archaeologist	'ālim 'āθār (m)	عالِم آثار
archaeological (adj)	aθariy	أثريّ
excavation site	mawqi' ḥafr (m)	موقع حفر
excavations	tanqīb (m)	تنقيب
find (object)	iktiʃāf (m)	إكتشاف
fragment	qiṭ'a (f)	قطعة

188. Middle Ages

people (ethnic group)	ʃa'b (m)	شعب
peoples	ʃu'ūb (pl)	شعوب
tribe	qabīla (f)	قبيلة
tribes	qabā'il (pl)	قبائل
barbarians	al barābira (pl)	البرابرة

Gauls	al ɣalyūn (pl)	الغاليون
Goths	al qūṭiyyūn (pl)	القوطيّين
Slavs	as silāf (pl)	السلاف
Vikings	al vaykinɣ (pl)	الفايكينغ

Romans	ar rūmān (pl)	الرومان
Roman (adj)	rumāniy	رومانيّ

Byzantines	bizanṭiyyūn (pl)	بيزنطيّين
Byzantium	bīzanṭa (f)	بيزنطة
Byzantine (adj)	bizanṭiy	بيزنطيّ

emperor	imbiraṭūr (m)	إمبراطور
leader, chief (tribal ~)	zaʿīm (m)	زعيم
powerful (~ king)	qawiy	قويّ
king	malik (m)	ملك
ruler (sovereign)	ḥākim (m)	حاكم

knight	fāris (m)	فارس
feudal lord	iqṭāʿiy (m)	إقطاعيّ
feudal (adj)	iqṭāʿiy	إقطاعيّ
vassal	muqṭaʿ (m)	مقطع

duke	dūq (m)	دوق
earl	īrl (m)	إيرل
baron	barūn (m)	بارون
bishop	usquf (m)	أسقف

armour	dirʿ (m)	درع
shield	turs (m)	ترس
sword	sayf (m)	سيف
visor	ḥāffa amāmiyya lil χūða (f)	حافة أماميّة للخوذة
chainmail	dirʿ az zarad (m)	درع الزرد

Crusade	ḥamla ṣalībiyya (f)	حملة صليبيّة
crusader	ṣalībiy (m)	صليبيّ

territory	arḍ (f)	أرض
to attack (invade)	haʒam	هجم
to conquer (vt)	fataḥ	فتح
to occupy (invade)	iḥtall	إحتلّ

siege (to be under ~)	ḥiṣār (m)	حصار
besieged (adj)	muḥāṣar	محاصر
to besiege (vt)	ḥāṣar	حاصر

inquisition	maḥākim at taftīʃ (pl)	محاكم التفتيش
inquisitor	mufattiʃ (m)	مفتّش
torture	taʿðīb (m)	تعذيب
cruel (adj)	qās	قاس
heretic	harṭūqiy (m)	هرطوقيّ
heresy	harṭaqa (f)	هرطقة

seafaring	as safar bil baḥr (m)	السفر بالبحر
pirate	qurṣān (m)	قرصان
piracy	qarṣana (f)	قرصنة

boarding (attack)	muhāӡmat safīna (f)	مهاجمة سفينة
loot, booty	ɣanīma (f)	غنيمة
treasure	kunūz (pl)	كنوز

discovery	iktiʃāf (m)	إكتشاف
to discover (new land, etc.)	iktaʃaf	إكتشف
expedition	ba'θa (f)	بعثة

musketeer	fāris (m)	فارس
cardinal	kardināl (m)	كاردينال
heraldry	ʃi'ārāt an nabāla (pl)	شعارات النبالة
heraldic (adj)	χāṣṣ bi ʃi'ārāt an nabāla	خاصّ بشعارات النبالة

189. Leader. Chief. Authorities

king	malik (m)	ملك
queen	malika (f)	ملكة
royal (adj)	malakiy	ملكيّ
kingdom	mamlaka (f)	مملكة

| prince | amīr (m) | أمير |
| princess | amīra (f) | أميرة |

president	ra'īs (m)	رئيس
vice-president	nā'ib ar ra'īs (m)	نائب الرئيس
senator	'uḍw maӡlis aʃ ʃuyūχ (m)	عضو مجلس الشيوخ

monarch	'āhil (m)	عاهل
ruler (sovereign)	ḥākim (m)	حاكم
dictator	diktatūr (m)	ديكتاتور
tyrant	ṭāɣiya (f)	طاغية
magnate	ra'smāliy kabīr (m)	رأسمالي كبير

director	mudīr (m)	مدير
chief	ra'īs (m)	رئيس
manager (director)	mudīr (m)	مدير
boss	ra'īs (m), mudīr (m)	رئيس, مدير
owner	ṣāḥib (m)	صاحب

leader	za'īm (m)	زعيم
head (~ of delegation)	ra'īs (m)	رئيس
authorities	suluṭāt (pl)	سلطات
superiors	ru'asā' (pl)	رؤساء

governor	muḥāfiẓ (m)	محافظ
consul	qunṣul (m)	قنصل
diplomat	diblumāsiy (m)	دبلوماسيّ
mayor	ra'īs al baladiyya (m)	رئيس البلديّة
sheriff	ʃarīf (m)	شريف

emperor	imbiraṭūr (m)	إمبراطور
tsar, czar	qayṣar (m)	قيصر
pharaoh	fir'awn (m)	فرعون
khan	χān (m)	خان

190. Road. Way. Directions

road	ṭarīq (m)	طريق
way (direction)	ṭarīq (m)	طريق
highway	ṭarīq sarīʿ (m)	طريق سريع
motorway	ṭarīq sarīʿ (m)	طريق سريع
trunk road	ṭarīq waṭaniy (m)	طريق وطني
main road	ṭarīq raʾīsiy (m)	طريق رئيسي
dirt road	ṭarīq turābiy (m)	طريق ترابي
pathway	mamarr (m)	ممرّ
footpath (troddenpath)	mamarr (m)	ممرّ
Where?	ayna?	أين؟
Where (to)?	ila ayna?	إلى أين؟
From where?	min ayna?	من أين؟
direction (way)	ittiʒāh (m)	إتّجاه
to point (~ the way)	aʃār	أشار
to the left	ilaʃ ʃimāl	إلى الشمال
to the right	ilal yamīn	إلى اليمين
straight ahead (adv)	ilal amām	إلى الأمام
back (e.g. to turn ~)	ilal warāʾ	إلى الوراء
bend, curve	munʿaṭif (m)	منعطف
to turn (e.g., ~ left)	inʿaṭaf	إنعطف
to make a U-turn	istadār lil xalf	إستدار للخلف
to be visible (mountains, castle, etc.)	ẓahar	ظهر
to appear (come into view)	ẓahar	ظهر
stop, halt (e.g., during a trip)	istirāḥa (f)	إستراحة
to rest, to pause (vi)	istarāḥ	إستراح
rest (pause)	istirāḥa (f)	إستراحة
to lose one's way	tāh	تاه
to lead to … (ab. road)	adda ila …	أدّى إلى...
to came out (e.g., on the highway)	waṣal ila …	وصل إلى...
stretch (of the road)	imtidād (m)	إمتداد
asphalt	asfalt (m)	اسفلت
kerb	ḥāffat ar raṣīf (f)	حافّة الرصيف
ditch	xandaq (m)	خندق
manhole	fatḥat ad duxūl (f)	فتحة الدخول
roadside (shoulder)	ḥāffat aṭ ṭarīq (f)	حافّة الطريق
pit, pothole	ḥufra (f)	حفرة
to go (on foot)	maʃa	مشى
to overtake (vt)	laḥiq bi	لحق بـ
step (footstep)	xaṭwa (f)	خطوة

on foot (adv)	māʃiyan	ماشيًا
to block (road)	sadd	سدّ
boom gate	ḥāʒiz ṭarīq (m)	حاجز طريق
dead end	ṭarīq masdūd (m)	طريق مسدود

191. Breaking the law. Criminals. Part 1

bandit	qāṭiʿ ṭarīq (m)	قاطع طريق
crime	ʒarīma (f)	جريمة
criminal (person)	muʒrim (m)	مجرم

thief	sāriq (m)	سارق
to steal (vi, vt)	saraq	سرق
stealing, theft	sirqa (f)	سرقة

to kidnap (vt)	xaṭaf	خطف
kidnapping	xaṭf (m)	خطف
kidnapper	xāṭif (m)	خاطف

| ransom | fidya (f) | فدية |
| to demand ransom | ṭalab fidya | طلب فدية |

to rob (vt)	nahab	نهب
robbery	nahb (m)	نهب
robber	nahhāb (m)	نهّاب

to extort (vt)	balṭaʒ	بلطج
extortionist	balṭaʒiy (m)	بلطجي
extortion	balṭaʒa (f)	بلطجة

to murder, to kill	qatal	قتل
murder	qatl (m)	قتل
murderer	qātil (m)	قاتل

gunshot	ṭalaqat nār (f)	طلقة نار
to fire (~ a shot)	aṭlaq an nār	أطلق النار
to shoot to death	qatal bir ruṣāṣ	قتل بالرصاص
to shoot (vi)	aṭlaq an nār	أطلق النار
shooting	iṭlāq an nār (m)	إطلاق النار

incident (fight, etc.)	ḥādiθ (m)	حادث
fight, brawl	ʿirāk (m)	عراك
Help!	sāʿidni	ساعدني!
victim	ḍaḥiyya (f)	ضحيّة

to damage (vt)	atlaf	أتلف
damage	xasāra (f)	خسارة
dead body, corpse	ʒuθθa (f)	جثّة
grave (~ crime)	ʿanīf	عنيف

to attack (vt)	haʒam	هجم
to beat (to hit)	ḍarab	ضرب
to beat up	ḍarab	ضرب
to take (rob of sth)	salab	سلب

to stab to death	ṭa'an ḥatta al mawt	طعن حتّى الموت
to maim (vt)	ʃawwah	شوّه
to wound (vt)	ʒaraḥ	جرح

blackmail	balṭaʒa (f)	بلطجة
to blackmail (vt)	ibtazz	إبتزّ
blackmailer	mubtazz (m)	مبتزّ

protection racket	naṣb (m)	نصب
racketeer	naṣṣāb (m)	نصّاب
gangster	raʒul 'iṣāba (m)	رجل عصابة
mafia	māfia (f)	مافيا

pickpocket	naʃʃāl (m)	نشّال
burglar	liṣṣ buyūt (m)	لصّ بيوت
smuggling	tahrīb (m)	تهريب
smuggler	muharrib (m)	مهرّب

forgery	tazwīr (m)	تزوير
to forge (counterfeit)	zawwar	زوّر
fake (forged)	muzawwar	مزوّر

192. Breaking the law. Criminals. Part 2

rape	iɣtiṣāb (m)	إغتصاب
to rape (vt)	iɣtaṣab	إغتصب
rapist	muɣtaṣib (m)	مغتصب
maniac	mahwūs (m)	مهووس

prostitute (fem.)	'āhira (f)	عاهرة
prostitution	da'āra (f)	دعارة
pimp	qawwād (m)	قوّاد

| drug addict | mudmin muxaddirāt (m) | مدمن مخدّرات |
| drug dealer | tāʒir muxaddirāt (m) | تاجر مخدّرات |

to blow up (bomb)	faʒʒar	فجّر
explosion	infiʒār (m)	إنفجار
to set fire	aʃ'al an nār	أشعل النار
arsonist	muʃ'il ḥarīq (m)	مشعل حريق

terrorism	irhāb (m)	إرهاب
terrorist	irhābiy (m)	إرهابيّ
hostage	rahīna (m)	رهينة

to swindle (deceive)	iḥtāl	إحتال
swindle, deception	iḥtiyāl (m)	إحتيال
swindler	muhtāl (m)	محتال

to bribe (vt)	raʃa	رشا
bribery	irtiʃā' (m)	إرتشاء
bribe	raʃwa (f)	رشوة
poison	samm (m)	سمّ
to poison (vt)	sammam	سمّم

to poison oneself	sammam nafsahu	سمّم نفسه
suicide (act)	intiḥār (m)	إنتحار
suicide (person)	muntaḥir (m)	منتحر

to threaten (vt)	haddad	هدّد
threat	tahdīd (m)	تهديد
to make an attempt	ḥāwal iɣtiyāl	حاول الإغتيال
attempt (attack)	muḥāwalat iɣtiyāl (f)	محاولة إغتيال

| to steal (a car) | saraq | سرق |
| to hijack (a plane) | iχtaṭaf | إختطف |

| revenge | intiqām (m) | إنتقام |
| to avenge (get revenge) | intaqam | إنتقم |

to torture (vt)	ʿaððab	عذّب
torture	taʿðīb (m)	تعذيب
to torment (vt)	ʿaððab	عذّب

pirate	qurṣān (m)	قرصان
hooligan	wabaʃ (m)	وبش
armed (adj)	musallaḥ	مسلّح
violence	ʿunf (m)	عنف
illegal (unlawful)	ɣayr qānūniy	غير قانونيّ

| spying (espionage) | taʒassas (m) | تجسّس |
| to spy (vi) | taʒassas | تجسّس |

193. Police. Law. Part 1

| justice | qaḍāʾ (m) | قضاء |
| court (see you in ~) | maḥkama (f) | محكمة |

judge	qāḍi (m)	قاض
jurors	muḥallafūn (pl)	محلّفون
jury trial	qaḍāʾ al muḥallafīn (m)	قضاء المحلّفين
to judge, to try (vt)	ḥakam	حكم

lawyer, barrister	muḥāmi (m)	محام
defendant	muddaʿa ʿalayh (m)	مدّعى عليه
dock	qafṣ al ittihām (m)	قفص الإتّهام

| charge | ittihām (m) | إتّهام |
| accused | muttaham (m) | متّهم |

| sentence | ḥukm (m) | حكم |
| to sentence (vt) | ḥakam | حكم |

guilty (culprit)	muðnib (m)	مذنب
to punish (vt)	ʿāqab	عاقب
punishment	ʿuqūba (f), ʿiqāb (m)	عقوبة، عقاب

| fine (penalty) | ɣarāma (f) | غرامة |
| life imprisonment | siʒn mada al ḥayāt (m) | سجن مدى الحياة |

death penalty	'uqūbat 'i'dām (f)	عقوبة إعدام
electric chair	kursiy kaharabā'iy (m)	كرسيّ كهربائيّ
gallows	maʃnaqa (f)	مشنقة

to execute (vt)	a'dam	أعدم
execution	i'dām (m)	إعدام

prison	siʒn (m)	سجن
cell	zinzāna (f)	زنزانة

escort (convoy)	ḥirāsa (f)	حراسة
prison officer	ḥāris siʒn (m)	حارس سجن
prisoner	saʒīn (m)	سجين

handcuffs	aṣfād (pl)	أصفاد
to handcuff (vt)	ṣaffad	صفّد

prison break	hurūb min as siʒn (m)	هروب من السجن
to break out (vi)	harab	هرب
to disappear (vi)	ixtafa	إختفى
to release (from prison)	axla sabīl	أخلى سبيل
amnesty	'afw 'āmm (m)	عفو عامّ

police	ʃurṭa (f)	شرطة
police officer	ʃurṭiy (m)	شرطيّ
police station	qism ʃurṭa (m)	قسم شرطة
truncheon	hirāwat aʃ ʃurṭiy (f)	هراوة الشرطيّ
megaphone (loudhailer)	būq (m)	بوق

patrol car	sayyārat dawrīyyāt (f)	سيّارة دوريّات
siren	ṣaffārat inðār (f)	صفّارة إنذار
to turn on the siren	atlaq sirīna	أطلق سرينة
siren call	ṣawt sirīna (m)	صوت سرينة

crime scene	masraḥ al ʒarīma (m)	مسرح الجريمة
witness	ʃāhid (m)	شاهد
freedom	ḥurriyya (f)	حرّيّة
accomplice	ʃarīk fil ʒarīma (m)	شريك في الجريمة
to flee (vi)	harab	هرب
trace (to leave a ~)	aθar (m)	أثر

194. Police. Law. Part 2

search (investigation)	baḥθ (m)	بحث
to look for ...	baḥaθ	بحث
suspicion	ʃubha (f)	شبهة
suspicious (e.g., ~ vehicle)	maʃbūh	مشبوه
to stop (cause to halt)	awqaf	أوقف
to detain (keep in custody)	i'taqal	إعتقل

case (lawsuit)	qaḍiyya (f)	قضيّة
investigation	taḥqīq (m)	تحقيق
detective	muḥaqqiq (m)	محقّق
investigator	mufattiʃ (m)	مفتّش

hypothesis	riwāya (f)	رواية
motive	dāfiʿ (m)	دافع
interrogation	istiʒwāb (m)	إستجواب
to interrogate (vt)	istaʒwab	إستجوب
to question (~ neighbors, etc.)	istantaq	إستنطق
check (identity ~)	faḥṣ (m)	فحص
round-up (raid)	ʒamʿ (m)	جمع
search (~ warrant)	taftīʃ (m)	تفتيش
chase (pursuit)	mutārada (f)	مطاردة
to pursue, to chase	tārad	طارد
to track (a criminal)	tābaʿ	تابع
arrest	iʿtiqāl (m)	إعتقال
to arrest (sb)	iʿtaqal	إعتقل
to catch (thief, etc.)	qabaḍ	قبض
capture	qabḍ (m)	قبض
document	waθīqa (f)	وثيقة
proof (evidence)	dalīl (m)	دليل
to prove (vt)	aθbat	أثبت
footprint	baṣma (f)	بصمة
fingerprints	baṣamāt al aṣābiʿ (pl)	بصمات الأصابع
piece of evidence	dalīl (m)	دليل
alibi	dafʿ bil ɣayba (f)	دفع بالغيبة
innocent (not guilty)	barīʾ	بريء
injustice	ẓulm (m)	ظلم
unjust, unfair (adj)	ɣayr ʿādil	غير عادل
criminal (adj)	iʒrāmiy	إجراميّ
to confiscate (vt)	ṣādar	صادر
drug (illegal substance)	muxaddirāt (pl)	مخدّرات
weapon, gun	silāḥ (m)	سلاح
to disarm (vt)	ʒarrad min as silāḥ	جرّد من السلاح
to order (command)	amar	أمر
to disappear (vi)	ixtafa	إختفى
law	qānūn (m)	قانون
legal, lawful (adj)	qānūniy, ʃarʿiy	قانونيّ، شرعيّ
illegal, illicit (adj)	ɣayr qanūniy, ɣayr ʃarʿi	غير قانونيّ، غير شرعيّ
responsibility (blame)	masʾūliyya (f)	مسؤوليّة
responsible (adj)	masʾūl (m)	مسؤول

NATURE

The Earth. Part 1

195. Outer space

space	faḍā' (m)	فضاء
space (as adj)	faḍā'iy	فضائيّ
outer space	faḍā' (m)	فضاء
world	'ālam (m)	عالم
universe	al kawn (m)	الكون
galaxy	al maӡarra (f)	المجرّة
star	naӡm (m)	نجم
constellation	burӡ (m)	برج
planet	kawkab (m)	كوكب
satellite	qamar ṣinā'iy (m)	قمر صناعيّ
meteorite	haӡar nayzakiy (m)	حجر نيزكيّ
comet	muðannab (m)	مذنّب
asteroid	kuwaykib (m)	كويكب
orbit	madār (m)	مدار
to revolve	dār	دار
(~ around the Earth)		
atmosphere	al ɣilāf al ӡawwiy (m)	الغلاف الجوّيّ
the Sun	aʃ ʃams (f)	الشمس
solar system	al maӡmū'a aʃ ʃamsiyya (f)	المجموعة الشمسيّة
solar eclipse	kusūf aʃ ʃams (m)	كسوف الشمس
the Earth	al arḍ (f)	الأرض
the Moon	al qamar (m)	القمر
Mars	al mirrīχ (m)	المرّيخ
Venus	az zahra (f)	الزهرة
Jupiter	al muʃtari (m)	المشتري
Saturn	zuḥal (m)	زحل
Mercury	'aṭārid (m)	عطارد
Uranus	urānus (m)	اورانوس
Neptune	nibtūn (m)	نبتون
Pluto	blūtu (m)	بلوتو
Milky Way	darb at tabbāna (m)	درب التبّانة
Great Bear (Ursa Major)	ad dubb al akbar (m)	الدبّ الأكبر
North Star	naӡm al 'quṭb (m)	نجم القطب
Martian	sākin al mirrīχ (m)	ساكن المرّيخ
extraterrestrial (n)	faḍā'iy (m)	فضائيّ

| alien | faḍā'iy (m) | فَضائِيّ |
| flying saucer | ṭabaq ṭā'ir (m) | طَبَق طائِر |

spaceship	markaba faḍā'iyya (f)	مَرْكَبة فَضائِيّة
space station	maḥaṭṭat faḍā' (f)	مَحَطّة فَضاء
blast-off	intilāq (m)	إِنْطِلاق

engine	mutūr (m)	موتور
nozzle	manfaθ (m)	مَنْفَث
fuel	wuqūd (m)	وَقود

cockpit, flight deck	kabīna (f)	كابِينة
aerial	hawā'iy (m)	هَوائِيّ
porthole	kuwwa mustadīra (f)	كُوّة مُسْتَدِيرة
solar panel	lawḥ ʃamsiy (m)	لَوْح شَمْسِيّ
spacesuit	baðlat al faḍā' (f)	بَذْلة الفَضاء

| weightlessness | in'idām al wazn (m) | إِنْعِدام الوَزْن |
| oxygen | uksiʒīn (m) | أَكْسِجِين |

| docking (in space) | rasw (m) | رَسْو |
| to dock (vi, vt) | rasa | رَسا |

observatory	marṣad (m)	مَرْصَد
telescope	tiliskūp (m)	تِلِسْكوب
to observe (vt)	rāqab	راقَب
to explore (vt)	istakʃaf	إِسْتَكْشَف

196. The Earth

the Earth	al arḍ (f)	الأَرْض
the globe (the Earth)	al kura al arḍiyya (f)	الكُرة الأَرْضِيّة
planet	kawkab (m)	كَوْكَب

atmosphere	al ɣilāf al ʒawwiy (m)	الغِلاف الجَوِّيّ
geography	ʒuɣrāfiya (f)	جِغْرافْيا
nature	ṭabī'a (f)	طَبِيعة

globe (table ~)	namūðaʒ lil kura al arḍiyya (m)	نَموذَج لِلكُرة الأَرْضِيّة
map	xarīṭa (f)	خَرِيطة
atlas	aṭlas (m)	أَطْلَس

| Europe | urūbba (f) | أوروبّا |
| Asia | 'āsiya (f) | آسْيا |

| Africa | afrīqiya (f) | أَفْرِيقْيا |
| Australia | usturāliya (f) | أُسْتْرالْيا |

America	amrīka (f)	أَمْرِيكا
North America	amrīka aʃ ʃimāliyya (f)	أَمْرِيكا الشَمالِيّة
South America	amrīka al ʒanūbiyya (f)	أَمْرِيكا الجَنوبِيّة

| Antarctica | al quṭb al ʒanūbiy (m) | القُطْب الجَنوبِيّ |
| the Arctic | al quṭb aʃ ʃimāliy (m) | القُطْب الشَمالِيّ |

197. Cardinal directions

north	ʃimāl (m)	شمال
to the north	ilaʃʃimāl	إلى الشمال
in the north	fiʃʃimāl	في الشمال
northern (adj)	ʃimāliy	شماليَ

south	ʒanūb (m)	جنوب
to the south	ilal ʒanūb	إلى الجنوب
in the south	fil ʒanūb	في الجنوب
southern (adj)	ʒanūbiy	جنوبي

west	ɣarb (m)	غرب
to the west	ilal ɣarb	إلى الغرب
in the west	fil ɣarb	في الغرب
western (adj)	ɣarbiy	غربي

east	ʃarq (m)	شرق
to the east	ilaʃ ʃarq	إلى الشرق
in the east	fiʃ ʃarq	في الشرق
eastern (adj)	ʃarqiy	شرقيَ

198. Sea. Ocean

sea	baḥr (m)	بحر
ocean	muḥīṭ (m)	محيط
gulf (bay)	xalīʒ (m)	خليج
straits	maḍīq (m)	مضيق

land (solid ground)	barr (m)	برَ
continent (mainland)	qārra (f)	قارَة
island	ʒazīra (f)	جزيرة
peninsula	ʃibh ʒazīra (f)	شبه جزيرة
archipelago	maʒmūʿat ʒuzur (f)	مجموعة جزر

bay, cove	xalīʒ (m)	خليج
harbour	mīnāʾ (m)	ميناء
lagoon	buḥayra ʃāṭiʾa (f)	بحيرة شاطئة
cape	raʾs (m)	رأس

| atoll | ʒazīra marʒāniyya istiwāʾiyya (f) | جزيرة مرجانيَة إستوائيَة |

reef	ʃiʿāb (pl)	شعاب
coral	murʒān (m)	مرجان
coral reef	ʃiʿāb marʒāniyya (pl)	شعاب مرجانيَة

deep (adj)	ʿamīq	عميق
depth (deep water)	ʿumq (m)	عمق
abyss	mahwāt (f)	مهواة
trench (e.g. Mariana ~)	xandaq (m)	خندق

| current (Ocean ~) | tayyār (m) | تيَار |
| to surround (bathe) | aḥāṭ | أحاط |

| shore | sāḥil (m) | ساحل |
| coast | sāḥil (m) | ساحل |

flow (flood tide)	madd (m)	مَدّ
ebb (ebb tide)	ʒazr (m)	جزر
shoal	miyāh ḍaḥla (f)	مياه ضحلة
bottom (~ of the sea)	qāʿ (m)	قاع

wave	mawʒa (f)	موجة
crest (~ of a wave)	qimmat mawʒa (f)	قمّة موجة
spume (sea foam)	zabad al baḥr (m)	زبد البحر

storm (sea storm)	ʿāṣifa (f)	عاصفة
hurricane	iʿṣār (m)	إعصار
tsunami	tsunāmi (m)	تسونامي
calm (dead ~)	hudūʾ (m)	هدوء
quiet, calm (adj)	hādiʾ	هادئ

| pole | quṭb (m) | قطب |
| polar (adj) | quṭby | قطبيّ |

latitude	ʿarḍ (m)	عرض
longitude	ṭūl (m)	طول
parallel	mutawāzi (m)	متواز
equator	xaṭṭ al istiwāʾ (m)	خط الإستواء

sky	samāʾ (f)	سماء
horizon	ufuq (m)	أفق
air	hawāʾ (m)	هواء

lighthouse	manāra (f)	منارة
to dive (vi)	ɣāṣ	غاص
to sink (ab. boat)	ɣariq	غرق
treasure	kunūz (pl)	كنوز

199. Seas & Oceans names

Atlantic Ocean	al muḥīṭ al aṭlasiy (m)	المحيط الأطلسيّ
Indian Ocean	al muḥīṭ al hindiy (m)	المحيط الهنديّ
Pacific Ocean	al muḥīṭ al hādiʾ (m)	المحيط الهادئ
Arctic Ocean	al muḥīṭ il mutaʒammid aʃʃimāliy (m)	المحيط المتجمّد الشماليّ

Black Sea	al baḥr al aswad (m)	البحر الأسود
Red Sea	al baḥr al aḥmar (m)	البحر الأحمر
Yellow Sea	al baḥr al aṣfar (m)	البحر الأصفر
White Sea	al baḥr al abyaḍ (m)	البحر الأبيض

Caspian Sea	baḥr qazwīn (m)	بحر قزوين
Dead Sea	al baḥr al mayyit (m)	البحر المَيِّت
Mediterranean Sea	al baḥr al abyaḍ al mutawassiṭ (m)	البحر الأبيض المتوسّط

| Aegean Sea | baḥr īʒah (m) | بحر إجة |
| Adriatic Sea | al baḥr al adriyatīkiy (m) | البحر الأدرياتيكيّ |

Arabian Sea	baḥr al 'arab (m)	بحر العرب
Sea of Japan	baḥr al yabān (m)	بحر اليابان
Bering Sea	baḥr biriŋʒ (m)	بحر بيرينغ
South China Sea	baḥr aṣ ṣīn al ʒanūbiy (m)	بحر الصين الجنوبيّ

Coral Sea	baḥr al marʒān (m)	بحر المرجان
Tasman Sea	baḥr tasmān (m)	بحر تسمان
Caribbean Sea	al baḥr al karībiy (m)	البحر الكاريبيّ

| Barents Sea | baḥr barints (m) | بحر بارينس |
| Kara Sea | baḥr kara (m) | بحر كارا |

North Sea	baḥr aʃ ʃimāl (m)	بحر الشمال
Baltic Sea	al baḥr al balṭīq (m)	البحر البلطيق
Norwegian Sea	baḥr an narwīʒ (m)	بحر النرويج

200. Mountains

mountain	ʒabal (m)	جبل
mountain range	silsilat ʒibāl (f)	سلسلة جبال
mountain ridge	qimam ʒabaliyya (pl)	قمم جبليّة

summit, top	qimma (f)	قمّة
peak	qimma (f)	قمّة
foot (~ of the mountain)	asfal (m)	أسفل
slope (mountainside)	munḥadar (m)	منحدر

volcano	burkān (m)	بركان
active volcano	burkān naʃiṭ (m)	بركان نشط
dormant volcano	burkān xāmid (m)	بركان خامد

eruption	θawrān (m)	ثوران
crater	fūhat al burkān (f)	فوهة البركان
magma	māɣma (f)	ماغما
lava	ḥumam burkāniyya (pl)	حمم بركانيّة
molten (~ lava)	munṣahira	منصهرة

canyon	tal'a (m)	تلمة
gorge	wādi ḍayyiq (m)	واد ضيّق
crevice	ʃaqq (m)	شقّ
abyss (chasm)	hāwiya (f)	هاوية

pass, col	mamarr ʒabaliy (m)	ممرّ جبليّ
plateau	haḍba (f)	هضبة
cliff	ʒurf (m)	جرف
hill	tall (m)	تلّ

glacier	nahr ʒalīdiy (m)	نهر جليديّ
waterfall	ʃallāl (m)	شلّال
geyser	fawwāra ḥārra (m)	فوّارة حارّة
lake	buḥayra (f)	بحيرة

| plain | sahl (m) | سهل |
| landscape | manẓar ṭabī'iy (m) | منظر طبيعيّ |

echo	ṣada (m)	صدى
alpinist	mutasalliq al ʒibāl (m)	متسلّق الجبال
rock climber	mutasalliq ṣuxūr (m)	متسلّق صخور
to conquer (in climbing)	taɣallab ʿala	تغلّب على
climb (an easy ~)	tasalluq (m)	تسلّق

201. Mountains names

The Alps	ʒibāl al alb (pl)	جبال الألب
Mont Blanc	mūn blūn (m)	مون بلون
The Pyrenees	ʒibāl al barānis (pl)	جبال البرانس
The Carpathians	ʒibāl al karbāt (pl)	جبال الكاربيات
The Ural Mountains	ʒibāl al ʾūrāl (pl)	جبال الأورال
The Caucasus Mountains	ʒibāl al qawqāz (pl)	جبال القوقاز
Mount Elbrus	ʒabal ilbrūs (m)	جبل إلبروس
The Altai Mountains	ʒibāl altāy (pl)	جبال ألتاي
The Tian Shan	ʒibāl tian ʃan (pl)	جبال تيان شان
The Pamirs	ʒibāl bamīr (pl)	جبال بامير
The Himalayas	himalāya (pl)	هيمالايا
Mount Everest	ʒabal ivirist (m)	جبل افرست
The Andes	ʒibāl al andīz (pl)	جبال الأنديز
Mount Kilimanjaro	ʒabal kilimanʒāru (m)	جبل كليمنجارو

202. Rivers

river	nahr (m)	نهر
spring (natural source)	ʿayn (m)	عين
riverbed (river channel)	maʒra an nahr (m)	مجرى النهر
basin (river valley)	ḥawḍ (m)	حوض
to flow into ...	ṣabb fi ...	صبّ في...
tributary	rāfid (m)	رافد
bank (river ~)	ḍiffa (f)	ضفّة
current (stream)	tayyār (m)	تيّار
downstream (adv)	f ittiʒāh maʒra an nahr	في إتجاه مجرى النهر
upstream (adv)	ḍidd at tayyār	ضدّ التيّار
inundation	ɣamr (m)	غمر
flooding	fayaḍān (m)	فيضان
to overflow (vi)	fāḍ	فاض
to flood (vt)	ɣamar	غمر
shallow (shoal)	miyāh ḍaḥla (f)	مياه ضحلة
rapids	munḥadar an nahr (m)	منحدر النهر
dam	sadd (m)	سدّ
canal	qanāt (f)	قناة
reservoir (artificial lake)	xazzān māʾiy (m)	خزّان مائيّ

sluice, lock	hawīs (m)	هويس
water body (pond, etc.)	masṭaḥ māʾiy (m)	مسطح مائيّ
swamp (marshland)	mustanqaʿ (m)	مستنقع
bog, marsh	mustanqaʿ (m)	مستنقع
whirlpool	dawwāma (f)	دوّامة

stream (brook)	ʒadwal māʾiy (m)	جدول مائيّ
drinking (ab. water)	aʃ ʃurb	الشرب
fresh (~ water)	ʿaðb	عذب

ice	ʒalīd (m)	جليد
to freeze over (ab. river, etc.)	taʒammad	تجمّد

203. Rivers names

Seine	nahr as sīn (m)	نهر السين
Loire	nahr al luaːr (m)	نهر اللوار

Thames	nahr at tīmz (m)	نهر التيمز
Rhine	nahr ar rayn (m)	نهر الراين
Danube	nahr ad danūb (m)	نهر الدانوب

Volga	nahr al vulɣa (m)	نهر الفولغا
Don	nahr ad dūn (m)	نهر الدون
Lena	nahr līna (m)	نهر لينا

Yellow River	an nahr al aṣfar (m)	النهر الأصفر
Yangtze	nahr al yanɣtsi (m)	نهر اليانغتسي
Mekong	nahr al mikunɣ (m)	نهر الميكونغ
Ganges	nahr al ɣānʒ (m)	نهر الغانج

Nile River	nahr an nīl (m)	نهر النيل
Congo River	nahr al kunɣu (m)	نهر الكونغو
Okavango River	nahr ukavanʒu (m)	نهر اوكافانجو
Zambezi River	nahr az zambizi (m)	نهر الزمبيزي
Limpopo River	nahr limbubu (m)	نهر ليمبوبو
Mississippi River	nahr al mississibbi (m)	نهر الميسيسيبي

204. Forest

forest, wood	ɣāba (f)	غابة
forest (as adj)	ɣāba	غابة

thick forest	ɣāba kaθīfa (f)	غابة كثيفة
grove	ɣāba ṣaɣīra (f)	غابة صغيرة
forest clearing	minṭaqa uzīlat minha al afʒār (f)	منطقة أزيلت منها الأشجار

thicket	aʒama (f)	أجمة
scrubland	ʃuʒayrāt (pl)	شجيرات
footpath (troddenpath)	mamarr (m)	ممرّ
gully	wādi ḍayyiq (m)	واد ضيّق

tree	ʃaʒara (f)	شجرة
leaf	waraqa (f)	ورقة
leaves (foliage)	waraq (m)	ورق
fall of leaves	tasāquṭ al awrāq (m)	تساقط الأوراق
to fall (ab. leaves)	saqaṭ	سقط
top (of the tree)	ra's (m)	رأس
branch	ɣuṣn (m)	غصن
bough	ɣuṣn (m)	غصن
bud (on shrub, tree)	burʻum (m)	برعم
needle (of the pine tree)	ʃawka (f)	شوكة
fir cone	kūz aṣ ṣanawbar (m)	كوز الصنوبر
tree hollow	ʒawf (m)	جوف
nest	ʻuʃʃ (m)	عش
burrow (animal hole)	ʒuḥr (m)	جحر
trunk	ʒiðʻ (m)	جذع
root	ʒiðr (m)	جذر
bark	liḥā' (m)	لحاء
moss	ṭuḥlub (m)	طحلب
to uproot (remove trees or tree stumps)	iqtalaʻ	إقتلع
to chop down	qaṭaʻ	قطع
to deforest (vt)	azāl al ɣābāt	أزال الغابات
tree stump	ʒiðʻ aʃ ʃaʒara (m)	جذع الشجرة
campfire	nār muxayyam (m)	نار مخيّم
forest fire	ḥarīq ɣāba (m)	حريق غابة
to extinguish (vt)	aṭfa'	أطفأ
forest ranger	ḥāris al ɣāba (m)	حارس الغابة
protection	ḥimāya (f)	حماية
to protect (~ nature)	ḥama	حمى
poacher	sāriq aṣ ṣayd (m)	سارق الصيد
steel trap	maṣyada (f)	مصيدة
to gather, to pick (vt)	ʒamaʻ	جمع
to lose one's way	tāh	تاه

205. Natural resources

natural resources	θarawāt ṭabīʻiyya (pl)	ثروات طبيعيّة
minerals	maʻādin (pl)	معادن
deposits	makāmin (pl)	مكامن
field (e.g. oilfield)	ḥaql (m)	حقل
to mine (extract)	istaxraʒ	إستخرج
mining (extraction)	istixrāʒ (m)	إستخراج
ore	xām (m)	خام
mine (e.g. for coal)	manʒam (m)	منجم
shaft (mine ~)	manʒam (m)	منجم

miner	'āmil manʒam (m)	عامل منجم
gas (natural ~)	ɣāz (m)	غاز
gas pipeline	χaṭṭ anābīb ɣāz (m)	خط أنابيب غاز

oil (petroleum)	naft (m)	نفط
oil pipeline	anābīb an naft (pl)	أنابيب النفط
oil well	bi'r an naft (m)	بئر النفط
derrick (tower)	ḥaffāra (f)	حفّارة
tanker	nāqilat an naft (f)	ناقلة النفط

sand	raml (m)	رمل
limestone	ḥaʒar kalsiy (m)	حجر كلسيّ
gravel	ḥaṣa (m)	حصى
peat	χaθθ faḥm nabātiy (m)	خثّ فحم نباتيّ
clay	ṭīn (m)	طين
coal	faḥm (m)	فحم

iron (ore)	ḥadīd (m)	حديد
gold	ðahab (m)	ذهب
silver	fiḍḍa (f)	فضّة
nickel	nikil (m)	نيكل
copper	nuḥās (m)	نحاس

zinc	zink (m)	زنك
manganese	manɣanīz (m)	منغنيز
mercury	zi'baq (m)	زئبق
lead	ruṣāṣ (m)	رصاص

mineral	ma'dan (m)	معدن
crystal	ballūra (f)	بلّورة
marble	ruχām (m)	رخام
uranium	yurānuim (m)	يورانيوم

The Earth. Part 2

206. Weather

weather	ṭaqs (m)	طقس
weather forecast	naʃra ʒawwiyya (f)	نشرة جوّيّة
temperature	ḥarāra (f)	حرارة
thermometer	tirmūmitr (m)	ترمومتر
barometer	barūmitr (m)	بارومتر
humid (adj)	raṭib	رطب
humidity	ruṭūba (f)	رطوبة
heat (extreme ~)	ḥarāra (f)	حرارة
hot (torrid)	ḥārr	حارّ
it's hot	al ʒaww ḥarr	الجوّ حارّ
it's warm	al ʒaww dāfiʾ	الجوّ دافئ
warm (moderately hot)	dāfiʾ	دافئ
it's cold	al ʒaww bārid	الجوّ بارد
cold (adj)	bārid	بارد
sun	ʃams (f)	شمس
to shine (vi)	aḍāʾ	أضاء
sunny (day)	muʃmis	مشمس
to come up (vi)	ʃaraq	شرق
to set (vi)	ɣarab	غرب
cloud	saḥāba (f)	سحابة
cloudy (adj)	ɣāʾim	غائم
rain cloud	saḥābat maṭar (f)	سحابة مطر
somber (gloomy)	ɣāʾim	غائم
rain	maṭar (m)	مطر
it's raining	innaha tamṭur	إنّها تمطر
rainy (~ day, weather)	mumṭir	ممطر
to drizzle (vi)	raðð	رذّ
pouring rain	maṭar munhamir (f)	مطر منهمر
downpour	maṭar ɣazīr (m)	مطر غزير
heavy (e.g. ~ rain)	ʃadīd	شديد
puddle	birka (f)	بركة
to get wet (in rain)	ibtall	إبتلّ
fog (mist)	ḍabāb (m)	ضباب
foggy	muḍabbab	مضبّب
snow	θalʒ (m)	ثلج
it's snowing	innaha taθluʒ	إنّها تثلج

207. Severe weather. Natural disasters

thunderstorm	'āṣifa ra'diyya (f)	عاصفة رعديّة
lightning (~ strike)	barq (m)	برق
to flash (vi)	baraq	برق
thunder	ra'd (m)	رعد
to thunder (vi)	ra'ad	رعد
it's thundering	tar'ad as samā'	ترعد السماء
hail	maṭar bard (m)	مطر برد
it's hailing	tamṭur as samā' bardan	تمطر السماء برداً
to flood (vt)	ɣamar	غمر
flood, inundation	fayaḍān (m)	فيضان
earthquake	zilzāl (m)	زلزال
tremor, shoke	hazza arḍiyya (f)	هزّة أرضيّة
epicentre	markaz az zilzāl (m)	مركز الزلزال
eruption	θawrān (m)	ثوران
lava	ḥumam burkāniyya (pl)	حمم بركانيّة
twister, tornado	i'ṣār (m)	إعصار
typhoon	ṭūfān (m)	طوفان
hurricane	i'ṣār (m)	إعصار
storm	'āṣifa (f)	عاصفة
tsunami	tsunāmi (m)	تسونامي
cyclone	i'ṣār (m)	إعصار
bad weather	ṭaqs sayyi' (m)	طقس سيّء
fire (accident)	ḥarīq (m)	حريق
disaster	kāriθa (f)	كارثة
meteorite	ḥaʒar nayzakiy (m)	حجر نيزكيّ
avalanche	inhiyār θalʒiy (m)	إنهيار ثلجيّ
snowslide	inhiyār θalʒiy (m)	إنهيار ثلجيّ
blizzard	'āṣifa θalʒiyya (f)	عاصفة ثلجيّة
snowstorm	'āṣifa θalʒiyya (f)	عاصفة ثلجيّة

208. Noises. Sounds

silence (quiet)	ṣamt (m)	صمت
sound	ṣawt (m)	صوت
noise	ḍawḍā' (f)	ضوضاء
to make noise	'amal aḍ ḍawḍā'	عمل الضوضاء
noisy (adj)	muz'iʒ	مزعج
loudly (to speak, etc.)	bi ṣawt 'āli	بصوت عال
loud (voice, etc.)	'āli	عال
constant (e.g., ~ noise)	mustamirr	مستمرّ
cry, shout (n)	ṣarxa (f)	صرخة

to cry, to shout (vi)	ṣaraχ	صرخ
whisper	hamsa (f)	همسة
to whisper (vi, vt)	hamas	همس

| barking (dog's ~) | nubāḥ (m) | نباح |
| to bark (vi) | nabaḥ | نبح |

groan (of pain, etc.)	anīn (m)	أنين
to groan (vi)	anna	أنّ
cough	su'āl (m)	سعال
to cough (vi)	sa'al	سعل

whistle	taṣfīr (m)	تصفير
to whistle (vi)	ṣaffar	صفّر
knock (at the door)	ṭarq, daqq (m)	طرق، دقّ
to knock (on the door)	daqq	دقّ

| to crack (vi) | farqa' | فرقع |
| crack (cracking sound) | farqa'a (f) | فرقعة |

siren	ṣaffārat inðār (f)	صفّارة إنذار
whistle (factory ~, etc.)	ṣafīr (m)	صفير
to whistle (ab. train)	ṣaffar	صفّر
honk (car horn sound)	tazmīr (m)	تزمير
to honk (vi)	zammar	زمر

209. Winter

winter (n)	ʃitā' (m)	شتاء
winter (as adj)	ʃitawiy	شتوي
in winter	fiʃ ʃitā'	في الشتاء

snow	θalʒ (m)	ثلج
it's snowing	innaha taθluʒ	إنّها تثلج
snowfall	tasāquṭ aθ θulūʒ (m)	تساقط الثلوج
snowdrift	rukma θalʒiyya (f)	ركمة ثلجيّة

snowflake	nudfat θalʒ (f)	ندفة ثلج
snowball	kurat θalʒ (f)	كرة ثلج
snowman	raʒul θalʒ (m)	رجل ثلج
icicle	qiṭ'at ʒalīd (f)	قطعة جليد

December	disimbar (m)	ديسمبر
January	yanāyir (m)	يناير
February	fibrāyir (m)	فبراير

| frost (severe ~, freezing cold) | ṣaqī' (m) | صقيع |
| frosty (weather, air) | ṣāqi' | صاقع |

below zero (adv)	taḥt aṣ ṣifr	تحت الصفر
first frost	ṣaqī' (m)	صقيع
hoarfrost	ṣaqī' (m)	صقيع
cold (cold weather)	bard (m)	برد
it's cold	al ʒaww bārid	الجوّ بارد

fur coat	mi'taf farw (m)	معطف فرو
mittens	quffāz muɣlaq (m)	قفّاز مغلق
to fall ill	maraḍ	مرض
cold (illness)	bard (m)	برد
to catch a cold	aṣābahu al bard	أصابه البرد
ice	ʒalīd (m)	جليد
black ice	ʒalīd (m)	جليد
to freeze over (ab. river, etc.)	taʒammad	تجمّد
ice floe	ṭāfiya ʒalīdiyya (f)	طافية جليديّة
skis	zallāʒāt (pl)	زلّاجات
skier	mutazalliʒ bil iski (m)	متزلّج بالإسكي
to ski (vi)	tazallaʒ	تزلّج
to skate (vi)	tazaḥlaq 'alal ʒalīd	تزحلق على الجليد

Fauna

210. Mammals. Predators

predator	ḥayawān muftaris (m)	حيوان مفترس
tiger	namir (m)	نمر
lion	asad (m)	أسد
wolf	ði'b (m)	ذئب
fox	θaʿlab (m)	ثعلب
jaguar	namir amrīkiy (m)	نمر أمريكيّ
leopard	fahd (m)	فهد
cheetah	namir ṣayyād (m)	نمر صيّاد
black panther	namir aswad (m)	نمر أسود
puma	būma (m)	بوما
snow leopard	namir aθ θulūʒ (m)	نمر الثلوج
lynx	waʃaq (m)	وشق
coyote	qayūṭ (m)	قيوط
jackal	ibn 'āwa (m)	ابن آوى
hyena	ḍabuʿ (m)	ضبع

211. Wild animals

animal	ḥayawān (m)	حيوان
beast (animal)	ḥayawān (m)	حيوان
squirrel	sinʒāb (m)	سنجاب
hedgehog	qumfuð (m)	قنفذ
hare	arnab barriy (m)	أرنب برّيّ
rabbit	arnab (m)	أرنب
badger	ɣarīr (m)	غرير
raccoon	rākūn (m)	راكون
hamster	qidād (m)	قداد
marmot	marmuṭ (m)	مرموط
mole	χuld (m)	خلد
mouse	fa'r (m)	فأر
rat	ʒurað (m)	جرذ
bat	χuffāʃ (m)	خفّاش
ermine	qāqum (m)	قاقم
sable	sammūr (m)	سمّور
marten	dalaq (m)	دلق
weasel	ibn 'irs (m)	إبن عرس
mink	mink (m)	منك

beaver	qundus (m)	قندس
otter	quḍā'a (f)	قضاعة
horse	ḥiṣān (m)	حصان
moose	mūz (m)	موظ
deer	ayyil (m)	أيَل
camel	ʒamal (m)	جمل
bison	bisūn (m)	بيسون
wisent	θawr barriy (m)	ثور برّيّ
buffalo	ʒāmūs (m)	جاموس
zebra	ḥimār zarad (m)	حمار زرد
antelope	ẓabiy (m)	ظبي
roe deer	yaḥmūr (m)	يحمور
fallow deer	ayyil asmar urubbiy (m)	أيَل أسمر أوروبّيّ
chamois	ʃamwāh (f)	شامواه
wild boar	xinzīr barriy (m)	خنزير برّيّ
whale	ḥūt (m)	حوت
seal	fuqma (f)	فقمة
walrus	faẓẓ (m)	فظّ
fur seal	fuqmat al firā' (f)	فقمة الفراء
dolphin	dilfīn (m)	دلفين
bear	dubb (m)	دبّ
polar bear	dubb quṭbiy (m)	دبّ قطبيّ
panda	bānda (m)	باندا
monkey	qird (m)	قرد
chimpanzee	ʃimbanzi (m)	شيمبانزي
orangutan	urangutān (m)	أورنغوتان
gorilla	ɣurīlla (f)	غوريلا
macaque	qird al makāk (m)	قرد المكاك
gibbon	ʒibbūn (m)	جيبون
elephant	fīl (m)	فيل
rhinoceros	xartīt (m)	خرتيت
giraffe	zarāfa (f)	زرافة
hippopotamus	faras an nahr (m)	فرس النهر
kangaroo	kanɣar (m)	كنغر
koala (bear)	kuala (m)	كوالا
mongoose	nims (m)	نمس
chinchilla	ʃinʃīla (f)	شنشيلة
skunk	ẓaribān (m)	ظربان
porcupine	nīṣ (m)	نيص

212. Domestic animals

cat	qiṭṭa (f)	قطّة
tomcat	ðakar al qiṭṭ (m)	ذكر القطّ
dog	kalb (m)	كلب

horse	ḥiṣān (m)	حصان
stallion (male horse)	faḥl al χayl (m)	فحل الخيل
mare	unθa al faras (f)	أنثى الفرس
cow	baqara (f)	بقرة
bull	θawr (m)	ثور
ox	θawr (m)	ثور
sheep (ewe)	χarūf (f)	خروف
ram	kabʃ (m)	كبش
goat	māʿiz (m)	ماعز
billy goat, he-goat	ðakar al māʿið (m)	ذكر الماعز
donkey	ḥimār (m)	حمار
mule	baɣl (m)	بغل
pig	χinzīr (m)	خنزير
piglet	χannūṣ (m)	خنّوص
rabbit	arnab (m)	أرنب
hen (chicken)	daʒāʒa (f)	دجاجة
cock	dīk (m)	ديك
duck	baṭṭa (f)	بطّة
drake	ðakar al baṭṭ (m)	ذكر البطّ
goose	iwazza (f)	إوزّة
tom turkey, gobbler	dīk rūmiy (m)	ديك رومي
turkey (hen)	daʒāʒ rūmiy (m)	دجاج رومي
domestic animals	ḥayawānāt dawāʒin (pl)	حيوانات دواجن
tame (e.g. ~ hamster)	alīf	أليف
to tame (vt)	allaf	ألّف
to breed (vt)	rabba	ربّى
farm	mazraʿa (f)	مزرعة
poultry	ṭuyūr dāʒina (pl)	طيور داجنة
cattle	māʃiya (f)	ماشية
herd (cattle)	qaṭīʿ (m)	قطيع
stable	isṭabl χayl (m)	إسطبل خيل
pigsty	ḥaẓīrat al χanāzīr (f)	حظيرة الخنازير
cowshed	zirībat al baqar (f)	زريبة البقر
rabbit hutch	qunn al arānib (m)	قنّ الأرانب
hen house	qunn ad daʒāʒ (m)	قنّ الدجاج

213. Dogs. Dog breeds

dog	kalb (m)	كلب
sheepdog	kalb raʿy (m)	كلب رعي
German shepherd	kalb ar rāʿi al almāniy (m)	كلب الراعي الألماني
poodle	būdli (m)	بودل
dachshund	daʃhund (m)	دشهند
bulldog	bulduɣ (m)	بلدغ

boxer	buksir (m)	بوكسر
mastiff	mastīf (m)	ماستيف
Rottweiler	rut vāylir (m)	روت فايلر
Doberman	dubirmān (m)	دوبرمان

basset	bāsit (m)	باسيت
bobtail	bubteyl (m)	بوبتيل
Dalmatian	kalb dalmāsiy (m)	كلب دلماسي
cocker spaniel	kukkir spaniil (m)	كوكر سبانيل

| Newfoundland | nyu faundland (m) | نيوفاوندلاند |
| Saint Bernard | san birnār (m) | سنبرنار |

husky	haski (m)	هاسكي
Chow Chow	tʃaw tʃaw (m)	تشاوتشاو
spitz	ʃbītz (m)	شبيتز
pug	bāk (m)	باك

214. Sounds made by animals

barking (n)	nubāḥ (m)	نباح
to bark (vi)	nabaḥ	نبح
to miaow (vi)	mā'	ماء
to purr (vi)	xarxar	خرخر

to moo (vi)	xār	خار
to bellow (bull)	xār	خار
to growl (vi)	damdam	دمدم

howl (n)	'uwā' (m)	عواء
to howl (vi)	'awa	عوى
to whine (vi)	'awa	عوى

to bleat (sheep)	ma'ma'	مأمأ
to oink, to grunt (pig)	qaba'	قبع
to squeal (vi)	ṣāḥ	صاح

to croak (vi)	naqq	نقّ
to buzz (insect)	ṭann	طنّ
to chirp (crickets, grasshopper)	zaqzaq	زقزق

215. Young animals

cub	ʒarw (m)	جرو
kitten	qiṭṭa sayīra (f)	قطّة صغيرة
baby mouse	fa'r ṣayīr (m)	فأر صغير
puppy	ʒarw (m)	جرو

leveret	xirniq (m)	خرنق
baby rabbit	arnab sayīr (m)	أرنب صغير
wolf cub	daɣfal ṣayīr að ði'ab (m)	دغفل صغير الذئب

| fox cub | haʒras ṣaɣīr aθ θaʿlab (m) | هجرس صغير الثعلب |
| bear cub | daysam ṣaɣīr ad dubb (m) | ديسم صغير الدبّ |

lion cub	ʃibl al asad (m)	شبل الأسد
tiger cub	ʃibl an namir (m)	شبل النمر
elephant calf	saɣīr al fīl (m)	صغير الفيل

piglet	xannūṣ (m)	خنّوص
calf (young cow, bull)	ʿiʒl (m)	عجل
kid (young goat)	ʒaday (m)	جدي
lamb	ḥaml (m)	حمل
fawn (young deer)	raʃaʾ ṣaɣīr al ayyil (m)	رشأ صغير الأيّل
young camel	ṣaɣīr al ʒamal (m)	صغير الجمل

| snakelet (baby snake) | ṣaɣīr aθ θuʿbān (m) | صغير الثعبان |
| froglet (baby frog) | ḍifḍaʿ saɣīr (m) | ضفدع صغير |

baby bird	farx (m)	فرخ
chick (of chicken)	katkūt (m)	كتكوت
duckling	farax baṭṭ (m)	فرخ بطّ

216. Birds

bird	ṭāʾir (m)	طائر
pigeon	ḥamāma (f)	حمامة
sparrow	ʿuṣfūr (m)	عصفور
tit (great tit)	qurquf (m)	قرقف
magpie	ʿaqʿaq (m)	عقعق

raven	ɣurāb aswad (m)	غراب أسود
crow	ɣurāb (m)	غراب
jackdaw	zāɣ (m)	زاغ
rook	ɣurāb al qayẓ (m)	غراب القيظ

duck	baṭṭa (f)	بطّة
goose	iwazza (f)	إوزّة
pheasant	tadarruʒ (m)	تدرج

eagle	nasr (m)	نسر
hawk	bāz (m)	باز
falcon	ṣaqr (m)	صقر
vulture	raxam (m)	رخم
condor (Andean ~)	kundūr (m)	كندور

swan	timma (m)	تمّ
crane	kurkiy (m)	كركي
stork	laqlaq (m)	لقلق

parrot	babaɣāʾ (m)	ببغاء
hummingbird	ṭannān (m)	طنّان
peacock	ṭāwūs (m)	طاووس

| ostrich | naʿāma (f) | نعامة |
| heron | balaʃūn (m) | بلشون |

| flamingo | nuḥām wardiy (m) | نحام وردي |
| pelican | baʒaʻa (f) | بجعة |

| nightingale | bulbul (m) | بلبل |
| swallow | sunūnū (m) | سنونو |

thrush	sumna (m)	سمنة
song thrush	summuna muɣarrida (m)	سمنة مغرّدة
blackbird	ʃaḥrūr aswad (m)	شحرور أسود

swift	samāma (m)	سمامة
lark	qubbara (f)	قبّرة
quail	sammān (m)	سمّان

woodpecker	naqqār al xaʃab (m)	نقّار الخشب
cuckoo	waqwāq (m)	وقواق
owl	būma (f)	بومة
eagle owl	būm urāsiy (m)	بوم أوراسي
wood grouse	dīk il xalanʒ (m)	ديك الخلنج
black grouse	ṭayhūʒ aswad (m)	طيهوج أسود
partridge	ḥaʒal (m)	حجل

starling	zurzūr (m)	زرزور
canary	kanāriy (m)	كناري
hazel grouse	ṭayhūʒ il bunduq (m)	طيهوج البندق
chaffinch	ʃurʃūr (m)	شرشور
bullfinch	diɣnāʃ (m)	دغناش

seagull	nawras (m)	نورس
albatross	al qaṭras (m)	القطرس
penguin	biṭrīq (m)	بطريق

217. Birds. Singing and sounds

to sing (vi)	ɣanna	غنّى
to call (animal, bird)	nāda	نادى
to crow (cock)	ṣāḥ	صاح
cock-a-doodle-doo	kukukuku	كوكوكوكو

to cluck (hen)	qaraq	قرق
to caw (crow call)	naʻaq	نعق
to quack (duck call)	baṭbaṭ	بطبط
to cheep (vi)	ṣaʻṣaʼ	صأصأ
to chirp, to twitter	zaqzaq	زقزق

218. Fish. Marine animals

bream	abramīs (m)	أبراميس
carp	ʃabbūṭ (m)	شبّوط
perch	farx (m)	فرخ
catfish	qarmūṭ (m)	قرموط
pike	samak al karāki (m)	سمك الكراكي

| salmon | salmūn (m) | سلمون |
| sturgeon | ḥaffʃ (m) | حفش |

herring	rinʒa (f)	رنجة
Atlantic salmon	salmūn aṭlasiy (m)	سلمون أطلسيّ
mackerel	usqumriy (m)	أسقمريّ
flatfish	samak mufalṭaḥ (f)	سمك مفلطح

zander, pike perch	samak sandar (m)	سمك سندر
cod	qudd (m)	قدّ
tuna	tūna (f)	تونة
trout	salmūn muraqqaṭ (m)	سلمون مرقّط

eel	ḥankalīs (m)	حنكليس
electric ray	ra"ād (m)	رعّاد
moray eel	murāy (m)	موراي
piranha	birāna (f)	بيرانا

shark	qirʃ (m)	قرش
dolphin	dilfīn (m)	دلفين
whale	ḥūt (m)	حوت

crab	salṭaʕūn (m)	سلطعون
jellyfish	qindīl al baḥr (m)	قنديل البحر
octopus	uxṭubūṭ (m)	أخطبوط

starfish	naʒmat al baḥr (f)	نجمة البحر
sea urchin	qumfuð al baḥr (m)	قنفذ البحر
seahorse	ḥiṣān al baḥr (m)	فرس البحر

oyster	maḥār (m)	محار
prawn	ʒambari (m)	جمبريّ
lobster	istakūza (f)	إستكوزا
spiny lobster	karkand ʃāik (m)	كركند شائك

219. Amphibians. Reptiles

| snake | θuʕbān (m) | ثعبان |
| venomous (snake) | sāmm | سامّ |

viper	afʕa (f)	أفعى
cobra	kūbra (m)	كوبرا
python	biθūn (m)	بيثون
boa	buwāʾ (f)	بواء

grass snake	θuʕbān al ʕuʃb (m)	ثعبان العشب
rattle snake	afʕa al ʒalʒala (f)	أفعى الجلجلة
anaconda	anakūnda (f)	أناكوندا

lizard	siḥliyya (f)	سحليّة
iguana	iɣwāna (f)	إغوانة
monitor lizard	waral (m)	ورل
salamander	samandar (m)	سمندر
chameleon	ḥirbāʾ (f)	حرباء

scorpion	ʿaqrab (m)	عقرب
turtle	sulaḥfāt (f)	سلحفاة
frog	ḍifḍaʿ (m)	ضفدع
toad	ḍifḍaʿ aṭ ṭīn (m)	ضفدع الطين
crocodile	timsāḥ (m)	تمساح

220. Insects

insect	ḥaʃara (f)	حشرة
butterfly	farāʃa (f)	فراشة
ant	namla (f)	نملة
fly	ðubāba (f)	ذبابة
mosquito	namūsa (f)	ناموسة
beetle	xunfusa (f)	خنفسة

wasp	dabbūr (m)	دبّور
bee	naḥla (f)	نحلة
bumblebee	naḥla ṭannāna (f)	نحلة طنّانة
gadfly (botfly)	naʿra (f)	نعرة

spider	ʿankabūt (m)	عنكبوت
spider's web	nasīʒ ʿankabūt (m)	نسيج عنكبوت

dragonfly	yaʿsūb (m)	يعسوب
grasshopper	ʒarād (m)	جراد
moth (night butterfly)	ʿitta (f)	عتّة

cockroach	ṣurṣūr (m)	صرصور
tick	qurāda (f)	قرادة
flea	burɣūθ (m)	برغوث
midge	baʿūḍa (f)	بعوضة

locust	ʒarād (m)	جراد
snail	ḥalzūn (m)	حلزون
cricket	ṣarrār al layl (m)	صرّار الليل
firefly	yarāʿa muḍīʾa (f)	يراعة مضيئة
ladybird	daʿsūqa (f)	دعسوقة
cockchafer	xunfusa kabīra (f)	خنفسة كبيرة

leech	ʿalaqa (f)	علقة
caterpillar	yasrūʿ (m)	يسروع
earthworm	dūda (f)	دودة
larva	yaraqa (f)	يرقة

221. Animals. Body parts

beak	minqār (m)	منقار
wings	aʒniḥa (pl)	أجنحة
foot (of the bird)	riʒl (f)	رجل
feathers (plumage)	rīʃ (m)	ريش
feather	rīʃa (f)	ريشة
crest	tāʒ (m)	تاج

gills	χayāʃim (pl)	خياشيم
spawn	bayḍ as samak (pl)	بيض السمك
larva	yaraqa (f)	يرقة
fin	ziʿnifa (f)	زعنفة
scales (of fish, reptile)	ḥarāfiʃ (pl)	حرافش
fang (canine)	nāb (m)	ناب
paw (e.g. cat's ~)	qadam (f)	قدم
muzzle (snout)	χaṭm (m)	خطم
mouth (cat's ~)	fam (m)	فم
tail	ðayl (m)	ذيل
whiskers	ʃawārib (pl)	شوارب
hoof	ḥāfir (m)	حافر
horn	qarn (m)	قرن
carapace	dirʿ (m)	درع
shell (mollusk ~)	maḥāra (f)	محارة
eggshell	qiʃrat bayḍa (f)	قشرة بيضة
animal's hair (pelage)	ʃaʿr (m)	شعر
pelt (hide)	ʒild (m)	جلد

222. Actions of animals

to fly (vi)	ṭār	طار
to fly in circles	ḥallaq	حلّق
to fly away	ṭār	طار
to flap (~ the wings)	rafraf	رفرف
to peck (vi)	naqar	نقر
to sit on eggs	qaʿad ʿalal bayḍ	قعد على البيض
to hatch out (vi)	faqas	فقس
to build a nest	bana ʿiʃʃa	بنى عشّة
to slither, to crawl	zaḥaf	زحف
to sting, to bite (insect)	lasaʿ	لسع
to bite (ab. animal)	ʿaḍḍ	عضّ
to sniff (vt)	taʃammam	تشمّم
to bark (vi)	nabaḥ	نبح
to hiss (snake)	hashas	هسهس
to scare (vt)	χawwaf	خوّف
to attack (vt)	haʒam	هجم
to gnaw (bone, etc.)	qaraḍ	قرض
to scratch (with claws)	χadaʃ	خدش
to hide (vi)	istaχbaʾ	إختبأ
to play (kittens, etc.)	laʿib	لعب
to hunt (vi, vt)	iṣṭād	إصطاد
to hibernate (vi)	kān di subāt aʃ ʃitāʾ	كان في سبات الشتاء
to go extinct	inqaraḍ	إنقرض

223. Animals. Habitats

habitat	mawṭin (m)	موطن
migration	hiʒra (f)	هجرة
mountain	ʒabal (m)	جبل
reef	ʃiʿāb (pl)	شعاب
cliff	ʒurf (m)	جرف
forest	ɣāba (f)	غابة
jungle	adɣāl (pl)	أدغال
savanna	savānna (f)	سافانا
tundra	tundra (f)	تندرا
steppe	sahb (m)	سهب
desert	ṣaḥrāʾ (f)	صحراء
oasis	wāḥa (f)	واحة
sea	baḥr (m)	بحر
lake	buḥayra (f)	بحيرة
ocean	muḥīṭ (m)	محيط
swamp (marshland)	mustanqaʿ (m)	مستنقع
freshwater (adj)	al miyāh al ʿaðba	المياه العذبة
pond	birka (f)	بركة
river	nahr (m)	نهر
den (bear's ~)	wakr (m)	وكر
nest	ʿuʃʃ (m)	عش
tree hollow	ʒawf (m)	جوف
burrow (animal hole)	ʒuḥr (m)	جحر
anthill	ʿuʃʃ naml (m)	عش نمل

224. Animal care

zoo	ḥadīqat al ḥayawān (f)	حديقة حيوان
nature reserve	maḥmiyya ṭabiʿiyya (f)	محمية طبيعية
breeder (cattery, kennel, etc.)	murabba (m)	مربى
open-air cage	qafṣ fil hawāʾ aṭ ṭalq (m)	قفص في الهواء الطلق
cage	qafṣ (m)	قفص
kennel	bayt al kalb (m)	بيت الكلب
dovecot	burʒ al ḥamām (m)	برج الحمام
aquarium (fish tank)	ḥawḍ samak (m)	حوض سمك
dolphinarium	ḥawḍ dilfīn (m)	حوض دلفين
to breed (animals)	rabba	ربّى
brood, litter	ðurriyya (f)	ذرّية
to tame (vt)	allaf	ألّف
to train (animals)	darrab	درّب
feed (fodder, etc.)	ʿalaf (m)	علف
to feed (vt)	aṭʿam	أطعم

pet shop	maḥall ḥayawānāt (m)	محلّ حيوانات
muzzle (for dog)	kimāma (f)	كمامة
collar (e.g., dog ~)	ṭawq (m)	طوق
name (of an animal)	ism (m)	إسم
pedigree (dog's ~)	silsilat an nasab (f)	سلسلة النسب

225. Animals. Miscellaneous

pack (wolves)	qaṭīʿ (m)	قطيع
flock (birds)	sirb (m)	سرب
shoal, school (fish)	sirb (m)	سرب
herd (horses)	qaṭīʿ (m)	قطيع
male (n)	ðakar (m)	ذكر
female (n)	unθa (f)	أنثى
hungry (adj)	ʒawʿān	جوعان
wild (adj)	barriy	بريّ
dangerous (adj)	χaṭir	خطير

226. Horses

horse	ḥiṣān (m)	حصان
breed (race)	sulāla (f)	سلالة
foal	muhr (m)	مهر
mare	unθa al faras (f)	أنثى الفرس
mustang	mustān (m)	موستان
pony	ḥiṣān qazam (m)	حصان قزم
draught horse	ḥiṣān an naql (m)	حصان النقل
mane	ʿurf (m)	عرف
tail	ðayl (m)	ذيل
hoof	ḥāfir (m)	حافر
horseshoe	naʿl (m)	نعل
to shoe (vt)	naʿʿal	نعّل
blacksmith	ḥaddād (m)	حدّاد
saddle	sarʒ (m)	سرج
stirrup	rikāb (m)	ركاب
bridle	liʒām (m)	لجام
reins	ʿinān (m)	عنان
whip (for riding)	kurbāʒ (m)	كرباج
rider	fāris (m)	فارس
to saddle up (vt)	asraʒ	أسرج
to mount a horse	rakib ḥiṣān	جلس على سرج
gallop	rimāḥa (f)	رماحة
to gallop (vi)	ʿada bil ḥiṣān	عدا بالحصان

trot (n)	ҳabab (m)	خبب
at a trot (adv)	ҳābban	خابًا
to go at a trot	inṭalaq rākiḍan	إنطلق راكضا
racehorse	ḥiṣān sibāq (m)	حصان سباق
horse racing	sibāq al ҳayl (m)	سباق الخيل
stable	isṭabl ҳayl (m)	إسطبل خيل
to feed (vt)	aṭʻam	أطعم
hay	qaʃʃ (m)	قش
to water (animals)	saqa	سقى
to wash (horse)	naẓẓaf	نظف
horse-drawn cart	ʻarabat ҳayl (f)	عربة خيل
to graze (vi)	irtaʻa	إرتعى
to neigh (vi)	ṣahal	صهل
to kick (to buck)	rafas	رفس

Flora

227. Trees

tree	ʃaʒara (f)	شجرة
deciduous (adj)	nafḍiyya	نفضيّة
coniferous (adj)	ṣanawbariyya	صنوبريّة
evergreen (adj)	dā'imat al χuḍra	دائمة الخضرة
apple tree	ʃaʒarat tuffāḥ (f)	شجرة تفّاح
pear tree	ʃaʒarat kummaθra (f)	شجرة كمّثرى
cherry tree	ʃaʒarat karaz (f)	شجرة كرز
plum tree	ʃaʒarat barqūq (f)	شجرة برقوق
birch	batūla (f)	بتولا
oak	ballūṭ (f)	بلّوط
linden tree	ʃaʒarat zayzafūn (f)	شجرة زيزفون
aspen	ḥawr raʒrāʒ (m)	حور رجراج
maple	qayqab (f)	قيقب
spruce	ratinaʒ (f)	راتينج
pine	ṣanawbar (f)	صنوبر
larch	arziyya (f)	أرزيّة
fir tree	tannūb (f)	تنّوب
cedar	arz (f)	أرز
poplar	ḥawr (f)	حور
rowan	ɣubayrā' (f)	غبيراء
willow	ṣafsāf (f)	صفصاف
alder	ʒār il mā' (m)	جار الماء
beech	zān (m)	زان
elm	dardār (f)	دردار
ash (tree)	marān (f)	مران
chestnut	kastanā' (f)	كستناء
magnolia	maɣnūliya (f)	مغنوليا
palm tree	naχla (f)	نخلة
cypress	sarw (f)	سرو
mangrove	ayka sāḥiliyya (f)	أيكة ساحليّة
baobab	bāubāb (f)	باوباب
eucalyptus	ukaliptus (f)	أوكاليبتوس
sequoia	siqūya (f)	سيكويا

228. Shrubs

bush	ʃuʒayra (f)	شجيرة
shrub	ʃuʒayrāt (pl)	شجيرات

grapevine	karma (f)	كرمة
vineyard	karam (m)	كرم

raspberry bush	tūt al 'ullayq al ahmar (m)	توت العليق الأحمر
redcurrant bush	kiʃmiʃ ahmar (m)	كشمش أحمر
gooseberry bush	'inab aθ θa'lab (m)	عنب الثعلب

acacia	sanṭ (f)	سنط
barberry	amīr barīs (m)	أمير باريس
jasmine	yāsmīn (m)	ياسمين

juniper	'ar'ar (m)	عرعر
rosebush	ʃuʒayrat ward (f)	شجيرة ورد
dog rose	ward ʒabaliy (m)	ورد جبليّ

229. Mushrooms

mushroom	fuṭr (f)	فطر
edible mushroom	fuṭr sālih lil akl (m)	فطر صالح للأكل
poisonous mushroom	fuṭr sāmm (m)	فطر سامّ
cap	ṭarbūʃ al fuṭr (m)	طربوش الفطر
stipe	sāq al fuṭr (m)	ساق الفطر

cep, penny bun	fuṭr bulīṭ ma'kūl (m)	فطر بوليط مأكول
orange-cap boletus	fuṭr ahmar (m)	فطر أحمر
birch bolete	fuṭr bulīṭ (m)	فطر بوليط
chanterelle	fuṭr kwīzi (m)	فطر كويزي
russula	fuṭr russūla (m)	فطر روسّولا

morel	fuṭr al ɣūʃna (m)	فطر الغوشنة
fly agaric	fuṭr amānīt aṭ ṭā'ir as sāmm (m)	فطر أمانيت الطائر السامّ
death cap	fuṭr amānīt falusyāniy as sāmm (m)	فطر أمانيت فالوسياني السامّ

230. Fruits. Berries

fruit	θamra (f)	ثمرة
fruits	θamr (m)	ثمر
apple	tuffāha (f)	تفّاحة
pear	kummaθra (f)	كمّثرى
plum	barqūq (m)	برقوق

strawberry (garden ~)	farawla (f)	فراولة
cherry	karaz (m)	كرز
grape	'inab (m)	عنب

raspberry	tūt al 'ullayq al ahmar (m)	توت العليق الأحمر
blackcurrant	'inab aθ θa'lab al aswad (m)	عنب الثعلب الأسود
redcurrant	kiʃmiʃ ahmar (m)	كشمش أحمر
gooseberry	'inab aθ θa'lab (m)	عنب الثعلب
cranberry	tūt ahmar barriy (m)	توت أحمر برّيّ

orange	burtuqāl (m)	برتقال
tangerine	yūsufiy (m)	يوسفي
pineapple	ananās (m)	أناناس
banana	mawz (m)	موز
date	tamr (m)	تمر

lemon	laymūn (m)	ليمون
apricot	miʃmiʃ (f)	مشمش
peach	durrāq (m)	دراق
kiwi	kiwi (m)	كيوي
grapefruit	zinbāʿ (m)	زنباع

berry	ḥabba (f)	حبّة
berries	ḥabbāt (pl)	حبّات
cowberry	ʿinab aθ θawr (m)	عنب الثور
wild strawberry	farāwla barriyya (f)	فراولة برّية
bilberry	ʿinab al aḥrāʒ (m)	عنب الأحراج

231. Flowers. Plants

| flower | zahra (f) | زهرة |
| bouquet (of flowers) | bāqat zuhūr (f) | باقة زهور |

rose (flower)	warda (f)	وردة
tulip	tulīb (f)	توليب
carnation	qurumful (m)	قرنفل
gladiolus	dalbūθ (f)	دلبوث

cornflower	turunʃāh (m)	ترنشاه
harebell	ʒarīs (m)	جريس
dandelion	hindibāʾ (f)	هندباء
camomile	babunʒ (m)	بابونج

aloe	aluwwa (m)	ألوّة
cactus	ṣabbār (m)	صبّار
rubber plant, ficus	tīn (m)	تين

lily	sawsan (m)	سوسن
geranium	ibrat ar rāʾi (f)	إبرة الراعي
hyacinth	zanbaq (f)	زنبق

mimosa	mimūza (f)	ميموزا
narcissus	narʒis (f)	نرجس
nasturtium	abu χanʒar (f)	أبو خنجر

orchid	saḥlab (f)	سحلب
peony	fawniya (f)	فاوانيا
violet	banafsaʒ (f)	بنفسج

pansy	banafsaʒ muθallaθ (m)	بنفسج مثلث
forget-me-not	ʾāðān al faʾr (pl)	آذان الفأر
daisy	uqhuwān (f)	أقحوان
poppy	χaʃχāʃ (f)	خشخاش
hemp	qinnab (m)	قنب

mint	na'nā' (m)	نعناع
lily of the valley	sawsan al wādi (m)	سوسن الوادي
snowdrop	zahrat al laban (f)	زهرة اللبن
nettle	qarrāṣ (m)	قرّاص
sorrel	ḥammāḍ (m)	حمّاض
water lily	nilūfar (m)	نيلوفر
fern	saraxs (m)	سرخس
lichen	uʃna (f)	أشنة
conservatory (greenhouse)	daffʼa (f)	دفيئة
lawn	'uʃb (m)	عشب
flowerbed	ȝunaynat zuhūr (f)	جنينة زهور
plant	nabāt (m)	نبات
grass	'uʃb (m)	عشب
blade of grass	'uʃba (f)	عشبة
leaf	waraqa (f)	ورقة
petal	waraqat az zahra (f)	ورقة الزهرة
stem	sāq (f)	ساق
tuber	darnat nabāt (f)	درنة نبات
young plant (shoot)	nabta saȝīra (f)	نبتة صغيرة
thorn	ʃawka (f)	شوكة
to blossom (vi)	nawwar	نوّر
to fade, to wither	ðabal	ذبل
smell (odour)	rāʼiḥa (f)	رائحة
to cut (flowers)	qaṭa'	قطع
to pick (a flower)	qaṭaf	قطف

232. Cereals, grains

grain	ḥubūb (pl)	حبوب
cereal crops	maḥāṣīl al ḥubūb (pl)	محاصيل الحبوب
ear (of barley, etc.)	sumbula (f)	سنبلة
wheat	qamḥ (m)	قمح
rye	ȝāwdār (m)	جاودار
oats	ʃūfān (m)	شوفان
millet	duxn (m)	دخن
barley	ʃaʼīr (m)	شعير
maize	ðura (f)	ذرّة
rice	urz (m)	أرز
buckwheat	ḥinṭa sawdā' (f)	حنطة سوداء
pea plant	bisilla (f)	بسلة
kidney bean	faṣūliya (f)	فاصوليا
soya	fūl aṣ ṣūya (m)	فول الصويا
lentil	'adas (m)	عدس
beans (pulse crops)	fūl (m)	فول

233. Vegetables. Greens

vegetables	xuḍār (pl)	خضار
greens	xuḍrawāt waraqiyya (pl)	خضروات ورقيّة
tomato	ṭamāṭim (f)	طماطم
cucumber	xiyār (m)	خيار
carrot	ʒazar (m)	جزر
potato	baṭāṭis (f)	بطاطس
onion	baṣal (m)	بصل
garlic	θūm (m)	ثوم
cabbage	kurumb (m)	كرنب
cauliflower	qarnabīṭ (m)	قرنبيط
Brussels sprouts	kurumb brūksil (m)	كرنب بروكسل
broccoli	brūkuli (m)	بروكلي
beetroot	banʒar (m)	بنجر
aubergine	bātinʒān (m)	باذنجان
marrow	kūsa (f)	كوسة
pumpkin	qarʿ (m)	قرع
turnip	lift (m)	لفت
parsley	baqdūnis (m)	بقدونس
dill	ʃabat (m)	شبت
lettuce	xass (m)	خسّ
celery	karafs (m)	كرفس
asparagus	halyūn (m)	هليون
spinach	sabānix (m)	سبانخ
pea	bisilla (f)	بسلّة
beans	fūl (m)	فول
maize	ðura (f)	ذرّة
kidney bean	faṣūliya (f)	فاصوليا
pepper	filfil (m)	فلفل
radish	fiʒl (m)	فجل
artichoke	xurʃūf (m)	خرشوف

REGIONAL GEOGRAPHY

234. Western Europe

Europe	urūbba (f)	أوروبا
European Union	al ittiḥād al urubbiy (m)	الإتّحاد الأوروبيّ
European (n)	urūbbiy (m)	أوروبيّ
European (adj)	urūbbiy	أوروبيّ
Austria	an nimsa (f)	النمسا
Austrian (masc.)	nimsāwy (m)	نمساويّ
Austrian (fem.)	nimsāwiyya (f)	نمساويّة
Austrian (adj)	nimsāwiy	نمساويّ
Great Britain	briṭāniya al 'uẓma (f)	بريطانيا العظمى
England	inʒiltirra (f)	إنجلترَا
British (masc.)	briṭāniy (m)	بريطانيّ
British (fem.)	briṭāniyya (f)	بريطانيّة
English, British (adj)	inʒlīziy	إنجليزيّ
Belgium	balʒīka (f)	بلجيكا
Belgian (masc.)	balʒīkiy (m)	بلجيكيّ
Belgian (fem.)	balʒīkiyya (f)	بلجيكيّة
Belgian (adj)	balʒīkiy	بلجيكيّ
Germany	almāniya (f)	ألمانيا
German (masc.)	almāniy (m)	ألمانيّ
German (fem.)	almāniyya (f)	ألمانيّة
German (adj)	almāniy	ألمانيّ
Netherlands	hulanda (f)	هولندا
Holland	hulanda (f)	هولندا
Dutch (masc.)	hulandiy (m)	هولنديّ
Dutch (fem.)	hulandiyya (f)	هولنديّة
Dutch (adj)	hulandiy	هولنديّ
Greece	al yūnān (f)	اليونان
Greek (masc.)	yunāniy (m)	يونانيّ
Greek (fem.)	yunāniyya (f)	يونانيّة
Greek (adj)	yunāniy	يونانيّ
Denmark	ad danimārk (f)	الدانمارك
Dane (masc.)	danimārkiy (m)	دانماركيّ
Dane (fem.)	dānimarkiyya (f)	دانماركيّة
Danish (adj)	danimārkiy	دانماركيّ
Ireland	irlanda (f)	أيرلندا
Irish (masc.)	irlandiy (m)	أيرلنديّ
Irish (fem.)	irlandiyya (f)	أيرلنديّة
Irish (adj)	irlandiy	أيرلنديّ

Iceland	'āyslanda (f)	آيسلندا
Icelander (masc.)	'āyslandiy (m)	آيسلنديّ
Icelander (fem.)	'āyslandiyya (f)	آيسلنديّة
Icelandic (adj)	'āyslandiy	آيسلنديّ

Spain	isbāniya (f)	إسبانيا
Spaniard (masc.)	isbāniy (m)	إسبانيّ
Spaniard (fem.)	isbāniyya (f)	إسبانيّة
Spanish (adj)	isbāniy	إسبانيّ

Italy	iṭāliya (f)	إيطاليا
Italian (masc.)	iṭāliy (m)	إيطاليّ
Italian (fem.)	iṭāliyya (f)	إيطاليّة
Italian (adj)	iṭāliy	إيطاليّ

Cyprus	qubruṣ (f)	قبرص
Cypriot (masc.)	qubruṣiy (m)	قبرصيّ
Cypriot (fem.)	qubruṣiyya (f)	قبرصيّة
Cypriot (adj)	qubruṣiy	قبرصيّ

Malta	malṭa (f)	مالطا
Maltese (masc.)	māltiy (m)	مالطيّ
Maltese (fem.)	malṭiyya (f)	مالطيّة
Maltese (adj)	māltiy	مالطيّ

Norway	an nirwīʒ (f)	النرويج
Norwegian (masc.)	nurwīʒiy (m)	نرويجي
Norwegian (fem.)	nurwīʒiyya (f)	نرويجيّة
Norwegian (adj)	nurwīʒiy	نرويجيّ

Portugal	al burtuɣāl (f)	البرتغال
Portuguese (masc.)	burtuɣāliy (m)	برتغاليّ
Portuguese (fem.)	burtuɣāliyya (f)	برتغاليّة
Portuguese (adj)	burtuɣāliy	برتغاليّ

Finland	finlanda (f)	فنلندا
Finn (masc.)	finlandiy (m)	فنلنديّ
Finn (fem.)	finlandiyya (f)	فنلنديّة
Finnish (adj)	finlandiy	فنلنديّ

France	faransa (f)	فرنسا
French (masc.)	faransiy (m)	فرنسيّ
French (fem.)	faransiyya (f)	فرنسيّة
French (adj)	faransiy	فرنسيّ

Sweden	as suwayd (f)	السويد
Swede (masc.)	suwaydiy (m)	سويديّ
Swede (fem.)	suwaydiyya (f)	سويديّة
Swedish (adj)	suwaydiy	سويديّ

Switzerland	swīsra (f)	سويسرا
Swiss (masc.)	swisriy (m)	سويسريّ
Swiss (fem.)	swisriyya (f)	سويسريّة
Swiss (adj)	swisriy	سويسريّ
Scotland	iskutlanda (f)	اسكتلندا
Scottish (masc.)	iskutlandiy (m)	اسكتلنديّ

| Scottish (fem.) | iskutlandiyya (f) | اسكتلندية |
| Scottish (adj) | iskutlandiy | اسكتلندي |

Vatican City	al vatikān (m)	الفاتيكان
Liechtenstein	liſtinſtāyn (m)	ليشتنشتاين
Luxembourg	luksimburɣ (f)	لوكسمبورغ
Monaco	munāku (f)	موناكو

235. Central and Eastern Europe

Albania	albāniya (f)	ألبانيا
Albanian (masc.)	albāniy (m)	ألباني
Albanian (fem.)	albāniyya (f)	ألبانية
Albanian (adj)	albāniy	ألباني

Bulgaria	bulɣāriya (f)	بلغاريا
Bulgarian (masc.)	bulɣāriy (m)	بلغاري
Bulgarian (fem.)	bulɣāriyya (f)	بلغارية
Bulgarian (adj)	bulɣāriy	بلغاري

Hungary	al maʒar (f)	المجر
Hungarian (masc.)	maʒariy (m)	مجري
Hungarian (fem.)	maʒariyya (f)	مجرية
Hungarian (adj)	maʒariy	مجري

Latvia	lātviya (f)	لاتفيا
Latvian (masc.)	lātviy (m)	لاتفي
Latvian (fem.)	lātviyya (f)	لاتفية
Latvian (adj)	lātviy	لاتفي

Lithuania	litwāniya (f)	ليتوانيا
Lithuanian (masc.)	litwāniy (m)	ليتواني
Lithuanian (fem.)	litwāniyya (f)	ليتوانية
Lithuanian (adj)	litwāny	ليتواني

Poland	bulanda (f)	بولندا
Pole (masc.)	bulandiy (m)	بولندي
Pole (fem.)	bulandiyya (f)	بولندية
Polish (adj)	bulandiy	بولندي

Romania	rumāniya (f)	رومانيا
Romanian (masc.)	rumāniy (m)	روماني
Romanian (fem.)	rumāniyya (f)	رومانية
Romanian (adj)	rumāniy	روماني

Serbia	ṣirbiya (f)	صربيا
Serbian (masc.)	ṣirbiy (m)	صربي
Serbian (fem.)	ṣirbiyya (f)	صربية
Serbian (adj)	ṣirbiy	صربي

Slovakia	sluvākiya (f)	سلوفاكيا
Slovak (masc.)	sluvākiy (m)	سلوفاكي
Slovak (fem.)	sluvākiyya (f)	سلوفاكية
Slovak (adj)	sluvākiy	سلوفاكي

Croatia	kruātiya (f)	كرواتيا
Croatian (masc.)	kruātiy (m)	كرواتيّ
Croatian (fem.)	kruātiyya (f)	كرواتيّة
Croatian (adj)	kruātiy	كرواتيّ

Czech Republic	atʃ tʃīk (f)	التشيك
Czech (masc.)	tʃīkiy (m)	تشيكيّ
Czech (fem.)	tʃīkiyya (f)	تشيكيّة
Czech (adj)	tʃīkiy	تشيكيّ

Estonia	istūniya (f)	إستونيا
Estonian (masc.)	istūniy (m)	إستونيّ
Estonian (fem.)	istūniyya (f)	إستونيّة
Estonian (adj)	istūniy	إستونيّ

Bosnia and Herzegovina	al busna wal hirsuk (f)	البوسنة والهرسك
North Macedonia	maqdūniya (f)	مقدونيا
Slovenia	sluvīniya (f)	سلوفينيا
Montenegro	al ӡabal al aswad (m)	الجبل الأسود

236. Former USSR countries

Azerbaijan	aðarbiӡān (m)	أذربيجان
Azerbaijani (masc.)	aðarbiӡāniy (m)	أذربيجانيّ
Azerbaijani (fem.)	aðarbiӡāniyya (f)	أذربيجانيّة
Azerbaijani, Azeri (adj)	aðarbiӡāniy	أذربيجانيّ

Armenia	armīniya (f)	أرمينيا
Armenian (masc.)	armaniy (m)	أرمنيّ
Armenian (fem.)	armaniyya (f)	أرمنيّة
Armenian (adj)	armaniy	أرمنيّ

Belarus	bilarūs (f)	بيلاروس
Belarusian (masc.)	bilarūsiy (m)	بيلاروسيّ
Belarusian (fem.)	bilārūsiyya (f)	بيلاروسيّة
Belarusian (adj)	bilarūsiy	بيلاروسيّ

Georgia	ӡūrӡiya (f)	جورجيا
Georgian (masc.)	ӡurӡiy (m)	جورجيّ
Georgian (fem.)	ӡurӡiyya (f)	جورجيّة
Georgian (adj)	ӡurӡiy	جورجيّ

Kazakhstan	kazaxstān (f)	كازاخستان
Kazakh (masc.)	kazaxstāniy (m)	كازاخستانيّ
Kazakh (fem.)	kazaxstāniyya (f)	كازاخستانيّة
Kazakh (adj)	kazaxstāniy	كازاخستانيّ

Kirghizia	qirɣizistān (f)	قيرغيزستان
Kirghiz (masc.)	qirɣizistāny (m)	قيرغيزستانيّ
Kirghiz (fem.)	qirɣizistāniyya (f)	قيرغيزستانيّة
Kirghiz (adj)	qirɣizistāniy	قيرغيزستانيّ

Moldova, Moldavia	muldāviya (f)	مولدافيا
Moldavian (masc.)	muldāviy (m)	مولدافيّ

| Moldavian (fem.) | muldāviyya (f) | مولدافيّة |
| Moldavian (adj) | muldāviy | مولدافيّ |

Russia	rūsiya (f)	روسيا
Russian (masc.)	rūsiy (m)	روسيّ
Russian (fem.)	rūsiyya (f)	روسيّة
Russian (adj)	rūsiy	روسيّ

Tajikistan	ṭaӡīkistān (f)	طاجيكستان
Tajik (masc.)	ṭaӡīkiy (m)	طاجيكيّ
Tajik (fem.)	ṭaӡīkiyya (f)	طاجيكيّة
Tajik (adj)	ṭaӡīkiy	طاجيكيّ

Turkmenistan	turkmānistān (f)	تركمانستان
Turkmen (masc.)	turkmāniy (m)	تركمانيّ
Turkmen (fem.)	turkmāniyya (f)	تركمانيّة
Turkmenian (adj)	turkmāniy	تركمانيّ

Uzbekistan	uzbikistān (f)	أوزبكستان
Uzbek (masc.)	uzbikiy (m)	أوزبكيّ
Uzbek (fem.)	uzbikiyya (f)	أوزبكيّة
Uzbek (adj)	uzbikiy	أوزبكيّ

Ukraine	ukrāniya (f)	أوكرانيا
Ukrainian (masc.)	ukrāniy (m)	أوكرانيّ
Ukrainian (fem.)	ukrāniyya (f)	أوكرانيّة
Ukrainian (adj)	ukrāniy	أوكرانيّ

237. Asia

| Asia | 'āsiya (f) | آسيا |
| Asian (adj) | 'āsyawiy | آسيويّ |

Vietnam	vitnām (f)	فيتنام
Vietnamese (masc.)	vitnāmiy (m)	فيتناميّ
Vietnamese (fem.)	vitnāmiyya (f)	فيتناميّة
Vietnamese (adj)	vitnāmiy	فيتناميّ

India	al hind (f)	الهند
Indian (masc.)	hindiy (m)	هنديّ
Indian (fem.)	hindiyya (f)	هنديّة
Indian (adj)	hindiy	هنديّ

Israel	isrā'īl (f)	إسرائيل
Israeli (masc.)	isra'īliy (m)	إسرائيليّ
Israeli (fem.)	isrā'īliyya (f)	إسرائيليّة
Israeli (adj)	isrā'īliy	إسرائيليّ

Jew (n)	yahūdiy (m)	يهوديّ
Jewess (n)	yahūdiyya (f)	يهوديّة
Jewish (adj)	yahūdiy	يهوديّ

| China | aṣ ṣīn (f) | الصين |
| Chinese (masc.) | ṣīniy (m) | صينيّ |

| Chinese (fem.) | ṣīniyya (f) | صينية |
| Chinese (adj) | ṣīniy | صيني |

Korean (masc.)	kūriy (m)	كوري
Korean (fem.)	kuriyya (f)	كورية
Korean (adj)	kūriy	كوري

Lebanon	lubnān (f)	لبنان
Lebanese (masc.)	lubnāniy (m)	لبناني
Lebanese (fem.)	lubnāniyya (f)	لبنانية
Lebanese (adj)	lubnāniy	لبناني

Mongolia	manɣūliya (f)	منغوليا
Mongolian (masc.)	manɣūliy (m)	منغولي
Mongolian (fem.)	manɣūliyya (f)	منغولية
Mongolian (adj)	manɣūliy	منغولي

Malaysia	malīziya (f)	ماليزيا
Malaysian (masc.)	malīziy (m)	ماليزي
Malaysian (fem.)	malīziyya (f)	ماليزية
Malaysian (adj)	malīziy	ماليزي

Pakistan	bakistān (f)	باكستان
Pakistani (masc.)	bakistāniy (m)	باكستاني
Pakistani (fem.)	bakistāniyya (f)	باكستانية
Pakistani (adj)	bakistāniy	باكستاني

Saudi Arabia	as saʿūdiyya (f)	السعودية
Arab (masc.)	ʿarabiy (m)	عربي
Arab (fem.)	ʿarabiyya (f)	عربية
Arabic, Arabian (adj)	ʿarabiy	عربي

Thailand	taylānd (f)	تايلاند
Thai (masc.)	taylāndiy (m)	تايلاندي
Thai (fem.)	taylandiyya (f)	تايلاندية
Thai (adj)	taylāndiy	تايلاندي

Taiwan	taywān (f)	تايوان
Taiwanese (masc.)	taywāniy (m)	تايواني
Taiwanese (fem.)	taywāniyya (f)	تايوانية
Taiwanese (adj)	taywāniy	تايواني

Turkey	turkiya (f)	تركيا
Turk (masc.)	turkiy (m)	تركي
Turk (fem.)	turkiyya (f)	تركية
Turkish (adj)	turkiy	تركي

Japan	al yabān (f)	اليابان
Japanese (masc.)	yabāniy (m)	ياباني
Japanese (fem.)	yabāniyya (f)	يابانية
Japanese (adj)	yabāniy	ياباني

Afghanistan	afɣanistān (f)	أفغانستان
Bangladesh	banʒladīʃ (f)	بنجلاديش
Indonesia	indunīsiya (f)	إندونيسيا
Jordan	al urdun (m)	الأردن

Iraq	al 'irāq (m)	العراق
Iran	'īrān (f)	إيران
Cambodia	kambūdya (f)	كمبوديا
Kuwait	al kuwayt (f)	الكويت

Laos	lawus (f)	لاوس
Myanmar	myanmār (f)	ميانمار
Nepal	nibāl (f)	نيبال
United Arab Emirates	al imārāt al 'arabiyya al muttahida (pl)	الإمارات العربيّة المتّحدة

Syria	sūriya (f)	سوريا
Palestine	filistīn (f)	فلسطين
South Korea	kuriya al ʒanūbiyya (f)	كوريا الجنوبيّة
North Korea	kūria aʃʃimāliyya (f)	كوريا الشماليّة

238. North America

United States of America	al wilāyāt al muttahida al amrīkiyya (pl)	الولايات المتّحدة الأمريكيّة
American (masc.)	amrīkiy (m)	أمريكيّ
American (fem.)	amrīkiyya (f)	أمريكيّة
American (adj)	amrīkiy	أمريكيّ

Canada	kanada (f)	كندا
Canadian (masc.)	kanadiy (m)	كنديّ
Canadian (fem.)	kanadiyya (f)	كنديّة
Canadian (adj)	kanadiy	كنديّ

Mexico	al maksīk (f)	المكسيك
Mexican (masc.)	maksīkiy (m)	مكسيكيّ
Mexican (fem.)	maksīkiyya (f)	مكسيكيّة
Mexican (adj)	maksīkiy	مكسيكيّ

239. Central and South America

Argentina	arʒantīn (f)	الأرجنتين
Argentinian (masc.)	arʒantīniy (m)	أرجنتينيّ
Argentinian (fem.)	arʒantīniyya (f)	أرجنتينيّة
Argentinian (adj)	arʒantīniy	أرجنتينيّ

Brazil	al brazīl (f)	البرازيل
Brazilian (masc.)	brazīliy (m)	برازيليّ
Brazilian (fem.)	brazīliyya (f)	برازيليّة
Brazilian (adj)	brazīliy	برازيليّ

Colombia	kulumbiya (f)	كولومبيا
Colombian (masc.)	kulumbiy (m)	كولومبيّ
Colombian (fem.)	kulumbiyya (f)	كولومبيّة
Colombian (adj)	kulumbiy	كولومبيّ
Cuba	kūba (f)	كوبا
Cuban (masc.)	kūbiy (m)	كوبيّ

Cuban (fem.)	kūbiyya (f)	كوبيّة
Cuban (adj)	kūbiy	كوبيّ
Chile	tʃīli (f)	تشيلي
Chilean (masc.)	tʃīliy (m)	تشيليّ
Chilean (fem.)	tʃīliyya (f)	تشيليّة
Chilean (adj)	tʃīliy	تشيليّ
Bolivia	bulīviya (f)	بوليفيا
Venezuela	vinizwiyla (f)	فنزويلا
Paraguay	baraɣwāy (f)	باراغواي
Peru	biru (f)	بيرو
Suriname	surinām (f)	سورينام
Uruguay	uruɣwāy (f)	الأوروغواي
Ecuador	al iqwadūr (f)	الإكوادور
The Bahamas	ʒuzur bahāmas (pl)	جزر باهاماس
Haiti	haīti (f)	هايتي
Dominican Republic	ʒumhūriyyat ad duminikan (f)	جمهوريّة الدومينيكان
Panama	banama (f)	بنما
Jamaica	ʒamāyka (f)	جامايكا

240. Africa

Egypt	miṣr (f)	مصر
Egyptian (masc.)	miṣriy (m)	مصريّ
Egyptian (fem.)	miṣriyya (f)	مصريّة
Egyptian (adj)	miṣriy	مصريّ
Morocco	al maɣrib (m)	المغرب
Moroccan (masc.)	maɣribiy (m)	مغربيّ
Moroccan (fem.)	maɣribiyya (f)	مغربيّة
Moroccan (adj)	maɣribiy	مغربيّ
Tunisia	tūnis (f)	تونس
Tunisian (masc.)	tūnisiy (m)	تونسيّ
Tunisian (fem.)	tūnisiyya (f)	تونسيّة
Tunisian (adj)	tūnisiy	تونسيّ
Ghana	ɣāna (f)	غانا
Zanzibar	zanʒibār (f)	زنجبار
Kenya	kiniya (f)	كينيا
Libya	lībiya (f)	ليبيا
Madagascar	madaɣaʃqar (f)	مدغشقر
Namibia	namībiya (f)	ناميبيا
Senegal	as siniɣāl (f)	السنغال
Tanzania	tanzāniya (f)	تنزانيا
South Africa	ʒumhūriyyat afrīqiya al ʒanūbiyya (f)	جمهوريّة أفريقيا الجنوبيّة
African (masc.)	afrīqiy (m)	أفريقيّ
African (fem.)	afrīqiyya (f)	أفريقيّة
African (adj)	afrīqiy	أفريقيّ

241. Australia. Oceania

Australia	usturāliya (f)	أستراليا
Australian (masc.)	usturāliy (m)	أستراليّ
Australian (fem.)	usturāliyya (f)	أستراليّة
Australian (adj)	usturāliy	أستراليّ
New Zealand	nyu zilanda (f)	نيوزيلندا
New Zealander (masc.)	nyu zilandiy (m)	نيوزيلنديّ
New Zealander (fem.)	nyu zilandiyya (f)	نيوزيلنديّة
New Zealand (as adj)	nyu zilandiy	نيوزيلنديّ
Tasmania	tasmāniya (f)	تاسمانيا
French Polynesia	bulinīziya al faransiyya (f)	بولينزيا الفرنسيّة

242. Cities

Amsterdam	amstirdām (f)	أمستردام
Ankara	anqara (f)	أنقرة
Athens	aθīna (f)	أثينا
Baghdad	bayḍād (f)	بغداد
Bangkok	bankūk (f)	بانكوك
Barcelona	barʃalūna (f)	برشلونة
Beijing	bikīn (f)	بيكين
Beirut	bayrūt (f)	بيروت
Berlin	birlīn (f)	برلين
Mumbai (Bombay)	bumbāy (f)	بومباى
Bonn	būn (f)	بون
Bordeaux	burdu (f)	بوردو
Bratislava	bratislāva (f)	براتيسلافا
Brussels	brūksil (f)	بروكسل
Bucharest	buxarist (f)	بوخارست
Budapest	budabist (f)	بودابست
Cairo	al qāhira (f)	القاهرة
Kolkata (Calcutta)	kalkutta (f)	كلكتا
Chicago	ʃikāɣu (f)	شيكاغو
Copenhagen	kubinhāʒin (f)	كوبنهاجن
Dar-es-Salaam	dar as salām (f)	دار السلام
Delhi	dilhi (f)	دلهي
Dubai	dibay (f)	دبي
Dublin	dablin (f)	دبلن
Düsseldorf	dusildurf (f)	دوسلدورف
Florence	flurinsa (f)	فلورنسا
Frankfurt	frankfurt (f)	فرانكفورت
Geneva	ʒinīv (f)	جنيف
The Hague	lahāy (f)	لاهاى
Hamburg	hamburɣ (m)	هامبورغ

Hanoi	hanuy (f)	هانوى
Havana	havāna (f)	هافانا
Helsinki	hilsinki (f)	هلسنكي
Hiroshima	hiruʃīma (f)	هيروشيما
Hong Kong	hunɣ kunɣ (f)	هونغ كونغ
Istanbul	isṭanbūl (f)	إسطنبول
Jerusalem	al quds (f)	القدس
Kyiv	kiyiv (f)	كييف
Kuala Lumpur	kuala lumpur (f)	كوالالمبور
Lisbon	liʃbūna (f)	لشبونة
London	lundun (f)	لندن
Los Angeles	lus anʒilis (f)	لوس أنجلوس
Lyons	liyūn (f)	ليون
Madrid	madrīd (f)	مدريد
Marseille	marsīliya (f)	مرسيليا
Mexico City	madīnat maksiku (f)	مدينة مكسيكو
Miami	mayāmi (f)	ميامي
Montreal	muntriyāl (f)	مونتريال
Moscow	musku (f)	موسكو
Munich	myūniҳ (f)	ميونخ
Nairobi	nayrūbi (f)	نيروبي
Naples	nabuli (f)	نابولي
New York	nyu yūrk (f)	نيويورك
Nice	nīs (f)	نيس
Oslo	uslu (f)	أوسلو
Ottawa	uttawa (f)	أوتاوا
Paris	barīs (f)	باريس
Prague	brāɣ (f)	براغ
Rio de Janeiro	riu di ʒaniyru (f)	ريو دي جانيرو
Rome	rūma (f)	روما
Saint Petersburg	sant bitirsburɣ (f)	سانت بطرسبرغ
Seoul	siūl (f)	سيول
Shanghai	ʃanɣhāy (f)	شانغهاي
Singapore	sinɣafūra (f)	سنغافورة
Stockholm	stukhūlm (f)	ستوكهولم
Sydney	sidniy (f)	سيدني
Taipei	taybay (f)	تايبيه
Tokyo	ṭukyu (f)	طوكيو
Toronto	turūntu (f)	تورونتو
Venice	al bunduqiyya (f)	البندقيّة
Vienna	vyīna (f)	فيينا
Warsaw	warsaw (f)	وارسو
Washington	wāʃinṭun (f)	واشنطن

243. Politics. Government. Part 1

politics	siyāsa (f)	سياسة
political (adj)	siyāsiy	سياسيّ

politician	siyāsiy (m)	سياسيّ
state (country)	dawla (f)	دولة
citizen	muwāṭin (m)	مواطن
citizenship	ʒinsiyya (f)	جنسية

| national emblem | ʃiʿār waṭaniy (m) | شعار وطنيّ |
| national anthem | naʃīd waṭaniy (m) | نشيد وطنيّ |

government	ḥukūma (f)	حكومة
head of state	ra's ad dawla (m)	رأس الدولة
parliament	barlamān (m)	برلمان
party	ḥizb (m)	حزب

| capitalism | ra'smāliyya (f) | رأسماليّة |
| capitalist (adj) | ra'smāliy | رأسماليّ |

| socialism | iʃtirākiyya (f) | إشتراكيّة |
| socialist (adj) | iʃtirākiy | إشتراكيّ |

communism	ʃuyūʿiyya (f)	شيوعيّة
communist (adj)	ʃuyūʿiy	شيوعيّ
communist (n)	ʃuyūʿiy (m)	شيوعيّ

democracy	dimuqraṭiyya (f)	ديموقراطيّة
democrat	dimuqrāṭiy (m)	ديموقراطيّ
democratic (adj)	dimuqrāṭiy	ديموقراطيّ
Democratic party	al ḥizb ad dimukrāṭiy (m)	الحزب الديموقراطيّ

liberal (n)	libirāliy (m)	ليبراليّ
Liberal (adj)	libirāliy	ليبراليّ
conservative (n)	muḥāfiẓ (m)	محافظ
conservative (adj)	muḥāfiẓ	محافظ

republic (n)	ʒumhūriyya (f)	جمهوريّة
republican (n)	ʒumhūriy (m)	جمهوريّ
Republican party	al ḥizb al ʒumhūriy (m)	الحزب الجمهوريّ

elections	intixābāt (pl)	إنتخابات
to elect (vt)	intaxab	إنتخب
elector, voter	nāxib (m)	ناخب
election campaign	ḥamla intixābiyya (f)	حملة إنتخابيّة

voting (n)	taṣwīt (m)	تصويت
to vote (vi)	ṣawwat	صوّت
suffrage, right to vote	ḥaqq al intixāb (m)	حقّ الإنتخاب

candidate	muraʃʃaḥ (m)	مرشّح
to run for (~ President)	raʃʃaḥ nafsahu	رشّح نفسه
campaign	ḥamla (f)	حملة

| opposition (as adj) | muʿāriḍ | معارض |
| opposition (n) | muʿāraḍa (f) | معارضة |

visit	ziyāra (f)	زيارة
official visit	ziyāra rasmiyya (f)	زيارة رسميّة
international (adj)	duwaliy	دوليّ

negotiations	mubāḥaθāt (pl)	مباحثات
to negotiate (vi)	aȝra mubāḥaθāt	أجرى مباحثات

244. Politics. Government. Part 2

society	muȝtama' (m)	مجتمع
constitution	dustūr (m)	دستور
power (political control)	sulṭa (f)	سلطة
corruption	fasād (m)	فساد
law (justice)	qānūn (m)	قانون
legal (legitimate)	qānūniy	قانوني
justice (fairness)	'adāla (f)	عدالة
just (fair)	'ādil	عادل
committee	laȝna (f)	لجنة
bill (draft law)	maʃrū' qānūn (m)	مشروع قانون
budget	mīzāniyya (f)	ميزانية
policy	siyāsa (f)	سياسة
reform	iṣlāḥ (m)	إصلاح
radical (adj)	radikāliy	راديكالي
power (strength, force)	quwwa (f)	قوّة
powerful (adj)	qawiy	قوي
supporter	mu'ayyid (m)	مؤيد
influence	ta'θīr (m)	تأثير
regime (e.g. military ~)	niẓām ḥukm (m)	نظام حكم
conflict	χilāf (m)	خلاف
conspiracy (plot)	mu'āmara (f)	مؤامرة
provocation	istifzāz (m)	إستفزاز
to overthrow (regime, etc.)	asqaṭ	أسقط
overthrow (of a government)	isqāṭ (m)	إسقاط
revolution	θawra (f)	ثورة
coup d'état	inqilāb (m)	إنقلاب
military coup	inqilāb 'askariy (m)	انقلاب عسكري
crisis	azma (f)	أزمة
economic recession	rukūd iqtiṣādiy (m)	ركود إقتصادي
demonstrator (protester)	mutaẓāhir (m)	متظاهر
demonstration	muẓāhara (f)	مظاهرة
martial law	al aḥkām al 'urfiyya (pl)	الأحكام العرفية
military base	qa'ida 'askariyya (f)	قاعدة عسكرية
stability	istiqrār (m)	إستقرار
stable (adj)	mustaqirr	مستقرّ
exploitation	istiɣlāl (m)	إستغلال
to exploit (workers)	istaɣall	إستغلّ
racism	'unṣuriyya (f)	عنصرية
racist	'unṣuriy (m)	عنصري

fascism	fāʃiyya (f)	فاشيّة
fascist	fāʃiy (m)	فاشيّ

245. Countries. Miscellaneous

foreigner	aʒnabiy (m)	أجنبيّ
foreign (adj)	aʒnabiy	أجنبيّ
abroad (in a foreign country)	fil χāriʒ	في الخارج

emigrant	nāziḥ (m)	نازح
emigration	nuziḥ (m)	نزوح
to emigrate (vi)	nazūḥ	نزح

the West	al ɣarb (m)	الغرب
the East	aʃ ʃarq (m)	الشرق
the Far East	aʃ ʃarq al aqṣa (m)	الشرق الأقصى

civilization	ḥaḍāra (f)	حضارة
humanity (mankind)	al baʃariyya (f)	البشريّة
the world (earth)	al ʿālam (m)	العالم
peace	salām (m)	سلام
worldwide (adj)	ʿālamiy	عالميّ

homeland	waṭan (m)	وطن
people (population)	ʃaʿb (m)	شعب
population	sukkān (pl)	سكّان
people (a lot of ~)	nās (pl)	ناس
nation (people)	umma (f)	أمّة
generation	ʒīl (m)	جيل
territory (area)	arḍ (f)	أرض
region	mintaqa (f)	منطقة
state (part of a country)	wilāya (f)	ولاية

tradition	taqlīd (m)	تقليد
custom (tradition)	ʿāda (f)	عادة
ecology	ʿilm al bīʾa (m)	علم البيئة

Indian (Native American)	hindiy aḥmar (m)	هنديّ أحمر
Gypsy (masc.)	ɣaʒariy (m)	غجريّ
Gypsy (fem.)	ɣaʒariyya (f)	غجريّة
Gypsy (adj)	ɣaʒariy	غجريّ

empire	imbiraṭuriyya (f)	امبراطوريّة
colony	mustaʿmara (f)	مستعمرة
slavery	ʿubūdiyya (f)	عبوديّة
invasion	ɣazw (m)	غزو
famine	maʒāʿa (f)	مجاعة

246. Major religious groups. Confessions

religion	dīn (m)	دين
religious (adj)	dīniy	دينيّ

faith, belief	ʾĪmān (m)	إيمان
to believe (in God)	ʾāman	آمن
believer	muʾmin (m)	مؤمن

| atheism | al ilḥād (m) | الإلحاد |
| atheist | mulḥid (m) | ملحد |

Christianity	al masīḥiyya (f)	المسيحيّة
Christian (n)	masīḥiy (m)	مسيحي
Christian (adj)	masīḥiy	مسيحي

Catholicism	al kaθūlikiyya (f)	الكاثوليكيّة
Catholic (n)	kaθulīkiy (m)	كاثوليكي
Catholic (adj)	kaθulīkiy	كاثوليكي

Protestantism	al brutistantiyya (f)	البروتستانتية
Protestant Church	al kanīsa al brutistantiyya (f)	الكنيسة البروتستانتيّة
Protestant (n)	brutistantiy (m)	بروتستانتي

Orthodoxy	urθuðuksiyya (f)	الأرثوذكسيّة
Orthodox Church	al kanīsa al urθuðuksiyya (f)	الكنيسة الأرثوذكسيّة
Orthodox (n)	urθuðuksiy (m)	أرثوذكسي

Presbyterianism	maʃīxiyya (f)	المشيخيّة
Presbyterian Church	al kanīsa al maʃīxiyya (f)	الكنيسة المشيخيّة
Presbyterian (n)	maʃīxiy (m)	مشيخي

| Lutheranism | al kanīsa al luθiriyya (f) | الكنيسة اللوثريّة |
| Lutheran (n) | luθiriy (m) | لوثري |

| Baptist Church | al kanīsa al maʿmadāniyya (f) | الكنيسة المعمدانيّة |
| Baptist (n) | maʿmadāniy (m) | معمداني |

| Anglican Church | al kanīsa al anʒlikāniyya (f) | الكنيسة الإنجليكانيّة |
| Anglican (n) | anʒlikāniy (m) | أنجليكاني |

| Mormonism | al murumūniyya (f) | المورمونيّة |
| Mormon (n) | masīḥiy murmūn (m) | مسيحي مرمون |

| Judaism | al yahūdiyya (f) | اليهودية |
| Jew (n) | yahūdiy (m) | يهودي |

| Buddhism | al būðiyya (f) | البوذيّة |
| Buddhist (n) | būðiy (m) | بوذي |

| Hinduism | al hindūsiyya (f) | الهندوسيّة |
| Hindu (n) | hindūsiy (m) | هندوسي |

Islam	al islām (m)	الإسلام
Muslim (n)	muslim (m)	مسلم
Muslim (adj)	islāmiy	إسلامي

Shiah Islam	al maðhab aʃ ʃīʿiy (m)	المذهب الشيعيّ
Shiite (n)	ʃīʿiy (m)	شيعي
Sunni Islam	al maðhab as sunniy (m)	المذهب السنّيّ
Sunnite (n)	sunniy (m)	سنّي

247. Religions. Priests

priest	qissīs (m), kāhin (m)	قسّيس, كاهن
the Pope	al bāba (m)	البابا
monk, friar	rāhib (m)	راهب
nun	rāhiba (f)	راهبة
pastor	qissīs (m)	قسّيس
abbot	ra'īs ad dayr (m)	رئيس الدير
vicar (parish priest)	viqār (m)	فيقار
bishop	usquf (m)	أسقف
cardinal	kardināl (m)	كاردينال
preacher	tabʃīr (m)	تبشير
preaching	χutba (f)	خطبة
parishioners	ra'iyyat al abraʃiyya (f)	رعية الأبرشيّة
believer	mu'min (m)	مؤمن
atheist	mulḥid (m)	ملحد

248. Faith. Christianity. Islam

Adam	'ādam (m)	آدم
Eve	ḥawā' (f)	حوّاء
God	allah (m)	الله
the Lord	ar rabb (m)	الربّ
the Almighty	al qadīr (m)	القدير
sin	ðamb (m)	ذنب
to sin (vi)	aðnab	أذنب
sinner (masc.)	muðnib (m)	مذنب
sinner (fem.)	muðniba (f)	مذنبة
hell	al ʒaḥīm (f)	الجحيم
paradise	al ʒanna (f)	الجنّة
Jesus	yasū' (m)	يسوع
Jesus Christ	yasū' al masīḥ (m)	يسوع المسيح
the Holy Spirit	ar rūḥ al qudus (m)	الروح القدس
the Saviour	al masīḥ (m)	المسيح
the Virgin Mary	maryam al 'aðrā' (f)	مريم العذراء
the Devil	aʃ ʃaytān (m)	الشيطان
devil's (adj)	ʃaytāniy	شيطانيّ
Satan	aʃ ʃaytān (m)	الشيطان
satanic (adj)	ʃaytāniy	شيطانيّ
angel	malāk (m)	ملاك
guardian angel	malāk ḥāris (m)	ملاك حارس
angelic (adj)	malā'ikiy	ملائكيّ

apostle	rasūl (m)	رسول
archangel	al malak ar ra'īsiy (m)	الملك الرئيسي
the Antichrist	al masīḥ ad daʒʒāl (m)	المسيح الدجّال

Church	al kanīsa (f)	الكنيسة
Bible	al kitāb al muqaddas (m)	الكتاب المقدّس
biblical (adj)	tawrātiy	توراتي

Old Testament	al ʿahd al qadīm (m)	العهد القديم
New Testament	al ʿahd al ʒadīd (m)	العهد الجديد
Gospel	inʒīl (m)	إنجيل
Holy Scripture	al kitāb al muqaddas (m)	الكتاب المقدّس
Heaven	al ʒanna (f)	الجنّة

Commandment	waṣiyya (f)	وصيّة
prophet	nabiy (m)	نبيّ
prophecy	nubū'a (f)	نبوءة

Allah	allah (m)	الله
Mohammed	muḥammad (m)	محمّد
the Koran	al qur'ān (m)	القرآن

mosque	masʒid (m)	مسجد
mullah	mulla (m)	ملّا
prayer	ṣalāt (f)	صلاة
to pray (vi, vt)	ṣalla	صلّى

pilgrimage	ḥaʒʒ (m)	حجّ
pilgrim	ḥāʒʒ (m)	حاجّ
Mecca	makka al mukarrama (f)	مكة المكرّمة

church	kanīsa (f)	كنيسة
temple	maʿbad (m)	معبد
cathedral	katidrā'iyya (f)	كاتدرائيّة
Gothic (adj)	qūṭiy	قوطيّ
synagogue	kanīs maʿbad yahūdiy (m)	كنيس معبد يهوديّ
mosque	masʒid (m)	مسجد

chapel	kanīsa saɣīra (f)	كنيسة صغيرة
abbey	dayr (m)	دير
convent	dayr (m)	دير
monastery	dayr (m)	دير

bell (church ~s)	ʒaras (m)	جرس
bell tower	burʒ al ʒaras (m)	برج الجرس
to ring (ab. bells)	daqq	دقّ

cross	ṣalīb (m)	صليب
cupola (roof)	qubba (f)	قبّة
icon	'īkūna (f)	ايقونة

soul	nafs (f)	نفس
fate (destiny)	maṣīr (m)	مصير
evil (n)	ʃarr (m)	شرّ
good (n)	χayr (m)	خير
vampire	maṣṣāṣ dimā' (m)	مصّاص دماء

witch (evil ~)	sāḥira (f)	ساحرة
demon	ʃayṭān (m)	شيطان
spirit	rūḥ (m)	روح
redemption (giving us ~)	takfīr (m)	تكفير
to redeem (vt)	kaffar ʿan	كفّر عن
church service	qaddās (m)	قدّاس
to say mass	alqa xuṭba bil kanīsa	ألقى خطبة بالكنيسة
confession	iʿtirāf (m)	إعتراف
to confess (vi)	iʿtaraf	إعترف
saint (n)	qiddīs (m)	قدّيس
sacred (holy)	muqaddas (m)	مقدّس
holy water	māʾ muqaddas (m)	ماء مقدّس
ritual (n)	ṭuqūs (pl)	طقوس
ritual (adj)	ṭuqūsiy	طقوسيّ
sacrifice	ðabīḥa (f)	ذبيحة
superstition	xurāfa (f)	خرافة
superstitious (adj)	muʾmin bil xurāfāt (m)	مؤمن بالخرافات
afterlife	al ʾāxira (f)	الآخرة
eternal life	al ḥayāt al abadiyya (f)	الحياة الأبدية

MISCELLANEOUS

249. Various useful words

background (green ~)	χalfiyya (f)	خلفيّة
balance (of the situation)	tawāzun (m)	توازن
barrier (obstacle)	ḥāʒiz (m)	حاجز
base (basis)	asās (m)	أساس
beginning	bidāya (f)	بداية
category	fi'a (f)	فئة
cause (reason)	sabab (m)	سبب
choice	iχtiyār (m)	إختيار
coincidence	ṣudfa (f)	صدفة
comfortable (~ chair)	murīḥ	مريح
comparison	muqārana (f)	مقارنة
compensation	taʿwīḍ (m)	تعويض
degree (extent, amount)	daraʒa (f)	درجة
development	tanmiya (f)	تنمية
difference	farq (m)	فرق
effect (e.g. of drugs)	ta'θīr (m)	تأثير
effort (exertion)	ʒuhd (m)	جهد
element	ʿunṣur (m)	عنصر
end (finish)	nihāya (f)	نهاية
example (illustration)	miθāl (m)	مثال
fact	ḥaqīqa (f)	حقيقة
frequent (adj)	mutakarrir (m)	متكرّر
growth (development)	numuww (m)	نموّ
help	musāʿada (f)	مساعدة
ideal	miθāl (m)	مثال
kind (sort, type)	nawʿ (m)	نوع
labyrinth	tayh (m)	تيه
mistake, error	χaṭa' (m)	خطأ
moment	laḥẓa (f)	لحظة
object (thing)	mawḍūʿ (m)	موضوع
obstacle	ʿaqba (f)	عقبة
original (original copy)	aṣl (m)	أصل
part (~ of sth)	ʒuz' (m)	جزء
particle, small part	ʒuz' (m)	جزء
pause (break)	istirāḥa (f)	إستراحة
position	mawqif (m)	موقف
principle	mabda' (m)	مبدأ
problem	muʃkila (f)	مشكلة
process	ʿamaliyya (f)	عمليّة

progress	taqaddum (m)	تقدّم
property (quality)	χaṣṣa (f)	خاصّة
reaction	radd fiʻl (m)	ردّ فعل
risk	muχāṭara (f)	مخاطرة

secret	sirr (m)	سرّ
series	silsila (f)	سلسلة
shape (outer form)	ʃakl (m)	شكل
situation	ḥāla (f), waḍʻ (m)	حالة, وضع
solution	ḥall (m)	حلّ

standard (adj)	qiyāsiy	قياسيّ
standard (level of quality)	qiyās (m)	قياس
stop (pause)	istirāḥa (f)	إستراحة
style	uslūb (m)	أسلوب

system	niẓām (m)	نظام
table (chart)	ӡadwal (m)	جدول
tempo, rate	surʻa (f)	سرعة
term (word, expression)	muṣṭalaḥ (m)	مصطلح
thing (object, item)	ʃayʾ (m)	شيء

truth (e.g. moment of ~)	ḥaqīqa (f)	حقيقة
turn (please wait your ~)	dawr (m)	دور
type (sort, kind)	nawʻ (m)	نوع
urgent (adj)	ʻāӡil	عاجل
urgently	ʻāӡilan	عاجلًا

utility (usefulness)	manfaʻa (f)	منفعة
variant (alternative)	ʃakl muχtalif (m)	شكل مختلف
way (means, method)	ṭarīqa (f)	طريقة
zone	mintaqa (f)	منطقة

250. Modifiers. Adjectives. Part 1

additional (adj)	iḍāfiy	إضافيّ
ancient (~ civilization)	qadīm	قديم
artificial (adj)	ṣināʻiy	صناعيّ
back, rear (adj)	χalfiy	خلفيّ
bad (adj)	sayyiʾ	سيئ

beautiful (~ palace)	ӡamīl	جميل
beautiful (person)	ӡamīl	جميل
big (in size)	kabīr	كبير
bitter (taste)	murr	مرّ
blind (sightless)	aʻma	أعمى

calm, quiet (adj)	hādiʾ	هادئ
careless (negligent)	muhmil	مهمل
caring (~ father)	muhtamm	مهتمّ
central (adj)	markaziy	مركزيّ

| cheap (low-priced) | raχīṣ | رخيص |
| cheerful (adj) | farḥān | فرحان |

children's (adj)	lil aṭfāl	للأطفال
civil (~ law)	madaniy	مدنيّ
clandestine (secret)	sirriy	سرّي
clean (free from dirt)	naẓīf	نظيف
clear (explanation, etc.)	wāḍiḥ	واضح
clever (intelligent)	ðakiy	ذكيّ
close (near in space)	qarīb	قريب
closed (adj)	muɣlaq	مغلق
cloudless (sky)	ṣāfi	صاف
cold (drink, weather)	bārid	بارد
compatible (adj)	mutawāfiq	متوافق
contented (satisfied)	rāḍi	راض
continuous (uninterrupted)	mutawāṣil	متواصل
cool (weather)	qarīr	قرير
dangerous (adj)	ҳaṭīr	خطير
dark (room)	muẓlim	مظلم
dead (not alive)	mayyit	ميّت
dense (fog, smoke)	kaθīf	كثيف
destitute (extremely poor)	mu'dim	معدم
different (not the same)	muҳtalif	مختلف
difficult (decision)	ṣa'b	صعب
difficult (problem, task)	ṣa'b	صعب
dim, faint (light)	bāhit	باهت
dirty (not clean)	wasiҳ	وسخ
distant (in space)	ba'īd	بعيد
dry (clothes, etc.)	ʒāff	جافّ
easy (not difficult)	sahl	سهل
empty (glass, room)	ҳāli	خال
even (e.g. ~ surface)	musaṭṭaḥ	مسطّح
exact (amount)	daqīq	دقيق
excellent (adj)	mumtāz	ممتاز
excessive (adj)	mufriṭ	مفرط
expensive (adj)	ɣāli	غال
exterior (adj)	ҳāriʒiy	خارجيّ
far (the ~ East)	ba'īd	بعيد
fast (quick)	sarī'	سريع
fatty (food)	dasim	دسم
fertile (land, soil)	ҳaṣib	خصب
flat (~ panel display)	musaṭṭaḥ	مسطّح
foreign (adj)	aʒnabiy	أجنبيّ
fragile (china, glass)	haʃʃ	هشّ
free (at no cost)	maʒʒāniy	مجّانيّ
free (unrestricted)	ḥurr	حر
fresh (~ water)	'aðb	عذب
fresh (e.g. ~ bread)	ṭāziʒ	طازج
frozen (food)	muʒammad	مجمّد
full (completely filled)	malɣān	مليان

gloomy (house, forecast)	muẓlim	مظلم
good (book, etc.)	ʒayyid	جيّد
good, kind (kindhearted)	ṭayyib	طيّب
grateful (adj)	ʃākir	شاكر

happy (adj)	saʕīd	سعيد
hard (not soft)	ʒāmid	جامد
heavy (in weight)	taqīl	ثقيل
hostile (adj)	muʕādin	معاد
hot (adj)	sāxin	ساخن

huge (adj)	ḍaxm	ضخم
humid (adj)	raṭib	رطب
hungry (adj)	ʒawʕān	جوعان
ill (sick, unwell)	marīḍ	مريض
immobile (adj)	θābit	ثابت

important (adj)	muhimm	مهمّ
impossible (adj)	mustaḥīl	مستحيل
incomprehensible	yayr wāḍiḥ	غير واضح
indispensable (adj)	ḍarūriy	ضروري
inexperienced (adj)	qalīl al xibra	قليل الخبرة

insignificant (adj)	yayr muhimm	غير مهمّ
interior (adj)	dāxiliy	داخلي
joint (~ decision)	muʃtarak	مشترك
last (e.g. ~ week)	māḍi	ماض

last (final)	’āxir	آخر
left (e.g. ~ side)	al yasār	اليسار
legal (legitimate)	qānūniy, ʃarʕiy	قانوني، شرعي
light (in weight)	xafīf	خفيف
light (pale color)	fātiḥ	فاتح

limited (adj)	maḥdūd	محدود
liquid (fluid)	sā’il	سائل
long (e.g. ~ hair)	ṭawīl	طويل
loud (voice, etc.)	ʕāli	عال
low (voice)	munxafiḍ	منخفض

251. Modifiers. Adjectives. Part 2

main (principal)	raʔīsi	رئيسي
matt, matte	munṭafi’	منطفئ
meticulous (job)	mutqan	متقن
mysterious (adj)	yarīb	غريب
narrow (street, etc.)	ḍayyiq	ضيّق

native (~ country)	aṣliy	أصلي
nearby (adj)	qarīb	قريب
needed (necessary)	lāzim	لازم
negative (~ response)	salbiy	سلبي
neighbouring (adj)	muʒāwir	مجاور
nervous (adj)	ʕaṣabiy	عصبي

new (adj)	ʒadīd	جديد
next (e.g. ~ week)	muqbil	مقبل
nice (agreeable)	laṭīf	لطيف

pleasant (voice)	laṭīf	لطيف
normal (adj)	ʿādiy	عادي
not big (adj)	ɣayr kabīr	غير كبير
not difficult (adj)	ɣayr ṣaʿb	غير صعب

obligatory (adj)	ḍarūriy	ضروري
old (house)	qadīm	قديم
open (adj)	maftūḥ	مفتوح
opposite (adj)	muqābil	مقابل
ordinary (usual)	ʿādiy	عادي

original (unusual)	aṣliy	أصلي
past (recent)	māḍi	ماض
permanent (adj)	dāʾim	دائم
personal (adj)	ʃaxṣiy	شخصي
polite (adj)	muʾaddab	مؤدب

poor (not rich)	faqīr	فقير
possible (adj)	mumkin	ممكن
present (current)	ḥāḍir	حاضر
previous (adj)	māḍi	ماض
principal (main)	asāsiy	أساسي

private (~ jet)	ʃaxṣiy	شخصي
probable (adj)	muḥtamal	محتمل
prolonged (e.g. ~ applause)	mumtadd	ممتد
public (open to all)	ʿāmm	عام

punctual (person)	daqīq	دقيق
quiet (tranquil)	hādiʾ	هادئ
rare (adj)	nādir	نادر
raw (uncooked)	nayy	ني

right (not left)	al yamīn	اليمين
right, correct (adj)	ṣaḥīḥ	صحيح
ripe (fruit)	nāḍiʒ	ناضج
risky (adj)	xaṭir	خطر
sad (~ look)	ḥazīn	حزين

sad (depressing)	ḥazīn	حزين
safe (not dangerous)	ʾāmin	آمن
salty (food)	māliḥ	مالح
satisfied (customer)	rāḍi	راض

second hand (adj)	mustaʿmal	مستعمل
shallow (water)	ḍaḥl	ضحل
sharp (blade, etc.)	ḥādd	حاد
short (in length)	qaṣīr	قصير

short, short-lived (adj)	qaṣīr	قصير
short-sighted (adj)	qaṣīr an naẓar	قصير النظر
significant (notable)	muhimm	مهم

similar (adj)	ʃabīh	شبيه
simple (easy)	basīṭ	بسيط

skinny	naḥīf	نحيف
small (in size)	ṣaɣīr	صغير
smooth (surface)	amlas	أملس
soft (~ toys)	ṭariy	طري
solid (~ wall)	matīn	متين

sour (flavour, taste)	ḥāmiḍ	حامض
spacious (house, etc.)	wāsiʿ	واسع
special (adj)	χāṣṣ	خاص
straight (line, road)	mustaqīm	مستقيم
strong (person)	qawiy	قوي

stupid (foolish)	ɣabiy	غبي
suitable (e.g. ~ for drinking)	ṣāliḥ	صالح
sunny (day)	muʃmis	مشمس
superb, perfect (adj)	mumtāz	ممتاز
swarthy (dark-skinned)	asmar	أسمر

sweet (sugary)	musakkar	مسكّر
tanned (adj)	asmar	أسمر
tasty (delicious)	laðīð	لذيذ
tender (affectionate)	ḥanūn	حنون

the highest (adj)	aʿla	أعلى
the most important	ahamm	أهم
the nearest	aqrab	أقرب
the same, equal (adj)	mumāθil	مماثل

thick (e.g. ~ fog)	kaθīf	كثيف
thick (wall, slice)	θaχīn	ثخين
thin (person)	naḥīf	نحيف
tight (~ shoes)	ḍayyiq	ضيق
tired (exhausted)	taʿbān	تعبان

tiring (adj)	mutʿib	متعب
transparent (adj)	ʃaffāf	شفاف
unclear (adj)	ɣayr wāḍiḥ	غير واضح
unique (exceptional)	farīd	فريد
various (adj)	muχtalif	مختلف

warm (moderately hot)	dāfiʾ	دافئ
wet (e.g. ~ clothes)	mablūl	مبلول
whole (entire, complete)	kāmil	كامل
wide (e.g. ~ road)	wāsiʿ	واسع
young (adj)	ʃabb	شاب

MAIN 500 VERBS

252. Verbs A-C

to accompany (vt)	rāfaq	رافق
to accuse (vt)	ittaham	إتّهم
to acknowledge (admit)	i'taraf	إعترف
to act (take action)	'amal	عمل
to add (supplement)	aḍāf	أضاف
to address (speak to)	χātab	خاطب
to admire (vi)	u'ʒab bi	أعجب بـ
to advertise (vt)	a'lan	أعلن
to advise (vt)	naṣaḥ	نصح
to affirm (assert)	aṣarr	أصرّ
to agree (say yes)	ittafaq	إتّفق
to aim (to point a weapon)	ṣawwab	صوّب
to allow (sb to do sth)	samaḥ	سمح
to amputate (vt)	batar	بتر
to answer (vi, vt)	aʒāb	أجاب
to apologize (vi)	i'taðar	إعتذر
to appear (come into view)	ẓahar	ظهر
to applaud (vi, vt)	ṣaffaq	صفّق
to appoint (assign)	'ayyan	عيّن
to approach (come closer)	iqtarab	إقترب
to arrive (ab. train)	waṣal	وصل
to ask (~ sb to do sth)	ṭalab	طلب
to aspire to ...	sa'a	سعى
to assist (help)	sā'ad	ساعد
to attack (mil.)	haʒam	هجم
to attain (objectives)	balaɣ	بلغ
to avenge (get revenge)	intaqam	إنتقم
to avoid (danger, task)	taʒannab	تجنّب
to award (give a medal to)	manaḥ	منح
to battle (vi)	qātal	قاتل
to be (vi)	kān	كان
to be a cause of ...	sabbab	سبّب
to be afraid	χāf	خاف
to be angry (with ...)	za'al	زعل
to be at war	ḥārab	حارب
to be based (on ...)	i'tamad	إعتمد
to be bored	ʃa'ar bil malal	شعر بالملل

to be convinced	iqtanaʿ	إقتنع
to be enough	kafa	كـفى
to be envious	ḥasad	حسد
to be indignant	istāʾ	إستاء
to be interested in ...	ihtamm	إهتمّ

to be lost in thought	ʃaṭaḥ bi muχayyilatih	شطح بمخيّلته
to be lying (~ on the table)	kān mawʒūdan	كان موجودًا
to be needed	kānat hunāk ḥāʒa ila	كانت هناك حاجة إلى
to be perplexed (puzzled)	iḥtār	إحتار

to be preserved	baqiya	بقي
to be required	kān maṭlūb	كان مطلوبًا
to be surprised	indahaʃ	إندهش
to be worried	qalaq	قلق

to beat (to hit)	ḍarab	ضرب
to become (e.g. ~ old)	aṣbaḥ	أصبح
to behave (vi)	taṣarraf	تصرّف
to believe (think)	iʿtaqad	إعتقد

to belong to ...	χaṣṣ	خصّ
to berth (moor)	rasa	رسا
to blind (other drivers)	aʿma	أعمى
to blow (wind)	habb	هبّ

to blush (vi)	iḥmarr	إحمرّ
to boast (vi)	tabāha	تباهى
to borrow (money)	istalaf	إستلف
to break (branch, toy, etc.)	kasar	كسر

to breathe (vi)	tanaffas	تنفّس
to bring (sth)	ata bi	أتى بـ
to burn (paper, logs)	ḥaraq	حرق
to buy (purchase)	iʃtara	إشترى

to call (~ for help)	istayāθ	إستغاث
to call (yell for sb)	nāda	نادى
to calm down (vt)	ṭamʾan	طمأن
can (v aux)	istaṭāʿ	إستطاع

to cancel (call off)	alɣa	ألغى
to cast off (of a boat or ship)	aqlaʿ	أقلع
to catch (e.g. ~ a ball)	amsak	أمسك
to change (~ one's opinion)	ɣayyar	غيّر
to change. (exchange)	ṣaraf	صرف

to charm (vt)	fatan	فتن
to choose (select)	iχtār	إختار
to chop off (with an axe)	qaṭaʿ	قطع
to clean (e.g. kettle from scale)	naẓẓaf	نظف

to clean (shoes, etc.)	naẓẓaf	نظف
to clean up (tidy)	rattab	رتّب
to close (vt)	aɣlaq	أغلق

to comb one's hair	tamaʃʃaṭ	تمشّط
to come down (the stairs)	nazil	نزل
to come out (book)	ṣadar	صدر
to compare (vt)	qāran	قارن
to compensate (vt)	ʿawwaḍ	عوّض

to compete (vi)	nāfas	نافس
to compile (~ a list)	ʒammaʿ	جمّع
to complain (vi, vt)	ʃaka	شكا
to complicate (vt)	ʿaqqad	عقّد

to compose (music, etc.)	laḥḥan	لحّن
to compromise (reputation)	faḍah	فضح
to concentrate (vi)	tarakkaz	تركّز
to confess (criminal)	iʿtaraf	إعترف

to confuse (mix up)	iχtalaṭ	إختلط
to congratulate (vt)	hannaʾ	هنّأ
to consult (doctor, expert)	istaʃār ...	إستشار...
to continue (~ to do sth)	istamarr	إستمرّ

to control (vt)	taḥakkam	تحكّم
to convince (vt)	aqnaʿ	أقنع
to cooperate (vi)	taʿāwan	تعاون
to coordinate (vt)	nassaq	نسّق

to correct (an error)	ṣaḥḥaḥ	صحّح
to cost (vt)	kallaf	كلّف
to count (money, etc.)	ʿadd	عدّ
to count on ...	iʿtamad ʿala ...	إعتمد على...

to crack (ceiling, wall)	taʃaqqaq	تشقّق
to create (vt)	χalaq	خلق
to crush, to squash (~ a bug)	faʿaṣ	فعص
to cry (weep)	baka	بكى
to cut off (with a knife)	qaṭaʿ	قطع

253. Verbs D-G

to dare (~ to do sth)	aqdam	أقدم
to date from ...	raʒaʿ tarīχuhu ila	رجع تاريخه إلى
to deceive (vi, vt)	χadaʿ	خدع
to decide (~ to do sth)	qarrar	قرّر

to decorate (tree, street)	zayyan	زيّن
to dedicate (book, etc.)	karras	كرّس
to defend (a country, etc.)	dāfaʿ	دافع
to defend oneself	dāfaʿ ʿan nafsih	دافع عن نفسه

to demand (request firmly)	ṭālib	طالب
to denounce (vt)	waʃa	وشى
to deny (vt)	ankar	أنكر
to depend on ...	taʿallaq bi ...	تعلّق بـ...
to deprive (vt)	ḥaram	حرم

to deserve (vt)	istaḥaqq	إستَحقَّ
to design (machine, etc.)	ṣammam	صمَّم
to desire (want, wish)	raɣib	رغب
to despise (vt)	iḥtaqar	إحتقر
to destroy (documents, etc.)	atlaf	أتلف
to differ (from sth)	iχtalaf	إختلف
to dig (tunnel, etc.)	ḥafar	حفر
to direct (point the way)	waʒʒah	وجَّه
to disappear (vi)	iχtafa	إختفى
to discover (new land, etc.)	iktaʃaf	إكتشف
to discuss (vt)	nāqaʃ	ناقش
to distribute (leaflets, etc.)	wazzaʿ	وزَّع
to disturb (vt)	azʿaʒ	أزعج
to dive (vi)	ɣāṣ	غاص
to divide (math)	qasam	قسم
to do (vt)	ʿamal	عمل
to do the laundry	ɣasal	غسل
to double (increase)	ḍāʿaf	ضاعف
to doubt (have doubts)	ʃakk fi	شكَّ في
to draw a conclusion	istantaʒ	إستنتج
to dream (daydream)	ḥalam	حلم
to dream (in sleep)	ḥalam	حلم
to drink (vi, vt)	ʃarib	شرب
to drive a car	qād sayyāra	قاد سيَّارة
to drive away (scare away)	ṭarad	طرد
to drop (let fall)	awqaʿ	أوقع
to drown (ab. person)	ɣariq	غرق
to dry (clothes, hair)	ʒaffaf	جفَّف
to eat (vi, vt)	akal	أكل
to eavesdrop (vi)	tanaṣṣat	تنصَّت
to emit (diffuse - odor, etc.)	fāḥ	فاح
to enjoy oneself	istamtaʿ	إستمتع
to enter (on the list)	saʒʒal	سجَّل
to enter (room, house, etc.)	daχal	دخل
to entertain (amuse)	salla	سلَّى
to equip (fit out)	ʒahhaz	جهَّز
to examine (proposal)	baḥas fi	بحث في
to exchange (sth)	tabādal	تبادل
to excuse (forgive)	ʿaðar	عذر
to exist (vi)	kān mawʒūd	كان موجودًا
to expect (anticipate)	tawaqqaʿ	توقَّع
to expect (foresee)	tanabba'	تنبَّأ
to expel (from school, etc.)	faṣal	فصل
to explain (vt)	ʃaraḥ	شرح
to express (vt)	ʿabbar	عبَّر
to extinguish (a fire)	aṭfa'	أطفأ

to fall in love (with ...)	ahabb	أحبَّ
to fancy (vt)	a'ʒab	أعجب
to feed (provide food)	at'am	أطعم
to fight (against the enemy)	qātal	قاتل
to fight (vi)	ta'ārak	تعارك
to fill (glass, bottle)	mala'	ملأ
to find (~ lost items)	waʒad	وجد
to finish (vt)	atamm	أتمّ
to fish (angle)	iṣṭād as samak	إصطاد السمك
to fit (ab. dress, etc.)	nāsab	ناسب
to flatter (vt)	ʒāmal	جامل
to fly (bird, plane)	ṭār	طار
to follow ... (come after)	taba'	تبع
to forbid (vt)	mana'	منع
to force (compel)	aʒbar	أجبر
to forget (vi, vt)	nasiy	نسي
to forgive (pardon)	'afa	عفا
to form (constitute)	ʃakkal	شكّل
to get dirty (vi)	tawassaχ	توسّخ
to get infected (with ...)	in'ada	إنعدى
to get irritated	inza'aʒ	إنزعج
to get married	tazawwaʒ	تزوّج
to get rid of ...	taχallaṣ min ...	تخلّص من...
to get tired	ta'ib	تعب
to get up (arise from bed)	qām	قام
to give (vt)	a'ṭa	أعطى
to give a bath (to bath)	hammam	حمّم
to give a hug, to hug (vt)	'ānaq	عانق
to give in (yield to)	istaslam	إستسلم
to glimpse (vt)	lamah	لمح
to go (by car, etc.)	sāfar	سافر
to go (on foot)	maʃa	مشى
to go for a swim	sabah	سبح
to go out (for dinner, etc.)	χaraʒ	خرج
to go to bed (go to sleep)	nām	نام
to greet (vt)	sallam 'ala	سلّم على
to grow (plants)	anbat	أنبت
to guarantee (vt)	daman	ضمن
to guess (the answer)	χamman	خمّن

254. Verbs H-M

to hand out (distribute)	wazza' 'ala	وزّع على
to hang (curtains, etc.)	'allaq	علّق
to have (vt)	malak	ملك

| to have a bath | istaḥamm | إستحمّ |
| to have a try | ḥāwal | حاول |

to have breakfast	afṭar	أفطر
to have dinner	ta'aʃʃa	تعشّى
to have lunch	taɣadda	تغدّى
to head (group, etc.)	ra's	رأس
to hear (vt)	sami'	سمع

to heat (vt)	saxxan	سخّن
to help (vt)	sā'ad	ساعد
to hide (vt)	xaba'	خبأ
to hire (e.g. ~ a boat)	ista'ʒar	إستأجر
to hire (staff)	waẓẓaf	وظّف

to hope (vi, vt)	tamanna	تمنّى
to hunt (for food, sport)	iṣṭād	إصطاد
to hurry (vi)	ista'ʒal	إستعجل
to imagine (to picture)	taṣawwar	تصوّر
to imitate (vt)	qallad	قلّد

to implore (vt)	tawassal	توسّل
to import (vt)	istawrad	إستورد
to increase (vi)	izdād	إزداد
to increase (vt)	zayyad	زيّد
to infect (vt)	a'da	أعدى

to influence (vt)	aθθar	أثّر
to inform	axbar	أخبر
(e.g. ~ the police about ...)		
to inform (vt)	axbar	أخبر
to inherit (vt)	wariθ	ورث
to inquire (about ...)	istafsar	إستفسر

to insert (put in)	adxal	أدخل
to insinuate (imply)	lamaḥ	لمح
to insist (vi, vt)	aṣarr	أصرّ
to inspire (vt)	alham	ألهم
to instruct (teach)	'allam	علّم

to insult (offend)	ahān	أهان
to interest (vt)	hamm	همّ
to intervene (vi)	tadaxxal	تدخّل
to introduce (sb to sb)	'arraf	عرّف

to invent (machine, etc.)	ixtara'	إخترع
to invite (vt)	da'a	دعا
to iron (clothes)	kawa	كوى
to irritate (annoy)	az'aʒ	أزعج
to isolate (vt)	'azal	عزل

to join (political party, etc.)	inḍamm ila	إنضمّ إلى
to joke (be kidding)	mazaḥ	مزح
to keep (old letters, etc.)	iḥtafaẓ	إحتفظ
to keep silent, to hush	sakat	سكت
to kill (vt)	qatal	قتل

to knock (on the door)	daqq	دقَ
to know (sb)	'araf	عرف
to know (sth)	'araf	عرف
to laugh (vi)	ḍaḥik	ضحك
to launch (start up)	aṭlaq	أطلق
to leave (~ for Mexico)	ɣādar	غادر
to leave (forget sth)	nasiya	نسي
to leave (spouse)	tarak	ترك
to liberate (city, etc.)	ḥarrar	حرر
to lie (~ on the floor)	raqad	رقد
to lie (tell untruth)	kaðib	كذب
to light (campfire, etc.)	aʃʻal	أشعل
to light up (illuminate)	aḍā'	أضاء
to limit (vt)	ḥaddad	حدّد
to listen (vi)	istamaʻ	إستمع
to live (~ in France)	sakan	سكن
to live (exist)	'āʃ	عاش
to load (gun)	ḥaʃa	حشا
to load (vehicle, etc.)	ʃaḥan	شحن
to look (I'm just ~ing)	naẓar	نظر
to look for ... (search)	baḥaθ	بحث
to look like (resemble)	kān ʃabīhan	كان شبيهًا
to lose (umbrella, etc.)	faqad	فقد
to love (e.g. ~ dancing)	aḥabb	أحبَ
to love (sb)	aḥabb	أحبَ
to lower (blind, head)	anzal	أنزل
to make (~ dinner)	ḥaḍḍar	حضّر
to make a mistake	axṭa'	أخطأ
to make angry	azʻal	أزعل
to make easier	sahhal	سهّل
to make multiple copies	ṣawwar	صوّر
to make the acquaintance	taʻarraf	تعرّف
to make use (of ...)	istanfaʻ	إستنفع
to manage, to run	adār	أدار
to mark (make a mark)	'allam	علّم
to mean (signify)	'ana	عنى
to memorize (vt)	ḥafaẓ	حفظ
to mention (talk about)	ðakar	ذكر
to miss (school, etc.)	ɣāb	غاب
to mix (combine, blend)	xalaṭ	خلط
to mock (make fun of)	saxar	سخر
to move (to shift)	ḥarrak	حرّك
to multiply (math)	ḍarab	ضرب
must (v aux)	kān yaʒib 'alayh	كان يجب عليه

255. Verbs N-R

to name, to call (vt)	samma	سمّى
to negotiate (vi)	aʒra mubāhaθāt	أجرى مباحثات
to note (write down)	katab mulāḥaẓa	كتب ملاحظة
to notice (see)	lāḥaẓ	لاحظ
to obey (vi, vt)	ṭāʕ	طاع
to object (vi, vt)	iʕtaraḍ	إعترض
to observe (see)	rāqab	راقب
to offend (vt)	asāʾ	أساء
to omit (word, phrase)	haðaf	حذف
to open (vt)	fataḥ	فتح
to order (in restaurant)	ṭalab	طلب
to order (mil.)	amar	أمر
to organize (concert, party)	naẓẓam	نظّم
to overestimate (vt)	bāliɣ fit taqdīr	بالغ في التقدير
to own (possess)	malak	ملك
to participate (vi)	iʃtarak	إشترك
to pass through (by car, etc.)	marr bi	مرّ بـ
to pay (vi, vt)	dafaʕ	دفع
to peep, to spy on	waṣwaṣ	وصوص
to penetrate (vt)	daχal	دخل
to permit (vt)	samaḥ	سمح
to pick (flowers)	qaṭaf	قطف
to place (put, set)	waḍaʕ	وضع
to plan (~ to do sth)	χaṭṭaṭ	خطّط
to play (actor)	maθθal	مثّل
to play (children)	laʕib	لعب
to point (~ the way)	aʃār	أشار
to pour (liquid)	ṣabb	صبّ
to pray (vi, vt)	ṣalla	صلّى
to prefer (vt)	faḍḍal	فضّل
to prepare (~ a plan)	aʕadd	أعدّ
to present (sb to sb)	qaddam	قدّم
to preserve (peace, life)	ḥafaẓ	حفظ
to prevail (vt)	ɣalab	غلب
to progress (move forward)	taqaddam	تقدّم
to promise (vt)	waʕad	وعد
to pronounce (vt)	naṭaq	نطق
to propose (vt)	iqtaraḥ, ʕaraḍ	إقترح , عرض
to protect (e.g. ~ nature)	ḥama	حمى
to protest (vi)	iḥtaʒʒ	إحتجّ
to prove (vt)	aθbat	أثبت
to provoke (vt)	istafazz	إستفزّ
to pull (~ the rope)	ʃadd	شدّ
to punish (vt)	ʕāqab	عاقب

to push (~ the door)	dafaʿ	دفع
to put away (vt)	ʃāl	شال
to put in order	naẓẓam	نظّم
to put, to place	waḍaʿ	وضع
to quote (cite)	istaʃhad	إستشهد
to reach (arrive at)	waṣal	وصل
to read (vi, vt)	qaraʾ	قرأ
to realize (a dream)	ḥaqqaq	حقّق
to recognize (identify sb)	ʿaraf	عرف
to recommend (vt)	naṣaḥ	نصح
to recover (~ from flu)	ʃufiy	شفي
to redo (do again)	aʿād	أعاد
to reduce (speed, etc.)	qallal	قلّل
to refuse (~ sb)	rafaḍ	رفض
to regret (be sorry)	nadim	ندم
to reinforce (vt)	ʿazzaz	عزّز
to remember (Do you ~ me?)	taðakkar	تذكّر
to remember (I can't ~ her name)	taðakkar	تذكّر
to remind of ...	ðakkar	ذكّر
to remove (~ a stain)	azāl	أزال
to remove (~ an obstacle)	azāl	أزال
to rent (sth from sb)	istaʾʒar	إستأجر
to repair (mend)	aṣlaḥ	أصلح
to repeat (say again)	karrar	كرّر
to report (make a report)	qaddam taqrīr	قدّم تقريراً
to reproach (vt)	lām	لام
to reserve, to book	ḥaʒaz	حجز
to restrain (hold back)	manaʿ	منع
to return (come back)	ʿād	عاد
to risk, to take a risk	χāṭar	خاطر
to rub out (erase)	masaḥ	مسح
to run (move fast)	ʒara	جرى
to rush (hurry sb)	aʿʒʒal	عجّل

256. Verbs S-W

to satisfy (please)	arḍa	أرضى
to save (rescue)	anqað	أنقذ
to say (~ thank you)	qāl	قال
to scold (vt)	wabbaχ	وبّخ
to scratch (with claws)	χadaʃ	خدش
to select (to pick)	iχtār	إختار
to sell (goods)	bāʿ	باع
to send (a letter)	arsal	أرسل
to send back (vt)	aʿād	أعاد

to sense (~ danger)	ʃaʿr bi	شعر بـ
to sentence (vt)	ḥakam	حكم
to serve (in restaurant)	χadam	خدم
to settle (a conflict)	sawwa	سوّى
to shake (vt)	hazz	هزّ
to shave (vi)	ḥalaq	حلق
to shine (gleam)	lamʿ	لمع
to shiver (with cold)	irtaʿaʃ	إرتعش
to shoot (vi)	aṭlaq an nār	أطلق النار
to shout (vi)	ṣaraχ	صرخ
to show (to display)	ʿaraḍ	عرض
to shudder (vi)	irtaʿaʃ	إرتعش
to sigh (vi)	tanahhad	تنهّد
to sign (document)	waqqaʿ	وقع
to signify (mean)	ʿana	عنى
to simplify (vt)	bassaṭ	بسّط
to sin (vi)	aðnab	أذنب
to sit (be sitting)	ʒalas	جلس
to sit down (vi)	ʒalas	جلس
to smell (emit an odor)	fāḥ	فاح
to smell (inhale the odor)	iʃtamm	إشتمّ
to smile (vi)	ibtasam	إبتسم
to snap (vi, ab. rope)	inqataʿ	إنقطع
to solve (problem)	ḥall	حلّ
to sow (seed, crop)	baðar	بذر
to spill (liquid)	dalaq	دلق
to spill out, scatter (flour, etc.)	saqaṭ	سقط
to spit (vi)	bazaq	بزق
to stand (toothache, cold)	taḥammal	تحمّل
to start (begin)	badaʾ	بدأ
to steal (money, etc.)	saraq	سرق
to stop (for pause, etc.)	waqaf	وقف
to stop (please ~ calling me)	tawaqqaf	توقّف
to stop talking	sakat	سكت
to stroke (caress)	masaḥ	مسح
to study (vt)	daras	درس
to suffer (feel pain)	ʿāna	عانى
to support (cause, idea)	ayyad	أيّد
to suppose (assume)	iftaraḍ	إفترض
to surface (ab. submarine)	ṣaʿid ilas saṭḥ	صعد إلى السطح
to surprise (amaze)	adhaʃ	أدهش
to suspect (vt)	iʃtabah fi	إشتبه في
to swim (vi)	sabaḥ	سبح
to take (get hold of)	aχað	أخذ
to take a rest	istarāḥ	إستراح

to take away (e.g. about waiter)	ðahab bi	ذهب بـ
to take off (aeroplane)	aqla'	أقلع
to take off (painting, curtains, etc.)	naza'	نزع
to take pictures	ṣawwar	صوّر
to talk to ...	takallam ma'a ...	تكلّم مع...
to teach (give lessons)	'allam	علّم
to tear off, to rip off (vt)	qaṭa'	قطع
to tell (story, joke)	haddaθ	حدّث
to thank (vt)	ʃakar	شكر
to think (believe)	i'taqad	إعتقد
to think (vi, vt)	ẓann	ظنّ
to threaten (vt)	haddad	هدّد
to throw (stone, etc.)	rama	رمى
to tie to ...	rabaṭ bi ...	ربط بـ...
to tie up (prisoner)	rabaṭ	ربط
to tire (make tired)	at'ab	أتعب
to touch (one's arm, etc.)	lamas	لمس
to tower (over ...)	irtafa'	إرتفع
to train (animals)	darrab	درّب
to train (sb)	darrab	درّب
to train (vi)	tadarrab	تدرّب
to transform (vt)	hawwal	حوّل
to translate (vt)	tarʒam	ترجم
to treat (illness)	'ālaʒ	عالج
to trust (vt)	waθiq	وثق
to try (attempt)	hāwal	حاول
to turn (e.g., ~ left)	in'aṭaf	إنعطف
to turn away (vi)	a'raḍ 'an	أعرض عن
to turn off (the light)	aṭfa'	أطفأ
to turn on (computer, etc.)	fataḥ, ʃaɣɣal	فتح، شغّل
to turn over (stone, etc.)	qalab	قلب
to underestimate (vt)	istaχaff	إستخفّ
to underline (vt)	waḍa' χaṭṭ taḥt	وضع خطّا تحت
to understand (vt)	fahim	فهم
to undertake (vt)	qām bi	قام بـ
to unite (vt)	waḥḥad	وحّد
to untie (vt)	fakk	فكّ
to use (phrase, word)	istaχdam	إستخدم
to vaccinate (vt)	laqqaḥ	لقّح
to vote (vi)	ṣawwat	صوّت
to wait (vt)	intaẓar	إنتظر
to wake (sb)	ayqaẓ	أيقظ
to want (wish, desire)	arād	أراد
to warn (of a danger)	haððar	حذّر

to wash (clean)	ɣasal	غسل
to water (plants)	saqa	سقى
to wave (the hand)	lawwaḥ	لوّح
to weigh (have weight)	wazan	وزن
to work (vi)	ʿamal	عمل
to worry (make anxious)	aqlaq	أقلق
to worry (vi)	qalaq	قلق
to wrap (parcel, etc.)	laff	لفّ
to wrestle (sport)	ṣāraʿ	صارع
to write (vt)	katab	كتب
to write down	katab	كتب